Praise for Never a dull Moment

"Jyl Lynn Felman rewrites feminist pedagogy as a vibrant, political, and self-critical performative practice. Felman connects theory to experience, knowledge to risk taking, and learning to the specificity of place and context. This is a book that equates pedagogy with courage, teaching with hope, and politics with particular bodies mutually crossing into uncharted territories where meaning, passion, justice, and critique open up new possibilities for critical learning and social change. *Never a Dull Moment* is a moving, cour   d insightful book that every teacher, student, adm   "

of *Impure Acts: The Practical
Politics of Cultural Studies*

"In her exciting ..... *ll Moment*, Felman reveals the deeper value of 'face-to-face' teaching, not simply as a means of getting information across, but as a way of exploring some of the most sensitive gender and racial issues we confront in the contemporary classroom."

—LILLIAN S. ROBINSON, author of *In the Canon's Mouth:
Dispatches from the Culture Wars*

"[E]nlivened and literary. . . . Readers are invited behind university scenes to ponder, from the inside out, a working portrait of the teacher. Felman animates a lively cast of characters, where even the curriculum seems to come alive to argue with the dilemmas and fantasies brought to a women's studies classroom. . . . Felman's . . . autobiography of pedagogy is also that of the teacher's own generation."

—DEBORAH P. BRITZMAN, author of *Lost Subjects, Contested
Objects: Toward a Psychoanalytic Inquiry of Learning*

never a dull moment

Never a dull moment

Teaching and the Art of Performance

Feminism Takes Center Stage

jyl Lynn felman

4/02
Routledge
New York and London

Published in 2001 by
Routledge
29 West 35th Street
New York, NY 10001

Published in Great Britain by
Routledge
11 New Fetter Lane
London EC4P 4EE

Routledge is an imprint of the Taylor & Francis Group.
Copyright © 2001 by Routledge
Printed in the United States of America on acid-free paper.

Rahel Chalfi, "'I Went to Work as an Ostrich' Blues," trans. Shirley
Kaufman, was published in *The Defiant Muse: Hebrew Feminist Poems from
Antiquity to the Present*, ed. Shirley Kaufman et al. (New York: Feminist
Press, 1999), and was reprinted with permission from the publisher.

Except for those people who have given permission to appear in this
book, all names and identifying details of individuals mentioned in this
book have been changed. In some instances, composite accounts have
been created based on the author's professional expertise.

10   9   8   7   6   5   4   3   2   1

Library of Congress Cataloging-in-Publication Data

Felman, Jyl Lynn, 1954–
    Never a dull moment : teaching and the art of performance /
Jyl Lynn Felman.
        p. cm.
    Includes bibliographical references (p.) and index.
    ISBN 0-415-92659-9 — ISBN 0-415-92660-2 (pbk.)
    1. Feminism and education. 2. women college teachers. I. title.
LC197 .F44 2001
    378.1'9822—dc21   00-051742

Contents

For my father

H. Marvin Felman

A teacher par excellence!

Through the performance ritual, the audience vicariously experiences the freedom, cultural risks, and utopian possibilities that society has denied them. Audience members are encouraged to touch us, smell us, feed us, defy us. In this strange millennial ceremony, the Pandora's box opens and the post-colonial demons are unleashed.

—*Guillermo Gómez-Peña*, Performance Diaries

Acknowledgments

The longer I write, the more I understand how much my ability to persevere through the protracted hours of self-doubt, loneliness, and sheer terror is dependent on the bonds of sisterhood and real friendships that have endured month after month, year after infinite writing year. Along the way, there are those people whose unconditional love continues to nurture me in ways far beyond my expectations. It becomes important then, at the end of the writing of this book, to publicly acknowledge the support of the following individuals. I am forever grateful for the presence of these unusual human beings in my life: Thom Hermann, Marianna Marguglio, Susan Tracy, Arlene Dallalfar, and Anne and Howard Irwin.

In addition, I want to honor several of my teaching assistants by name. Working as a team in the fall of 1999, we taught 5A together, and experienced all the turbulence and exhilaration that occurs in an introductory Women's Studies class. Many of these individuals are quoted extensively throughout the book; without them, *Never a Dull Moment* would be a very short act indeed. Thank you, Daniel J. Franklin, Jilly Gross, Rachel Boyer, Ariel Chesler, Samantha Joo, Antje Ellermann, and Carmen Nge. You have enriched my life more than you will ever know.

As a teacher I am often blessed with the most powerful support of all, my Women's Studies students. I look forward to long friendships with Patricia Desir, Maureen Dimino, Autumn Wiley, Jane Kahuth,

Jason W. Freeman, Michael Stepansky, Gardy Guiteau, and Marsha Pierre-Jacques.

And a special thank you to Dr. Sharon Washington, who understands the sheer power of feminist pedagogy to transform the classroom and who has performed dazzling feats of her own in my Brandeis classes.

To Ilene Kalish, editor extraordinaire and butterfly catcher of incomparable talent, thank you from your very own Monarch. The flight has been fantastic, first class all the way. What's next?

To Linda Randall, my sister spirit, comrade, and no-limits buddy, thank you is simply not enough.

Finally, *merci beaucoup, pour les bon temps*! To Lynne S. Brandon, who has always known that *le style est l'homme même*, and who after twenty years has filled in the strange, mysteriously missing pieces of my quite puzzling life with unimaginable passion and joy: *vraiment, je t'aime sans pareil.*

Preface: Dress Rehearsal

Academic Agitprop

*AGITPROP: adj. Of or for agitating. A term origi-
nally used in the Communist movement, for certain
plays, leaflets, etc.*

the night before open-
ing night, the first day of my Introduction to Women's Studies class, I
plan to go to bed early, very early. But it doesn't happen that way. By
mistake, I walk into my walk-in closet, which is full of all the styles of
the last twenty-five years. I don't throw anything out. Because I never
know when the baggy, black silk pants with the double-hipped zippers
will come back in style or whether or not I will ever wear my red leather
miniskirt again. It helps that I now view my closet as a valuable, historical site of archival fabrics worthy of an ethnographic study—The
Contemporary Female Professor's Institutional Wardrobe in Transition.
I no longer wear clothes to class, I costume.

Like aging, the revolution from clothing toward costuming was
gradual. As a teaching assistant, I began in multiple shades of black:
jet-black turtlenecks, a coal-black watch band, a smoky black corduroy
blazer with matching gaucho pants, and smooth, black, extremely cool,
knee-high Italian leather boots. Week after week, I wore black. Until
the end of the semester, when I read my anonymous student evaluations, and one student whose bold, block-letter handwriting I recognized

immediately (and never forgot), wrote, "Why does she always wear B-L-A-C-K?" Spring semester, I added a bright red handwoven, Mexican shawl draped around my long neck and slung dramatically over my left shoulder, without realizing that I now resembled a walking billboard for Che Guevara. The big gold hoop earrings came later. Much later.

In the beginning, when I was still teaching "freshpeople's" English, long before I began the performance of teaching, I viewed my wardrobe simply as clothes—not yet understanding the deeper and radical significance of clothes as costume, and the magnificent power that was embedded in the very fibers of the fabric itself. But before I could decide what to wear to class, I had a more pressing, acutely female problem. I had to decide if I was going to shave my underarms and my extremely short legs. (In the 1970s and 1980s, this was more a professional question than a political dilemma.) The fact is, I have more hair under my arms than on top of my head, and my legs, left untouched, would look unattractively hirsute. I worried obsessively that if I didn't shave, I would lose my audience appeal. I imagined the students as they spent the entire first hour staring hard at all that thick brown hair.

Instantly, I made two decisions, since I could not decide whether or not to shave. Standing in the middle of my wardrobe, staring into the full-length mirror on the inside of the closet door, I decided that in my Intro to Women's Studies class, the now infamous 5A, we would spend a good part of the semester studying hair and its multiple historical meanings. And that I would make the following announcement within an hour of the first class. Raising both arms, turning my head to the right and then to the left, and enunciating perfectly, I would say, "Yes, it's true, you may have noticed that I do not shave under my arms, but I do shave my legs even though you can't tell by looking because I am wearing black opaque stockings. So you can stop wondering and start learning." When I actually do this the next day and everyone laughs, and I even hear some scattered applause, I realize that the show has begun. I have found the way in, *not* to lecture, but to *perform*.

A star is born. She is not Judy Garland; she is Professor Jyl Lynn Felman. At the moment of my academic theatrical rebirth, I began intuitively to construct the theories that ultimately became this book. Over the years, I perfected these fledgling ideas until *Teaching Is Performing* and *Performing Is Teaching* became the guiding pedagogical practice of my weekly foray into the classroom and in addition, a truly personal, life-saving mantra, as I had found my authentic voice. When I taught a bad class, which I inevitably was doomed to do, I comforted myself with the hard-won knowledge that as surely as the curtain draws to a close at the end of each performance, so it also rises—the next day, the next week, month after month, year after academic year. I had a dramatic mission.

To understand myself as a woman playing the *role* of professor became the basis of my intellectual inquiry. I sought out the various ramifications and covert signifiers of this methodology, all the while articulating a new feminist pedagogy of performance wherein the classroom became my permanent stage. That this methodology was sometimes suspect, often misunderstood, and on occasion publicly maligned by highly esteemed colleagues continues to be a challenge that I welcome with all the relish of sitting down at my favorite corner table at my favorite San Francisco restaurant, Chez Panisse, where Alice Waters, master chef extraordinaire—Ms. Organic Epicurean herself—understands that the heart and soul of a good meal—from the lush descriptions on the menu, to the simple country elegance of the settings on the table, to the presentation of the food itself—is and must be great theater. That's what keeps the people coming back for more.

Twenty years later, I find myself still reading those formidable anonymous student evaluations. When, recognizing the slant of a particular student's horrible handwriting, I read out loud, to no one in particular, "Felman is a performance not to be missed!", I realize that performance has truly become the praxis and axis on which the turn of my feminist pedagogy revolves. What makes this performance Feminist and not Patriarchal is the fact that I too am transformed, even while in the process of transforming. There is continuous reciprocity on *this* stage between actor and audience, teacher and student. For this is live performance at its most electrifying, where the denouement depends on the students themselves, rather than on the professor, s/he who often remains isolated and alone, tucked neatly behind a podium peculiarly academic in nature, peering at impeccably prepared notes, and waiting for the staccato sounds of sufficiently respectful applause.

This book addresses the postmodern predicament of how to educate at the fin de siècle, in this the age of the cosmopolitan virtual realist, where a relationship with an electronic monitor is often more passionate and erotic than a relationship with a human mentor, where the computer is on its way to usurping the role of the traditional classroom. In this context, the live, indigenous academic performance becomes a matter of virtual survival and an imperative if the professor is not to be left standing naked behind the podium, alone and forever isolated with all those highly meticulous esoteric notes.

Guerrilla theater is the vehicle for assuming intellectual command in chapter 1, "All the Classroom's a Stage," as the feminist classroom itself becomes a revolving proscenium—one that is in constant motion. Then the revolutionary border crossers take over, pushing wide open the once static boundaries between the professor and the students that become instantly fluid. At this moment, intellectual activism by way of theatrical performance challenges the traditional status quo, as the classroom is magnificently transformed into an artistic site of resistance and the center of political community. Learning then becomes dynamic, intentionally dramatic and fully alive, as it was always meant to be. No one is left behind, bored or disinterested.

Students are the Best Supporting Actors and Actresses rather than traditional passive audience receptors in chapter 2, "Long Day's Journey into the Classroom." The Star of the Show, a.k.a. La Professora, must help the students feel at home, at ease, and safe enough to take unexpected risks in this new, wholly unrecognizable—even frightening—academic environment. All the cast—students, teaching assistants, as well as the professor—become intellectually open and vulnerable. And, at some point midsemester, there will be a spontaneous combustion right in the middle of the show. Then, the Professor as Leading Lady assisted by her TAs must be prepared to assist her audience the moment the academic volcanic eruption spews the hot molten lava of active, scintillating education around the room, covering everyone in sight.

"Lee Strasberg Comes to Class" in chapter 3, bringing with him his infamous, ground-breaking acting method, which then causes ambivalent feelings and emotions to move theatrically forward, front and center stage. But this is not therapy in dramatic academic drag. *This* student *and* teacher performance is about making real connections to the material and really connecting to each other, so that the student audience becomes critically engaged and emotionally invested in the intellectual performance. The entire room is thus transformed by "Lee Strasberg's" visit to the academic scene. In the end the mind-body split so commonplace in the academy is repaired through the performance of learning with a whole self as modeled by Strasberg, a.k.a. the professor.

Chapter 4, "GI Joe in the Last Row: Performing Masculinities," looks at what to do with all the guys in Women's Studies. How do the males perform their many expressions of masculinities in their various roles as students, teaching assistants, or professors on the feminist stage? How does the gender of the performer impact the performance itself? Is the expression and presence of all that testosterone an impediment to a successful feminist show? Or is the performance enhanced? Does it matter if the male actors are gay or straight, Black or White or Asian, or some other variant on the male continuum? Just what is masculinity anyway? Go ask GI Joe.

Sometimes the damsels are dragging their robes behind them and tripping on their way to sit down. In chapter 5, "Damsels in Distress: Performing Femininities," the women become "girls" once again as they get angry, starve themselves, or refuse to speak loud enough to be heard, reverting back to their ambivalent adolescent selves. They resent all the new roles this unfamiliar academic performance demands of them. Instead, they long for the simple days, when the door on the passenger side of the sleek new Chrysler convertible is open and shut for them by GI Joe himself. As the curtain of the classroom is raised and lowered, many of "the girls" sit back, passively applauding the professor's performance. What to do with all the fair maidens and their frightful maladies? And what of *Las Professoras* who inhabit the stage?

What happens when the performance in the classroom is "hot and bothered"? Or when the professor is an out lesbian and the erotic flows effortlessly between the performer and her audience? In chapter 6, "A Classroom Named Desire: Academic Bodies in Motion," all the audience—gay, straight, trans, or bi—is in love with the performer and her performance. Relying on the words of the African-American poet Audre Lorde, "The erotic is the nurturer or nursemaid of all our deepest knowledge," the professor plays to the forbidden and suppressed but ever-present desire running throughout the room. The erotic is the dramatic, taut narrative tension always moving effortlessly through the cool academic stream between the professor and student, and from student to student. Learning to use the erotic in the classroom rather than losing or forgetting it is just one of the challenges of active, engaged learning.

In chapter 7, "A Midsemester's Day Dream," the professor becomes a postmodern Puck, a fluid and queer performance artist. And the students in their own unplanned, inexplicable ways mirror Puck's changing selves, as they too experiment with new personas. The chapter considers the question of the "classroom as theater" by asking: *Where does Dr. Puck draw the curtain between performance and entertainment? How do Dr. Puck's various disguises, all in the name of gender variance, affect or effect the show? What turns the feminist classroom into Professor Puck's performance space and how do voice and agency improve the professor's acting?* Finally, the professor directly addresses the drama that has been brewing all semester by asking the class: *How and why does the methodology make the madness?*

After spending hours practicing and prepping in chapter 8, "If It's Tuesday It Must Be Improv," the professor has to throw away all her meticulously prepared lesson plans five minutes into the main show. She must rely instead on instinct born of experience, and improvisation as the way to reach the students. Here, the professor learns to lead by following the content of the classroom as it unfolds, rather than the form she had previously planned. This means that she may have to dramatically change or jettison the finished script at the last minute. Chapter 8 confronts the professor's reality of *not* knowing what exactly is going to happen on stage and the fact that giving up a certain amount of control is necessary for a thriving, feminist learning environment. This is truly "theater of the absurd" at its best. Just as the audience starts to nod off, resist, or explode with anger, the professor dares to explore the unexpected. Intellectual improvisation and pioneering inquiry is the answer.

In chapter 9 the "Backers and Flackers behind the Scenes" arrive in full academic regalia. These are the show makers and breakers: the producers, stagehands, directors, and technicians—that is, the students, faculty, and administration playing their appropriate, classically prescribed roles. This chapter asks, *Just what are the politics behind an administrative decision to make or cancel the classroom performance? And how does the professor keep the show going in spite of the institutional obstacles that suspicious colleagues continually throw in the way?* The backers-and-flackers chapter discusses how censorship of the script and style control—all issues that crowd and/or inhibit the academic performance—silence those brave, creative transgressors. What happens when the academy refuses to award the performance? The show must go on!

One of the hardest roles to play in the academy is that of mentor.

What are the boundaries and implications of mentoring in a feminist classroom? Chapter 10, "Power Plays in the Master Class," discusses the question of mentoring and how it relates to academic leadership: *to lead or not to lead, to be a role model or not to care at all*. Furthermore, what are the benefits and burdens of teaching students how to "act"? What qualities enhance the mentor's performance; what behaviors are over-reaching? And when is enough assistance too much, and thus a reflection of harmful, stereotypical maternalism? This chapter looks at the power the professor has to "call back" some students for that highly coveted second audition, while ignoring others who are less flamboyant or dramatic in the classroom. But in the feminist classroom, everybody is a "work in progress," including the mentor herself, who is also in need of mentoring. (Some) students, then, can be the unacknowledged mentors of their professors in the traditional academy, just as they wrestle (most likely for the first time) with their newly defined and publicly acknowledged position of importance evoked by feminist pedagogy.

To those who are listening, I say: Let the show begin.

Act 1

Warm-up

All the Classroom's a Stage

i was born in 1954, a good year. Three important events occurred in the year of my birth that forty-five years later continue to influence my behavior in the classroom. I begin with the most politically salient of events, the monumental Supreme Court decision of *Brown v. Board of Education*, which decided once and for all that separate is never equal. Around the same time this decision was handed down, the first official broadcast of color TV occurred in the United States. Until then, color chrome transmission was incompatible with the ubiquitous black-and-white, flat monochrome broadcasts. Third was the introduction of frozen TV dinners into busy households all across North America. That desegregation, color TV, frozen TV dinners, and I were all "born" the same year is not unrelated to how the classroom became my permanent stage of preference. Or to the performance of feminist pedagogy

As Henry Miller said, "Whenever a taboo is broken, something good happens, something vitalizing. . . . Taboos after all are only hangovers, the products of diseased minds, you might say, of fearsome people who hadn't the courage to live and who under the guise of morality and religion have imposed things upon us" (interview, Plimpton 1963). The year of my birth was a year of taboo breaking: for the first time, Black and White children were to be educated in the same classroom. Gorgeous nappy hair sat next to shining golden locks, beautiful brown eyes shared the new view with luminescent baby blues; the images we received ceased to be represented in multiple shades of black and white, while the dinners we ate were suddenly, orgasmically popped into over-heated, preheated ovens, thus freeing our preciously gendered but exhausted mothers from hours of preparation. All the while leaving a population at large in the perpetual political state of needing a good leg-islative thaw. *Brown v. Board of Education* turned the classroom into a performance space of race and rage to be acted *out* and *upon* forever into the future of these un-United States.

I was precipitously born into a world in which the classroom was radicalized, politicized, and polarized. The classroom became the national stage to rehearse desegregation for the next fifty years. Historically these events are intricately bound together in my imagination, until death do us part. The various meanings of "colored," as in colored TV or colored person who was to be miraculously transformed into person of color by the current nonpermanent, ever-changing lexicon, successfully impressed upon me this country's pernicious obsession with all things colored.

I too became obsessed with color and all her variant and sundry human performances. Color forever remains an important signifier in my role as a feminist professor—from what I wear to who sits in class, looking blankly, staring intently, or peering impassively, all the while lo-cating me at the center of an already decentered gaze. By now, there are a few things I know for sure. That color communicates across barriers of power in the classroom. That a red-and-green velveteen dress on a Jewish lesbian femme professor is never just a red-and-green dress. (About roses, Gertrude was right; about dresses, she didn't understand a damn thing.) And that I can use or abuse this color-coded knowledge as I so choose; and so can my Anglo, African-American, Chicano, Caribbean, Sephardic, Mizrachi, Ashkenazi, Hispanic or Latino, Irish, Korean, Hmong, Vietnamese, and Indian students. The stage is set for guerilla theater long before I ever enter the ivy league.

So what if all the classroom is a colored-coded stage? What does this mean for the professor professing feminism directly as the subject matter of the course itself, as in my Introduction to Women's Studies ("5A") class, or indirectly in the style of the pedagogy? It means that our classrooms are not stable sites sanctimoniously blessed with the security of the professors' infinite wisdom, and that our students are never har-nessed in their seats, taking copious notes minute by indefatigable minute. The movement is continuous, the exchange always contiguous, back and forth, from student to teacher, teacher to student, and student to student. Fluid by nature, not nurture.

When the stage is set, the classroom is live, not static; from every orifice the drama oozes. It is precisely this free-floating tension that most professors have traditionally suppressed, reined in the first day, from the moment the first page of the intricately prepared syllabus that hasn't changed in years is read out loud in a megaphone of a voice. It's a known, truly quantifiable fact that in the traditional undergraduate classroom stasis "feels" secure and retains the appearance of absolute control. But in theater—academic and non—there is electricity; the charge on stage ignites the audience sitting on the edge of their upholstered seats. In theater tension is a must, a necessary precursor to the transformative moment. I have fitfully come to understand that in the classroom a lack of tension equals an almost total lack of true learning.

At this point I am reminded of the frozen TV dinners in need of a good thaw. That is how I understand the moment of my own successful rebirth into a performance artist and the consequent birth of my students. By the time they walk, slouch, crouch, tear ten minutes late into class, they have often already been frozen by the ice of conservatism, Disneyed into swirls of pastel-colored pops who want to move to towns called Celebration, and then Mac'd through their adolescent years into perfectly shaped, uniform cubes of automatic, automated McStudents. In short, students today need to chill. Out. They need to reattach their detached selves. (And so do we, their not so benevolent, often still frozen, professors.) The students will be the first to say so, given a real live opportunity. Just ask.

I do. From the stage, I look directly, intently, dramatically into the first row. With a gaze that is both serious and insistent I make the rounds, row by row, to the back of the room.

"Where are you?" I ask. "Tell me, I want to know." The automation of their minds is stopped by the very realness of the question itself. That's when the stage comes into focus and how the traditional classroom becomes one of many necessary sites of resistance to the future of the status quo.

Of course this means that the professor has already melted to some degree or is ready for the M&M challenge, when the well-rehearsed lecture melts in the mouth, not in the hand that holds the notes. Each fall, reprinting my 5A course syllabus, I understand this formidable challenge. Because I know that no one (except me, myself, and I) will ever know if I don't change a word on the page or off. It's so deliciously tempting not to change a single solitary thing. But if I long for my students to thaw out long enough to resist the repetition of the well-established, all-too-familiar dominant paradigm, I too have to participate in the terrifying act of the intellectual meltdown. I simply cannot ask the students to do anything I do not ask of myself. And so I have come to accept that when I open my mouth, having over the years polished my introductory remarks to near perfection, I must admit that I know not entirely from whence I speak. When in the middle of a Maslow peak experience I lift mine eyes from the valley of my glorious and sacred field notes to look out unto the groundswell of new arrivals, I know that last year's anecdotes just won't work. I must risk something new.

Just ask Marilyn Monroe, who like my students longed for stability off the Hollywood stage. She married Joe DiMaggio. (1954 was also the year of their wedding.) To Marilyn I am forever grateful. She was postmodern before postmodern. She was fluid and mercurial and moody and tragic; modified by herself and commodified by everybody else. She had no structure. While tragic figures make good history they do not ultimately make good teachers. What Marilyn craved was not unlike the academic cravings of many of my colleagues and students at home and across the nation: security and *macho* stability. Sprinkled with the oregano of a life based on nuclear predictability and a string of home runs, Joe wanted status and beauty. He wanted to be envied for his brilliant taste in the opposite sex. But the marriage of opposing opposites failed one year later because neither Marilyn nor Joe understood the exact role *Marilyn* was supposed to play. And that is the current classroom dilemma. What is the role of the classroom professor if not to transform the lecture hall into a contemporary performance space, to move completely away from the singular act of the magnificent monologue while simultaneously embracing a full-bodied discourse based on uneven, fragmented, prodigious dialogue? To follow that infamous yellow-booked road, not to the Emerald City, but into the City of the Unknown. This takes courage, a brain, and most of all a good, compassionate heart.

Enter guerilla theater stage left. Enter the feminist professor who understands that good pedagogy is up close and personal, rather than intimidating and detached. It is the most intimate of exchanges between actors and actresses whose diverse and discordant narratives are in great need of contextualization. In order for the stage to be set properly, the boundaries between personal space and national state must be collapsed. Students arrive on campus from disparate sites both domestic and international. Exile is not a theoretical construct. My students are far closer to Genet and Algiers than Hemingway and Africa. Their families fled the former Soviet Union; a brother was killed in a drive-by shooting in the Bronx; Orthodox Jewish parents refuse to acknowledge their lesbian daughter; in India, the family was rich, while in the States the father is jobless and depressed as the mother barters social capital for food in the underground economy. Their narratives continue unabated, refusing homogenization, as entire Hmong communities relocate by sheer force of will to the freezing temperatures of Minnesota; a mother raises three children all alone in a one-bedroom apartment while the father remains behind in Korea; a daughter left Vietnam for a refugee camp when she was six, and two years later travelled alone to New York City; Jewish students whose grandparents died in Dachau sit next to Cambodian students who speak of Pol Pot's regime as "the Holocaust"; and African Americans don't understand Jamaicans who don't understand the Cape Verdean students. The locations by themselves are confusing; context is everything as students from India call some people "colored" with all the acceptable cultural familiarity of their homeland, without recognizing that in the United States they offend African Americans for whom the word *colored* is degrading; and the Israelis have all carried guns and served in the army—an anathema to many other Brandeis students. As the classroom becomes a surreal microcosm of international border disputes, theater becomes the only sensible response. The borders of race and rage, color and class, gender and sex must be acted out within the drama of the moment.

Simultaneously the border between the "head" of the seminar and the heads of the participants must be opened for frequent, unencumbered travel. The traffic of ideas must be permitted to flow uninhibited. This does not mean a chaotic free-for-all. Eye contact is essential. Good theater depends on connection. In many different languages, I learn my students' names, (and demand they do the same) from Daveka to Hahn from Rachim to Yasmin, from over seventy in a single class to as few as fifteen. As though this were a grand accomplishment, I am heralded all over campus. Not for the skill of my rigorous teaching, but for my now infamous ability to recall the first and last names of every student. But names are basic to our humanity.

Last semester, in teaching a course on Blacks and Jews, it took the Black students almost half the semester to say my name out loud, F2F, to me, whenever we spoke. Week after week, I waited for the familiar sound of my name. I would have patience. One day, when I least expected it, I heard the words themselves spoken out loud. My name. Turning around, I smiled when I saw the speaker waiting impatiently for me to answer the question. I knew then that I had ceased to be just another person of whiteness, one of those ubiquitous, anonymous professors. It is in guerilla theater, when we cease to be that anonymous population at large, that the humanity of the community is being preserved, not usurped for some greater institutional good.

To turn the classroom from lecture hall to center stage is to risk being misunderstood by both colleagues and students. "Staging" the classroom is often trivialized or exoticized. But that's the challenge. To embrace the risk with gusto and relish. To risk being misunderstood goes against the training of both my Hebraic culture and female sex. As an Ashkenazi Jew, assimilation into American culture after the *Shoah* had been the performance of choice. To not stand out or call attention to myself or my family in any particular way. To lose *the accent* yesterday was the goal. As a Jewish woman, it was always better to be seen and not heard, a role I had the most difficulty learning to play. But it is an indisputable fact that Jews and women have been performing before kings and czars, presidents and prime ministers, for centuries; our very survival depended upon just such a grand showing. So when I make my entrance, which I am sure to do, circling around the proscenium with arms raised high, calling the class to undivided attention, I understand: I have been in training for transforming the classroom. It is uniquely genetic, an inherited, political condition that I have finally accepted with all the grace and skill of a seasoned Amazon. I too must resist the seductive, all too familiar, and comforting pull of the omnipresent ideology of the dominant, paradigmatic classroom.

The problem comes from not being recognized and accepted; when what I'm doing is held suspect inside all that climbing ivy. "She doesn't lecture, she performs." My teaching has become unrecognizable to most everyone but the students themselves, who spend semester after semester with me. With this I must make my peace. I understand that when I walk to class, I must walk as though through an underground tunnel, so as not to be diverted from my path by all those quizzical, highly academic glances. I must trust that I will arrive at my destination unscathed. I enter the room alone, before a single student arrives. I need the quiet of the empty space. Because soon, I know, it will be full to brimming with an energy too hot to touch. When the first student enters and the invisible curtain rises, the class is mine and I am theirs.

First Movement

The preperformance begins with resistance—not mine, but the students'. For this I am now prepared. Holding my breath, I scan the audience. "How many of you consider yourselves feminists?" Out of seventy-plus, fifteen female hands with fingernails painted in all the new, raging shades, plus a few unpainted male ones, stick straight up into the unfiltered air. I wait before taking a quick count. If it's a good semester, I count twenty hands. Their eyes are watching me. "What's a feminist?" The dialogue begins. Moments later, there is the crescendo of deep academic silence, spreading fast throughout the room like a highly contagious disease that no one wants to catch. (Feminism is ultimately, feverishly contagious.) No one wants to answer or misanswer as the case may be. I wait. The students are very concerned, to the point of major preoccupation with the right answer. I wait. But I won't tell them, as if I know the absolute, most correct definition of this totally misunderstood and abused term. "Write down whatever you think a feminist is." There is the rustle of papers, followed by multiple sounds of annoyance, and then, finally, the quiet I have come to love and others fear. No one has ever asked them this question before. The electricity works. We are plugged in to each other. I know I have their complete attention because I feel the tension that used to scare me so very much. I have decentered the classroom right before their own eyes and mine. The house lights are turned off me, the professor, and directly onto the students, who rapidly fill center stage. What the students think, matters.

Now what? I tell them to turn to the person on the right, and compare notes. I wait for the buzz that heats up the room. "First, introduce yourself, make sure you know who you're sitting next to, what their name is." *This doesn't feel like college. It's too easy.* I know what they're thinking. Although I see them talking to each other, I am not interested in monitoring their conversations. They are free to say whatever they want, even to waste time gossiping. But already something significant has occurred. I have trusted them, without saying so explicitly. Without warning them to take this exercise seriously, I establish a certain synergy in the classroom. Slowly, the students realize, not without a small amount of trepidation, that this exercise is for real. They will be asked to discuss publicly their ideas, to agree, to disagree. The script writes itself. This is not a touchy, feel-good workshop.

I write the stage directions in my class notes. Where do I want to go, which way do I want to take the class? For the next thirty minutes, I call on students at random whether or not they raise their hands. (How unfeminist of me, one female student says. On the contrary, is my adamant reply.) I read names from the roster because it is after all the first day. I am less concerned with any one particular answer than with the drama of a succinct, successful interrogation. Intentionally, I set the tone for the entire semester. I want the class engaged. I want them to care and to learn to listen not just to me, but to each other. The resistance begins to shift, ever so slightly, away from me and the material. This is an unpredictable process that I have come to trust implicitly. Like and actor on opening night, I have a strong sense of what will happen as future performances unfold.

Guerilla theater then, is not *on* Broadway; it is *off* the beaten path. It is the classroom politicized. It is recognizing that neutrality is a fiction and agendas are endemic to the academic experience. And that dialogue, the "act" of talking and talking back, is a must. At first students think it's fun, not serious, this dialogue thing. They keep waiting for me to lecture, as 5A meets for *three hours* once a week. I don't. I rarely talk for more than ten minutes at once, and then it's usually in the form of questions, which is the way Jewish scholars study Torah. There are no answers, of this I am sure. With this lack of any one specific answer they are always frustrated and furious.

Second Movement

I give the students the article "A Wedding on a Caribbean Mountaintop" to read in class the first day, program notes of performances to come. It is a personal essay, a story. Their confusion is total.

This is not a complicated, highly theoretical essay that they will be quizzed on in fifteen minutes. It is the story of a Jewish family, written by the mother, who travel to an island in the Caribbean for the daughter's wedding. The key elements of the story include: a woman rabbi flown in for the ceremony, teaching the Caribbeans about Jewish wedding customs, building a *chupah*, flying the guests in from all across the United States, requesting that the French chef make a round, braided challah, stuffed with raisins, for the ceremony, and the specific name of the resort itself as listed in the marketing brochures. "Please underline anything that has to do with Women's Studies or feminism," I tell the class. *This is too easy. What is she talking about?* They are bewildered, my students. I do not help them out of their confusion. "Check in with your neighbor," I say.

I want them to learn from each other, to take their cues and clues not from me, but from their classmates. Finally, I address the room. "Let's talk."

"About what?" someone in the front row asks.

Raising my eyebrows and moving stage left, I gallop across the proscenium in my red-and-green velveteen dress. The students stare as if I have morphed into a wild-eyed, uncontrollable mare right before their very eyes, a *vilde chaye*.

"I know what you're thinking," they laugh when I throw back my short, just-dyed-the-color-of-Beaujolais, clipped mane.

This is performing. No, this is teaching. Actually it is performing teaching. But the form is unrecognizable. I want the students to understand that it is the *content* that defines the form and not the other way around as we have all been led to believe.

Someone says that the fact that the rabbi is a woman relates to this class.

"Why?" I want to know, knowing that I will not say another word.

"It doesn't matter," a small nervous voice speaks into the cavernous hall.

"Yes it does!" A woman with fantastic silver and gold piercings stubbornly shakes her head.

Content, not form, I think to myself while looking back at a totally exasperated audience. *How long can I tolerate that they are no longer with me?*

"The rabbi isn't doing anything different than a male rabbi does." In a thick Russian accent, the student pronounces each syllable slowly.

The entire class shifts in their seats as though a religious earth-quake of seismic proportion just ripped through Lown Auditorium on the Brandeis campus, canceling Yom Kippur for the year 5758.

I see that the tension has become unbearable; the students want me to be the professor and intervene. To explain immediately how it is a woman rabbi can be exactly the same as a male rabbi. It's the perfect time to continue.

I wait. The students wait. *This is Intro to Women's Studies, isn't it? And the rabbi's a woman.* They mumble just loud enough for me to hear. They are angry, but at what they don't know exactly.

Finally it is time for intermission. But I want to give them some-thing to think about, to feel as they rush from the room to inhale their nicotine in fits. According to the stage directions, by now I have moved myself to the far right, decentering my position as professor.

Later, one of the students will come to see me privately, to confess that she doesn't think I really listen to the class because I am never standing in the middle of the room, looking directly at the students. I nod, surprised that this complaint would come from a student with ex-tremely short orange hair and a pierced left eyebrow. Here the content truly doesn't match the form. Her behavior doesn't match her costume. So it's true: looks are ultimately deceiving. The roles students play don't always match the lines they say. What is the subtext here, the private, personal drama of this indignant female student? She is playing protec-tress, caring for the entire class out of her own discomfort; she is per-forming the traditional female role of caretaker while dressing the part of a woman warrior.

How to explain that I actually listen better standing off to the side and so do the students? (I'm not the one she should be watching.) For her, authority figures are infinitely desirable and die a hard, slow, ex-tremely drawn-out death. I have performed badly and have temporarily failed this woman. I am disappointed that her only feedback was about a decentered center. But I understand that the noble pull for a heroic leader is stronger than the student can bear.

The students are desperate for a break. A few have started coughing.

"What's the name of the resort?" I will let go in a minute.

"Plantation Inn." Three rows back from the front, it is the nervous voice again.

"What is being suggested by the name of the inn?"

They are caught off guard. This is getting too hard, too confusing. In my first years of teaching, at this point I was sure the entire class hated me, and that I could predict exactly what they would write in their evaluations. Now, I refuse to perform for the evaluations.

The dialogue continues as we deconstruct the word *plantation* and discuss why it might be used to describe a Caribbean resort catering to wealthy White North Americans. The only two Black students are smiling as the White kids struggle to comprehend what's being acted out. A couple of students have been to this resort, including one of my teaching assistants, who hasn't stopped taking notes since class began.

Swallowing hard before speaking, and choosing my words carefully, I ask a question. "What if the resort was called the Auschwitz Inn?"

There is absolute silence. And horror. I reach for the Mogen David, the Star of David, around my neck. *It's in the stage notes.* I must remind the majority of the students that I am one of them, that I understand their discomfort.

I glance down at the page.

Intermission.

Finally.

Intermezzo: The Space Between

It took me a long time to understand the students' resentment. That although they came to enjoy or even look forward to the weekly three-hour performances in 5A, they didn't know what to do when they left class. I didn't understand what they were saying. What exactly were they so upset about? "Are you bored?" I asked. *No. Never.* "Then what's the problem?" They didn't recognize the form anywhere else on campus and they felt betrayed. By me. I was shocked. *By me?* They had come to like, appreciate, the style of the class. But sitting in their other classrooms became a nightmare. They were restless and uninterested. The status quo was disrupted and they didn't know what to do. This is the consequence of a good performance.

In a good performance the audience feels just as important as the performer because the performer is only as good as the audience. That is, there is no authentic performance without the audience. And because it's so good, the audience never wants the show to end. You want more. You want to stuff yourself because it tastes so scrumptious that you feel fantastically satisfied. And you want everyone else to stuff themselves too. The whole world should be full. Their impatience mirrors my own. A student raises her hand. She tells the class that in her History 10A class the professor consistently lectures nonstop for an hour and thirty minutes. The students silently take notes the entire time. She can't listen anymore; she's afraid of failing the midterm. And it's all my fault. The rest of the class nods in agreement.

The classroom has become an activist community center where learning is a dynamic force. The classroom is a community of multiple protagonists playing multiple roles simultaneously. I want to tell this student that her rage is misdirected, but I don't. I nod, smiling slightly. This is part of the dramatic tension. She doesn't know it but her performance is stupendous: the damsel in distress finds her voice. The roles keep changing from Ophelia to Antigone, forward and backward. Toward the middle of the semester, students want to bring their friends, brothers, sisters, mothers, fathers, uncles, and aunts. They want everyone to see the performance and to see them perform.

I feel protective. I'm not sure what to do. I do not want to objectify the class or commodify the experience. Especially challenging are the women students who want to bring their boyfriends. "Tell them to take the class." They shake their heads. One semester I compromise, and after a brief discussion the class votes. They decide to call the day "bring your 'boyfriends' (*sic*) to class." The day was a fiasco. I should have known. We are not a traveling troupe—*la grande cirque du soleil*—on exhibition. There is a difference between performance for the sake of entertainment and performance that is integral to the process of learning. The students for a long time confuse the two. In the beginning, it's all a really good show to them. The best three hours of the week. Until they begin to understand. Then they get it, utterly and completely. No more requests for visitors. It doesn't work for them. The integrity of the classroom is at stake.

Fiascoes must be integrated into the performance with an appropriate response following quickly. Unlike recently in Belgium and France, when some people got sick from drinking Coca-Cola. The company made the grave mistake of not immediately acknowledging what had happened. Instead, they pretended it was nothing. But the sickness spread across the borders, and anti-American sentiment grew strong. The company could not contain the fiasco. When it was too late, they apologized to the public and pledged to do better in the future. But in the classroom, pretense always fails. The performance (and apology when necessary) has to be real and fully realized or the audience will refuse to applaud—and demand a refund.

This way of teaching is exhausting yet exhilarating. But good, satisfying, hard work *is* always exhausting. The whole self is pulled in, mind and body, spirit and soul. While teaching from the neck up is often easier, the result is usually extreme back pain. I bend and stretch and tell the students to do the same. When they are sleeping, I say, "Stand up." They think I'm kidding. But this is live theater. I do not want them to get too comfortable. Although the unexpected and unplanned consequence of this is that I too often feel uncomfortable while in the act of performing.

Then why do it? Why teach 'til you drop? Colleagues question both my motives and my credibility, which count for a lot in the academy. Sometimes I want to win an Academy Award, as if that would settle the question once and for all. But the problem is, at most universities those highly coveted teaching awards are quietly understood to be the end of the life of the tenure-track professor. So public recognition is not a guarantee of acceptance after all. And I am reminded of all those blue eyes that Toni Morrison's young Black female protagonist craved. She didn't realize that acceptance is mercurial and unreliable. Blue eyes are not the solution or exoneration. Blue eyes are simply blue.

If the classroom is going to be a stage, then all the performers must understand the nature of the risk involved. This means that teaching on the edge is edgy. The rewards of a good performance are almost always internal, not external. To desire otherwise is to misunderstand. To perform week after week is to walk out on the edge and know that you will neither fail nor fall. The key is to recognize that you are an intellectually, dramatically, totally committed trapeze artist possessing a rare and unique talent that is not quantifiable. That walking out on the academic tight rope, balanced precariously between the institutional status quo and the unrecognizable future, you will know that the ground beneath you will not break your bones, severing forever your spinal chord at the base of the neck. I trust that I will not end up paralyzed for the rest of my academic life. If I fall, I will float to the ground with a graceful ease. I know, because I have fallen and the students have risen to catch me.

Like a dazzling *pas de deux,* the teacher falls, her students cradle her descent; the students fall, the teacher reaches out, extending both arms, cushioning their crash to earth. It is a silent fall, deep and mysterious. Terrifying in its own right. Because once the pretense is gone, the students sense the professor's vulnerability. That is the greatest fear: to allow oneself to be truly naked in the performance of teaching. At this moment, the student's gaze extends well beyond the lines of my red-and-green velveteen dress. There is a communion of sorts when they understand that if the professor's costume is not permanent or fixed then neither is their own. There is relief and there is terror as the house lights come on. By the end, they understand that I never know exactly what to wear to class; it depends on the topic of the day.

After teaching a particularly arduous class, I go home to my color TV. Removing the frozen TV dinner from its sealed packaging, I pop it into the microwave and switch channels until the news comes on. Ward Connerly is on NBC raving about his plan to dismantle affirmative action across this great country of ours. About how it's the quality of the performance not the color of the skin that counts. Eating the steaming vegetarian lasagna, I put my fork down. Just which performance is Ward talking about?

Forty-five years after the year I was born, my obsession with all things colored is flying still, sky high. In the street, I stare into windows. Gorgeous nappy heads are sitting farther and father away from those shining golden locks. Beautiful brown eyes stare at rows of empty seats while luminescent baby blues are nowhere in sight. The performance of *Brown v. Board of Education* has become a farce, but with color TV we have been much more successful. The image travels easier than the reality. Instantaneously we move from the Sudan to Belfast, from New York City to Tel Aviv. It's the classroom that is frozen in time and all the inhabitants therein.

The curtain has failed to rise on a different kind of stage. And the performance has yet to begin. If Ward Connerly has his way, by tomorrow there will be more color on TV than in the academy. We will return to a stage set in black or white—a flat monochrome of an image. The dialogue will cease to be, and the monologue will return to center stage. We will rehearse the old scripts, changing very little. The dramatic moment will fizzle out, replaced with the familiarity of repetition.

I refuse this scenario. Scene after scene, I will continue to play the roles I am in training for. My own integrity is on the line. When I rise in the morning, before I have my coffee. I close my eyes one more time. I see a single wire hanging taut, limb to limb, tree to tree, spread all across the Brandeis campus. I choose my costume carefully. It is late September, after all, and a cool New England breeze fills the air. I am trying out a new trick, a balancing act of extreme proportions, and I am not sure exactly what to wear to get the point across.

I settle on black from head to toe, with a handmade shawl entwined with threads of silver and gold. Stepping gingerly out onto the wire, I decide to let go, once and for all. I fly across campus with gusto. I fly through the air, confident that my students are flying right beside me. We are on the tightrope together and have stopped looking back at Mr. Connerly, whose most recent appearance was on *The Tonight Show* with Jay Leno. I open my eyes, drink my coffee, and leave for school.

It is the last class of the semester, no one wants to leave even though this particular performance is over. *Finis.*

"What meant the most to you?" I say to the student on my right.

"Names." Her eyes are meeting mine.

"Names?" I'm thinking *plantation, Auschwitz.*

"That you learned all our names. That was just awesome."

I take a slight, almost imperceptible bow when the last student leaves Lown Auditorium.

Curtain

Long Day's Journey into the Classroom

The words *spectator*, *spectacle*, and *spectacular* have been linked together in my imagination since 1963, the year John F. Kennedy was assassinated. Recall, if you will, the media production: the long line of slowly moving black limousines, convertible in style—top down, as the presidential couple waved nonstop to the crowd, who eagerly waved back. The cameras rolled. Jackie was in pearls and pink, matching from head to toe, top to bottom. (Her blood-stained dress is now part of the permanent Smithsonian collection to be viewed and reviewed.) Auburn-haired Jack smiled broadly and boyishly, each cheek big as a ripe Georgia peach; Dallas belonged to him. The streets were lined with nuclear families; local schools were closed and the Stars and Stripes blew free in the cool fall air, topping every Texas mast. It was the quintessential American moment: patriotic and monumental.

Without warning a single bullet soared through Camelot and into the homes of millions of Americans. This was a tragedy of epic proportion in living, breathing color. And all colors mourned the loss of the president, as though he and they had been intimately, intricately bound up in the daily minutiae of each others' lives. They had and they were. That's how the assassination became a *coup de théâtre* and much later an Oliver Stone "spectacle" to be replayed over and over again. The entire citizenry, coast to coast, played the wide-eyed spectators, while the grief itself was a spectacular, infinite, and uncontrollable outpouring of genuine, unaffected sorrow. This was a spontaneous combustion on a naïve domestic front. Nearly four decades later, the hold on the national imagination is a permanent visegrip of the mind.

On a single day in Dallas all lines were blurred between the personal and the political. In an instant, the public space of a downtown Texas city blurred with all the private, psychedelic orange shag-carpeted living rooms across America. There was little difference between the grieving national widow, so young, bright, and stunningly beautiful, and all other Americans, who themselves were simultaneously widowed without warning. Teachers dropped the yellow chalk in their hands, stopped algebra lessons in the middle, or abruptly ended class discussion on *The Old Man and the Sea*. They started sobbing hysterically, right in front of their students, as the news that the President of the United States of America had been shot and killed came piping into the classroom through the PA system. It was a magnificent, spellbinding production of huge historical *and* theatrical importance. Classes were immediately dismissed. Ten years old, I watched the whole show dramatically unfold on TV. Regular programming was interrupted for the rest of the week. The whole country sat *shivah* for years to come.

This is how it is in the classroom when there is an intellectual crisis of pedagogical importance. Regular programming is interrupted as the preplanned lesson is dropped. The professor is forced to stop. She must attend to the spectacle unfolding in front of her, and the spectacular outpouring of emotion coming from the students instantaneously turned spectators. (Spectators are not to be confused with bystanders who simply stand by, or witnesses, who watch, remember, and later often record.) The spectacle can come from the outside as in the O.J. Simpson verdict, or it can originate organically and unintentionally, as a consequence of the class material itself. Either way, the situation must be confronted; spectacles will not be ignored. This is what happened (in my class) thirty-five years after John F. Kennedy was assassinated.

The topic for the day was *Transforming Masculinity and Structural Violence Against Women*. In the first hour of class, a Brandeis student who listens to gangsta rap and belongs to an off-campus (and officially banned) fraternity talked about being male and feminist; about how important feminism is in his relationships with men and women;

and the contradiction of being a feminist man and a rap aficionado, which meant he could not ignore the misogyny and violence against women pervading the music he listened to nonstop. The students listened appreciatively as Eric discussed the contradictions in his life. Applauding when he finished, they asked a lot of questions.

Seguéing into the concept of structural violence and how the state responds, I showed a British film on a staged police investigation of an alleged date rape. Although the alleged rape is never shown, the film proved to be far more traumatic for the class as a whole than I had prepared for. In the video, which describes an alleged date rape and the immediate aftermath, friends who went out together to a London pub for the evening are interviewed by the police. From a teaching point of view, I thought the depiction of the process of a police investigation and interrogation would be demystifying for the students. It was my hope that students (who had been or would be) involved socially either by association or as victims themselves could learn to speak up, to get help finding their voices through watching the video and then deconstructing it. I was wrong; we never got that far. Almost immediately, I realized that the students' reaction was as if they were viewing an actual rape unfolding right in front of them rather than a simulation drama of a police investigation of a date rape. As the alleged victim described her confusion over how an evening out with good friends could turn so violent, some women students walked out of class.

At first, the interval between departures was paced at ten minutes apart, but gradually the speed picked up, until the students went from leaving the room abruptly to absolute flight in less than five minutes. No one said a word. I was stunned. Let's be clear: this was not an imitation 1960s-style protest. *This* had never happened before in twenty years of teaching. Oh, occasionally a single student might walk out, go to the bathroom, and then return, slipping unobtrusively back into her seat. But this was entirely different. What felt like a mass female exodus occurred in my own Women's Studies class.

My first thought was to contain the great gendered departure before word leaked out from one end of bucolic Brandeis to the other. I was panicked and felt extremely unprofessorial. Looking out at the "patriotic" spectators who remained in their seats allowed me to relax and calm down slightly. In a flash, I realized this was all part of the show. And that the show must go on. But what was the show *now*, and how should I continue? This premature all-female departure before the performance had ended was not written anywhere in the script. But spontaneous combustion is a feminist moment of performance pedagogy *not* to be missed or misunderstood. On the contrary, it must be inventively reworked immediately as the drama itself unfolds. Just as in the death of JFK, when the media instantaneously reframed the assassination in terms of the ironic and tragic consequences of life in a democratic state. The script, after all, is live, not static.

Anna Deavere Smith, the performance artist, talks about creating a new civic dialogue where the artist and the community meet at a new location of aesthetic excellence and social concern (for more information, see the Institute on the Arts and Civic Dialogue at Harvard in association with the American Repertory Theatre and the W. E. B. Du Bois Institute). Smith urges the artist to leave the safety of her studio and the public to take leave of their own familiar outposts. Both parties should move to someplace different. Applying Smith's new aesthetic to the classroom experience means that the professor and the student(s)—like the solo artist and the community—must travel together to destinations previously unknown. A risky proposition. But in the classroom risk is essential to a good performance.

I wondered when some women walked out of the room how we could "safely" travel to destinations new and unknown and what civic dialogue was possible. And what specifically had so disrupted their sense of equilibrium in the classroom that they had actually felt the need to physically remove themselves from the offending space. I had to rethink my own pedagogical assumptions about *safety*. I knew that in their anonymous written evaluations students always wrote that "Felman's classes are safe," and that I create an atmosphere for them to explore difficult topics. But in retrospect, and after discussing what had happened with many of my colleagues, it seems obvious that there are different and multiple levels of safety operating simultaneously. It is the *performance of safety* in the feminist classroom that I didn't understand clearly before the walk-out. In leaving abruptly, without even the briefest explanation, the students were actually *performing safety* on their terms. The students (by leaving the room) felt safe enough to perform (for me and their classmates) their very real discomfort, formidable rage, and/or sheer terror at what was happening in the present moment. They understood intuitively that they would not be punished, have their grades lowered, or be reprimanded in any way. Ultimately, there would be no negative repercussions. They were performing feminist pedagogy in action, only I didn't recognize it at the time. They were in essence exercising their full rights and responsibilities as spectators to reject the show and create their own spectacle instead. I had prepared for the students to have strong reactions to the material—but not this strong! And I had chosen the reading assignments carefully. We were to have an in-depth discussion following the video, first in pairs, and then as a group. I understand now that I could never have prepared for just how strong the reactions were that day. That is exactly the point, treacherous as it is from the teacher's perspective.

At Brandeis, when I entered Lown Auditorium I had left the safety of the artist's studio and had assumed that the students too had eagerly left the security of their dorm rooms so that we could meet at a new site of transformation and civic discourse. *Why else had they "elected" to take the course?* I asked myself. Instead, the students played an unexpected role, literally running out on me *and* the performance. Because their comfort zone had been dislodged, they had to get out. This was not what the students had expected in 5A. So they had to return to the familiarity of their dorm rooms. Every year I struggle with how to teach this particular class. I have invited specialists in the field of violence against women to address the students. I have shown other videos. In every case, there is some kind of unexpected reaction that requires immediate attention.

I have come to accept (not without trepidation) that the spontaneous departure was inevitable and will happen again. And again. Professors who *perform* rather than *profess* must be prepared for just such explosions. The content of the course that day was in large part the issue. Violence against women, in theory and practice, is explosive. And explosions in class are often content-specific, as well as personal, in the sense that the students felt close enough to me to show their true reactions. There was no pretense in their performance. Explosions are also a consequence of blurring the boundaries. Whenever the public, fixed borders are broken (as in the JFK assassination), both professors and students cease to "perform" in expected, predictable ways. This is good. The challenge is to prepare the students (and yourself, the professor) as much as possible for a dislodging of the self and the resulting emotional and intellectual discomfort that is sure to follow, while recognizing the contradictory reality that there is no absolute prophylactic preparation that will dissolve a disruption before it ever happens. That's the nature of spontaneous combustion. Besides, discomfort is intrinsic to any revolutionary learning process. If I am to take performing in the classroom seriously, I need to prepare the students to walk on the edge of their own particularized, socially constructed and culturally influenced "safe" zones. For it is at the center of the disarmed moment that a new civic dialogue is possible. Students need help sitting with their own discomfort as the performance edges closer and closer to the veritable edge, erasing the demarcations between "them" and "us." You and me. Professor and non.

While writing the above section, a student who had not walked out of class, but was furious with me at the time, wrote to me via e-mail. On impulse I asked her to discuss how she saw the class now, over six months later. Rachel responded with the following long, thoughtful answer, edited only for spelling.

> The difficult class—I was so angry at first. And unfortunately, I had fuel for the fire that came from students who had taken the class before and other students who were just as angry if not angrier than I was. I didn't stop to think about the point of the class or the fact that I had not done the readings, I was just angry. I was angry, I felt taken advantage of. I felt that Professor Felman had abused her power as the leader of the class and put us all in a situation we were not prepared for and did not know how to handle. It took me a long time to recognize the lessons of that class.
>
> If you take the statements out of context: "abuse of power," "put in a situation one is not prepared for and does not know how to handle" these are statements one might make when one is raped, and though it is still a hard topic to talk about and when speaking, I find I still stutter a bit or just hesitate to say "rape" or lower my voice, I am finding it important and therefore easier to talk about because it is a subject that needs to be discussed. I am very fortunate to say that I have never been raped. I don't know what it is like to have someone use their power against me so violently and to violate me so much. But

because of the "5A" class on rape, I understand better what it means to have someone misuse their power and take advantage of that. Again, that sounds funny . . . Why would anyone want to be in that kind of atmosphere and why would they come to appreciate it? Too many people are raped every day, every minute and like I said, I am very fortunate to not know what that is like. But now, at least, I have some however tiny feeling of what it is like to be in a very uncomfortable, difficult situation where I felt that I had no voice, no power to change things and no means to deal with what had happened.

Fortunately, . . . Felman made herself available to talk about the difficult experience and I was eventually able to find a voice (in the company of others who had gone through the same experience) and to speak up and say that I thought it was wrong what happened to our class. Too often, someone who has been raped is not able to understand that she/he can speak up can understand that what happened to her or him was not right and not his or her fault and never does the rapist make himself/herself available to discuss what happened. I am in no way comparing Professor Felman to a rapist but I do understand now that she wanted us to understand how a person with more power can very easily use that power in an unfair way and she wanted us to understand how difficult it is to address that misuse of power. I, for example, wasn't even going to speak to Professor Felman at first. I was just going to be angry. And then when I did decide to speak with her, I went with the comfort and support of three other women. It was still difficult to address the person that I felt had violated me in some way.

I think . . . Felman gave a lot of people more courage after that class—even if it took that person(s) a long time to recognize it. And I think Professor Felman taught an invaluable lesson (with that class). I still struggle with it because I don't know what it would have been like if I had ever been raped and had to sit (through that class) and relive my experience and I am nervous about this class for next year and the years to follow, but I think that is okay and I think it is still a necessary class to teach.

Again, it is important to take that risk and to make people uncomfortable and to talk about difficult issues. We can learn so much by doing so.

Reading Rachel's response now, and remembering her (six months ago) sitting in my office, angry and visibly hurting, reminds me how important it is to teach toward the edge. For when our students arrive at the precipice, the learning is profound.

This risk taking and lack of orderliness are distasteful to many of my colleagues. At this point, retreating behind the hard-won podium seems like a welcome relief for students and professors alike. But don't be fooled. This rupture of the classroom is what Anna Deavere Smith understands and what I myself continue to seek as a "necessary frenzy," which is something like keeping a pot of water at the boiling-over point, while not turning the heat down.

Each September, as I peruse my 5A syllabus with all the confidence of a well-seasoned performer who has learned from her own past miscues, I know with absolute certainty that there will be a disruption at some point, probably midsemester. When, exactly, I never can tell. But students will refuse to go along with the script that plays too close to the edge. As soon as a topic reaches the boiling-over point, they will walk out, and Smith's necessary frenzy will begin. The question is, will I the professor be ready whenever the eruption comes? Yes: I can hardly wait.

But it has taken years to prepare. And to not panic the moment the explosion (or exodus) begins. I think back: How did I come to make peace with the process of (dis)rupture? It has a lot to do with my own personal biography, the well-traveled terrain of a nonurban, decentralized, observant Jew born and bred in the "Buckeye" heartlands of a gentile Midwest, where rainstorms hit the flat city of Dayton, Ohio, in such gigantic proportions that everyone assumes they are postmodern plagues, the reaction of a very angry god. The electricity inevitably goes out for hours at a time. I used to be scared of the dark. Not believing that the lights would ever truly come back on. (This is a vengeful, punitive god.) But they always did. After the biblical storm there was always relief and the most wonderful calm imaginable. This became my metaphor when I stopped teaching and started performing. I tell myself today that after the storm that is sure to come, so will the calm spread like a warm afterglow, seeping gently, soothingly, into the very pores of my students' human existence.

The explosion in the feminist classroom is an intense emotional reaction that cannot be prevented or ignored. It must neither be feared nor thwarted by academic perfidy. It helps to understand "the outburst" as a theatrical equilateral triangle consisting of three parts, of *spectacle*, *spectator*, and *spectacular*. Otherwise the emotions left behind will infuse the classroom with high *drama* rather than the *dramatic* high that it ultimately can be. In the academy, "high drama" is *not* what I'm after but often what I'm mistaken for.

To understand that the students are *spectators* means that they come to participate and to perform and not to passively observe or preserve. To view the professor in terms of performance is to break the professorial mold, which then turns the classroom into a "spectacle" in the dramatic sense, *not* in a Disney-cartooned but predictable sensibility. And when the entire production is viewed as such, the explosion, disruption, and/or departure becomes a spectacular, pedagogical fireworks display—an event to watch, appreciate, and applaud in all its colorful, insightful splendor but not to take too personally (that response would be basic Freudian narcissism and not credible behavior in the classroom). The truth is, "shit" happens. Why pretend otherwise?

In the days following the walk-out, students stopped me in the halls and in Parking Lot E to urgently report that everyone on campus was talking about what had happened in 5A. Even a few colleagues e-mailed wondering what all the ruckus was about. It was disturbing. I spent the rest of the week searching for a way to contextualize what had happened. Significantly, on that day only the White women ran out of 5A, and the students of color didn't understand why. *"What was the big deal?"* they asked. I could only assume that their threshold of safety is much different from that of the students (all women) who fled.

The next Tuesday at the beginning of class, Thomas, an African-American student, raised his hand to speak. He was genuinely confused.

"None of us walked out two weeks ago when the topic was race," he said. "It didn't occur to me and I wasn't exactly comfortable with the way the discussion was going. With what was being said by the White students and all. . . ." The other students of color nodded in agreement. I waited. The class was stunned into a silence that spread thick and fast throughout the room. It was a wordless spectacle—and uncomfortable. There was little eye contact between the students. Everyone stared at me. I waited before wading into the stunning silence, choosing to let the students feel the full impact of Thomas's spontaneous words. It was important not to interrupt the silence too soon. Then, as that moment edged toward total discomfort, I spoke to my students. "So, is it true then, that one person's safety is another's terror, possibly even abuse?" A few students nodded. "Give me an example." Thomas raised his hand; I nodded and he spoke. "The police. The minute I see these guys or hear a siren, my whole body tenses and I know my time's coming." We moved slowly out of the silence as many White students acknowledged how they had always looked to the police for protection, while the students of color talked about being terrorized and routinely (and randomly) stopped on the street. As last week's fear dissipated, some of the Black students talked about their own experiences in other classrooms and exactly what safety meant for them. Christina, a woman from Cape Verde, said that if she walked out of the class every time she felt at risk, she would never be in class at all and that safety for her was different from what it meant for the White women who had walked out. And she said she personally had no positive feelings for the police. This was the other side of the (l)edge. The students had taken us there, themselves. Even though the memory of last week's combustion would linger on, we had successfully inched forward together. This time no one walked out!

The modern dancer Bill T. Jones created a new civic dialogue with his extraordinary choreographed composition *Still/Here*. He traveled around the country holding workshops for nondancers with terminal illnesses. Correspondingly, he was duplicating Anna Deavere Smith's new aesthetic, her "necessary frenzy," her boiling-over point. He took himself out of the safety of his own dancer's studio and requested that the terminally ill take themselves out of their familiar sickbeds. As a Black HIV-positive gay man, Jones many times before had left the safety of his own home. But on the country road, facing others who face imminent death, he had no idea what he would find. The result is stunning. Jones incorporated the eloquent words and the elegiac movements of those he met on the road into a major balletic tour de force that culminated with a MacArthur "genius award."

I show the Bill Moyers video of Jones working on *Still/Here* in all my Women's Studies classes. I want the students to understand *risk taking*, and that safety is an illusion, socially and politically constructed for the security of the White middle class. I want to prepare the students to go to the edge with me, stand on the ledge, and leap off. The people who participated in Jones's workshop, total strangers to each other, agreed to dance toward that edge. The risks were many. Most of the participants were White, and Jones, as an African American, had no idea what his reception as "teacher" would be. Most of the participants were heterosexual; Jones, an out, HIV-positive gay man, would be "touching" them. The risk was reciprocal; the dislodgment went both ways. No one ran away. How did Jones accomplish this with terminally ill people? How did he get the participants to sit with their own discomfort for the duration of the workshop and not flee instead?

He said he wanted to choreograph a dance based on *living* with a terminal illness, not dying, that in itself challenges the status quo. He made himself as vulnerable as his participants. In order to move the students forward, to get nondancers to dance and not fear ridicule, the professor has to set the scene, create the mood, and prepare the spectators for what they are about to partake. And yet there is no real preparation. Jones knows this, as does Anna Deavere Smith. You can only set the stage, create the space for the spectacle to happen. (You can't make the spectacle happen your way.) But understanding ahead of time that something *will* happen, which these two prodigious artists understand, is what it's all about.

I have learned most of my feminist performance pedagogy from the arts rather than from the theory of education itself. What I am after is the realization of the peak dramatic experience: when in *Angels in America* Roy Cohn, emaciated and dying, begs a weary Ethel Rosenberg not for forgiveness, but to say the Kaddish for him, the audience is left awestruck and uneasy. Some Jews were unsettled, brought too close to the revelatory edge, and wanted to walk out of the theater. How could the Jew-hating, self-loathing Cohn dare ask anything of Ethel Rosenberg? This offended the moral sensibility of many in the audience. But for those who stayed, on stage occurred the transformation that I seek in my classroom. The release from a flat, black or white, intellectual binary and a persistent emotional strait/straight jacket. Ethel of course refused Cohn's request, but that is not the point. Cohn's asking was where the discomfort was lodged. In the feminist classroom the performance comes as close to the edge as the professor can handle and as close as the students willingly permit while still participating.

I am always nervous when I show the Bill T. Jones video in class. The "moving text" makes me cry. The images are so powerful and speak to me on such a deep level that I feel vulnerable and exposed when it's over. But that's the point. Why show the class a video in which I myself am not engaged? Why not let *my* process be part of *their* process? The students watch me watching Bill T. Jones and there is yet another performance occurring in the room. Always, we end up, the class and I, men and women, in tears together. Not because the narrative is sad, but because it is powerfully evocative of where each of us longs to go in our own lives. There is a nonverbal, highly intimate exchange that occurs between us when the students are free to cry without shame and when they see me, their feminist professor, blowing her nose, and crying along with them.

It is not just explosions and unexpected departures that are part of the spontaneous combustion of spectatorship. It is the chilling moment when no one is talking and everyone is wiping their eyes. This is a combustion, spontaneous in its own right as it springs forth, of another kind: that which is often repressed in the traditional classroom as "much too much." Just how much is too much? And for whom, I want to ask. Usually it's the professor for whom all this is too much. The students continue to talk about Bill T. Jones long after the course is over. This itself is enough affirmation for me that the "performance" of the video in class is critical to the process of transformation, an absolute "necessary frenzy."

There is another rupture that in many ways is more difficult for me to integrate simultaneously as it intrudes into the performance. It has to do with the *content* of the performance itself. The rupture occurs when some spectators voice publicly—because a safe, secure space has been created—their loud and vociferous objection to the material that is being covered in class at any particular, totally unspectacular moment. This inevitably happens when I show the video *Juggling Gender*, an autobiographical exploration of a bearded Jewish lesbian who is a real, live circus performer. The objections are not about the obvious. That the narrator is a lesbian, extremely butch, and has chosen not to continue the forced, painful electrolysis of her childhood does not raise a single multicultural eyebrow. Many of the female spectators sympathize with Jennifer Miller's uniquely gendered "problem." They too are blessed with the socially unaccepted and rigorously stigmatized dark facial hair that mysteriously grows out of the pores of the heretofore unblemished, perfect feminine faces. The rupture in the performance of the video comes from students in their role as spectators reacting to a spectacle. They reject Jennifer at her most vulnerable moment, alone in the bathtub, which represents their most intolerable site of gender confusion and discomfort. They cannot sit still with the tension.

There is a scene three-quarters of the way through in which Jennifer is relaxing and rejuvenating herself in the clear waters of a warm bath. The camera zooms in on her totally nude, open, exposed body with shots of her full breasts, round hairy belly, and dark black pubic hair the exact color of her untrimmed and "manly" beard. At this point, some students cough loudly, flinch, and move around in their seats. That they simply do not want to see Jennifer naked, floating freely in her own bathtub caught me, a seasoned performer in the feminist classroom, way off guard. (*This is the generation that loved all those obscene images in* Pulp Fiction, I thought.)

I thought, *Oh no, it's happening again.* Now what? My first thought was that I'd be called down to the dean's office and reprimanded for showing "pornography" in class; or worse, that I, the only out Jewish lesbian professor on campus, would be accused of sexually harassing an entire introductory Women's Studies class with outrageous, offensive, overtly homosexual images. A permanent memo would be placed in my file. I had to think quickly and remember that this was all part of the process. I reminded myself of what performance artist David Sedaris always says, that "the stage is a state of mind, not any one specific location." But the vulnerability I felt that day was different from anything I'd felt in the classroom before. Because somehow my own naked and, at the time, unshaven lesbian body was implicated in the student's objections. If Jewish Jennifer could have body hair and still be a woman, what did that mean for me? Although I did what I always do, incorporate the outburst into the performance of the feminist discourse itself, I remained uneasy.

First, I let the silence in. In fact, I worked the silence like a baker kneading dough so that later it will not fail to rise. Back and forth, side to side, I walked, engaging the spectators in the spectacle of the silent, wordless performer. I let them have some time.

"What is it about the bathtub scene that bothers you?" I turned and looked directly, straight into the room without blinking, holding their gaze until someone spoke.

"It's gratuitous. And unnecessary." The student sounded just like my father, Marvin, back in the Midwest.

Before the bathtub scene, Jennifer Miller had performed bare-breasted with her all-female circus troupe. She is a fire eater and master juggler. No one objected to the exposure of all those breasts. It was the great balls of swirling fire that had caught their eyes.

Waiting for someone to speak in a silent classroom is an arduous act of eternal faith. I continued to wait as the Brandeis University motto wafted across my brain: "Truth unto its innermost parts" was what I hoped the students could understand when viewing Jennifer Miller.

Way in the back row, a Mizrachi student fluent in English, Hebrew, and Farsi spoke with utter confidence. "The nudity is necessary. Jennifer is telling the viewer something about herself in that bathtub." Several students nodded vigorously in agreement while those in disagreement flinched hard, shaking their heads in disgust.

A shy, quiet student, a modern Orthodox Jew who rarely spoke unless called on raised her hand. "The bathtub scene is necessary because the narrator is saying through the camera that she is whole."

"Whole?" Students performed spontaneously. All eyes stared at the speaker.

"Wholly female," the woman added. "We have to see her naked with all her body hair, whether we want to or not, so that her female-ness is not obscured by her beard."

"I already know she's female," somebody says.

We had been inching toward that edge, where reality is dislodged, where a woman with a full beard and thick body hair remains still fully female. That we had to straddle that contradictory, gendered edge to-gether, not entirely agreeing or disagreeing, was part of the perform-ance. At the end of class, I did not neatly sum up (as we professors are often tempted to do) the many multiple meanings of the Jewish bearded lady who could easily pass as a middle-aged Chasid in Crown Heights hurrying home from shul to celebrate Shabbat. Instead, I told the class to write a reaction to what they viewed, and to articulate what questions were raised for them as spectators. After that semester, I didn't show *Juggling Gender* for a while, although I knew that the decision was a highly privileged, academic cop-out that I would regret. Recently, I began showing it again, ready to confront my own discomfort.

Performing is always precarious. Professing, on the other hand, is much more reliable and far less controversial.

Students tell me that 5A has a reputation that has reached the awkward status of a "new religious order." (Colleagues tease me about all the young zealots I personally convert to feminism.) The students describe walking around the campus, catching the eyes of the other "5A'ers." "We smile, nod conspiratorially and continue on to The Stein or Usden to eat lunch together. It's an attitude thing," they tell me. "You've changed us forever." This could sound like theocratic brainwashing; but that's not the goal of the pedagogy. Change is about agency—the ability to act and not just react—and voice—speaking one's own truth regardless of the consequences. And being in the body or having attitude is one of the most basic skills a performer needs to master before stepping out of the status quo and onto the stage. Before agency or voice, there is attitude. It's in the carriage, the actual physical manifestation of the self. It's a corporeal kind of thing; the body doesn't lie.

"You've changed us forever" haunts me like the smell of burnt raisin toast filling the whole first floor of my house. It stinks. "My parents think I need deprogramming," one student tells me. I remember watching Harvey Fierstein's *Torch Song Trilogy* on Broadway more than twenty years ago. I was changed forever, not brainwashed. I had been brought to the boiling point and then boiled over into that "necessary frenzy." I had never seen Jewish and homosexual woven together so seamlessly. Of course I was hot. The performance filled me with new possibilities, with *hope* not *fear*, with the possibility of transformation. (I did not join a cult.) But fear is what happens in the middle of a good performance, the fear of transformation. We are not taught that the goal of a good, successful, liberal arts education is transformation. Rather, we're taught that the goal is to become professional, to compete in the global marketplace of ideas and the IMF, and to earn much more than an hourly wage. We are taught not to feel or express emotions, and definitely not to explode or to be creative, or to participate in questioning the dominant ideological paradigm. Rather, we are taught the importance of scrupulous note taking in preparation for midterms and final exams, instead of the imperative of active listening.

But transformation (not brainwashing) is crucial to the preservation of the imagination, to the very spirit of creativity. So, I have come to understand the function of describing 5A as similar to a "new religious order," or a cultlike experience. It is a way for the students and some colleagues to conceptualize *and* compartmentalize the radical, deeply spiritual reactions that the students have to the class. It is a way to contain the virus, to mark it publicly and politically with the scarlet letter of academic deviance. I was profoundly disturbed that the work I was doing in the classroom would be described as creating the atmosphere of a cult. In the end, the professor who performs walks a tightrope, not just with her students but with her colleagues and the administration in general.

A standard lecture ends when the class is officially over and students walk out. But a spectacle is never finished; the show continues. On and on. This is what happened when JFK was shot. There was the painfully long procession to the rotunda, while the entire nation watched, transfixed as little John said a last goodbye to his father with a small, stately salute, which he must have practiced over and over again, ahead of time. That single solitary gesture was replayed on the news, hour after hour. (And again, for days after John Jr. himself died, everywhere that small hand saluting his father goodbye was replayed and reprinted.) We couldn't get enough. The grief of a bereft nation was held in that small masculine hand. We were already changed forever.

What is the problem with change? By its very nature it implicates those who do not participate. That's what happened with the Anita Hill–Clarence Thomas hearings. There were those of us who watched the "performance" and were changed forever. We were transformed by the process, the role playing and the role defying. By all the prerehearsed, senatorial lines and the unexpected, unrehearsed appearance of all of Hill's family walking solemnly, stately, to their preassigned seats. It is within spectacle that meanings are coded, decoded, and recoded again. Where the spectators become personally invested in the spectacle in such a way that the privacy of their lives is forever changed. The classroom ought to be just such a place: where students are taught to recognize a de facto code, to decode and recode it with their own newly found voices.

I always assume that my students have a voice, whether they know it or not. What I don't know is to what use this voice will be put. Will it implicate the status quo or preserve it? Which voices will collide with which other voices? Who will shriek the loudest, and to whom? Anita

Hill found her voice in the middle of the hearings. She was transformed by her own performance (and is now writing a treatise on sexual harassment in the workplace). This is what I want for my students, that within the combustion of their minds, a new voice emerges; that they find the courage to perform live with me on stage; and that they learn new lines without fear of leaving the old ones behind.

Last year there was a huge storm in the capital. The electricity went out all across the District of Columbia. At Arlington National Cemetery, for the first time since Ted Kennedy had lit it thirty-five years ago, the eternal flame at the base of the simple silver-plated bowl memorializing his brother John Fitzgerald went out. No one knows why; the flame is sustained by gas, not electricity. It should not have gone out. To me, the temporary loss of the permanent flame was a metaphor about not forgetting. I think back on my many years of education. Decade by decade, I remember the names of those passionate, engaged professors who ignited an eternal flame in my young, unharnessed spirit, charging me with the burning flame of fearless transformation.

In elementary school my first-grade teacher, Mrs. Jean Greassou, took the entire class to visit one of the now extinct midwestern dairy farms to see firsthand rows and rows of full-bellied cows, waiting to be milked. I remember the taste of freshly churned butter. In second grade Mrs. Miller took our class away for a week to a magical retreat in the woods, the Glen at Antioch College in Yellow Springs, Ohio. We learned to walk on tiptoes through huge, silent pine forests and to distinguish animal tracks and read the signs of snakes weaving through high grass. Before that week, I had hated studying the natural sciences.

In high school there was Miss Minton, who made us act out every Shakespearean drama we studied, line by line, dressed in Elizabethan costumes. At Syracuse University, David Owens could make a four-hundred-page book, *The Big Rock Candy Mountain*, by Wallace Stegner (an author none of us had ever heard of), come alive with full force. I understand now that he did not lecture—he performed. His colleagues thought him brilliant but overly dramatic—eccentric. Many of my classmates were terrified of the tall, gaunt, chain-smoking, nonstop hacking professor. I was not. I was ignited forever by the intensity of his gaze, and his commitment to a power of storytelling that I had thought belonged only to the Chasidic master, the *Baal Shem Tov* and his followers. Ironically (sadly?), as I became an ever more engaged student, going on for one advanced degree after another, I recall less and less any one class or the name of any one particular professor. Out of nine years of graduate and postgraduate work I recall the names of only two professors: Lee R. Edwards, who wrote a book I never forgot, *Woman as Hero*, and my creative writing professor, Jay Neugeboren, who told me to vary the structure of my sentences—they were too short. Why does the fervor in higher education so often diminish, the longer the student spends inside the ivy-covered walls?

Walking into my own classroom, I understand both the power and the politic of pedagogical light. And that it must never be allowed to extinguish. That when the spontaneous combustion comes, if I wait without fear, a light so fierce that it can never go out permanently will ignite the minds of my students. I understand too that the flame at Arlington National Cemetery is essential to the act of spectatorship, not only to the memory of a beloved assassinated president. For the burning flame allows us to grieve *and* to rise again. It is the symbol of a nation transformed by its own catastrophe.

So I will keep showing Bill T. Jones pirouetting to the edge with his terminally ill dancers. Although I remain nervous, I will also show Jennifer Miller and her Chasidic beard. And I will find a way to perform the hard, difficult questions of "Structural Masculinity and Violence Against Women." I want to look into the eyes of my students and continue to see the passion of my own hunger reflected back to me. It is in the reciprocity of the performance itself that the eternal flame is lit. We ignite each other, professor to student and student to professor, burning with a glowing heat that refuses to burn out. If I stop teaching tomorrow, I know with deep satisfaction that my students will not forget my name or the fire in my eyes. Long after they are gone, I continue to call forth their names and the questions we used to ponder together each semester: Why at the end of the twentieth century is taking a Women's Studies course still such a big deal? Why does everyone assume that the subject is soft-core? I remember laughing with the class at the end of last semester when we had finally made it to the edge and stepped nervously out onto that short, slender ledge, ready to leap forward together. There is nothing soft-core about transformation. It is the most treacherous act of learning that I know.

Lee Strasberg
Comes to Class

g rowing up, I watched the TV show *I Dream of Jeannie*. I was fascinated by the wide-bottomed, thin-necked green bottle and its resident female genie. Coded into this early-1960s sitcom was the stereotypical view that men were strong and masculine, while women were soft and had all the feelings. Once the cork was pulled, the bottled-up emotions flowed freely, both for the turban-headed blond, blue-eyed maiden inside and the Major himself, whose own life "on the outside" thrived on military precision. Now, in the late 1990s as I walk into Lown Auditorium at Brandeis University I often feel like a character in *I Dream of Jeannie*, preparing to pop a tightly fitted cork. Looking out at my students, I imagine all eighty corks popping at once, spraying the entire Introduction to Women's Studies class with layers of emotional confetti.

I have come to understand that part of my role as professor is to incite and ignite the emotions of my students. When I don't, everyone—me included—suffers. Like a skilled actor who makes the audience feel deeply, so too the professor needs to bring forth a range of emotions in the students. Emotional incitement, however, is not a traditional requirement for life in the academy. Most of my own academic preparation actually functioned to obfuscate any emotional responses while relying instead on an overabundance of facts and statistics. One challenge with inciting emotion in the feminist classroom is that the outcome can never be predicted and is often a precursor to the "spontaneous combustion" discussed in chapter 2. When students are permitted the space to both think and feel simultaneously, the professor must recognize her own complicated and contradictory feelings. Otherwise, the professor's unexamined feelings interfere and then dominate the direction of the discourse. This integration of feelings into the presentation of the course material is a pedagogical balancing act that requires a high degree of intentionality.

Knowing my own emotional investment in the material allows me to recognize those places where the students themselves will also have a range of emotional responses. It allows me to pose questions and organize the material in such a way that enough space is created for students to feel *and* think. A certain amount of distrust is triggered as soon as students start to have feelings in the process of learning, and this suspicion continues until students get used to the methodology. Nowhere else is emotional expression welcomed into their classroom experiences. Despite the risks involved, feelings and emotions belong at center stage in the feminist classroom, not bottled up, corked tightly, and stacked neatly, row after intellectual row. This is about the professor performing with her feelings intact, and letting the spectators, the students, have theirs too.

Acknowledging the possibility of the skeptical reaction, I ask the students to examine their feelings in context. *What is it that bothers them about feminism? Why is a beard on a woman so funny? So disturbing? Why does talking about race make you nervous?* When these topics are studied in isolation or on the purely theoretical plane students end up with a distorted, limited view of the material in question. And if students compartmentalize their feelings, the thinking itself becomes fragmentary and incomplete, just as relying solely on their feelings limits their understanding of the topics. But once the student is permitted to connect his or her feelings to the material, a whole person emerges. In the end, the analysis benefits as students articulate a more complex and informed synthesis.

One of the biggest challenges confronting the professor who intentionally seeks to emotionally engage students is that feelings have been socially assigned and culturally imbedded according to gender. Until recently, all real (read: heterosexual) boys had muscles and all girls had feelings—a holdover from the 1950s, an equation split equally down the middle, nice, neat, and supremely ordered. Rational minds never crossed the gender barrier unless it was to parody the men and women who publicly "crossed" gender themselves. Complaints abound that Hillary Rodham Clinton is always too rational, too masculine, and too tough to be one of the "girls," while David Bowie and Dennis Rodman are just frilly, froufrou girls who love lace. But everybody adores "Liddy" Dole, who dances the two-step with microphone in hand and works the crowd at the same time—such a multitalented gal! The only men who have their feelings are gay; but the price they pay is very high indeed, including death on the whipping post at the end of a long, winding, solitary country road in the middle of a dark, dry Wyoming night. Gay men are routinely, negatively feminized by the names they're called: sissy, fairy, fey, *feygelah*, and worse. And girls with muscles (my women students complain) are forever called tomboys.

Although gender expression is becoming more fluid, thinking is still rigidly "read" male and interpreted as neutral, rational, and consistent. Never subject to the unpredictable, frenzied, feeling state of those who are "read" female. Yet emotional intelligence—thinking and feeling with your body, mind, spirit, and soul—is not the irrational, solipsistic, unevolved, and adolescent behavior it is so often stereotyped as. Rather, it raises IQ levels. In twenty years of teaching, I've observed that the men and women in my classes who are the least successful are the ones who repeatedly try to quantify, rationalize, and intellectualize every issue discussed. They are also the students for whom *contradictory realities* and the *navigation of multiplicities* are the most difficult concepts to grasp. For those particular students who dwell in monochrome, relying on a flat, basic, black-and-white analysis, static cerebral binaries are the foundations on which they interpret the universe.

But for the students who risk feeling while they think about the theories discussed and the facts disseminated, learning is provocative, exhilarating, and fully satisfying. What's more, the learning itself endures, long after the facts themselves are forgotten. Unfortunately there are students in the beginning of every semester who become overly concerned when feelings, not just facts, enter the "feminized" (as opposed to feminist) classroom. They mistakenly conflate feelings with therapy (as if they are one and the same) as soon as the genie pops out of her bottle. In the feminist classroom, popping the emotional cork is an essential part of the performance.

What is it about feelings in the classroom that is so very frightening? That the necessary "act of feeling" is forcibly and intellectually separated from the more highly valued "act of critical inquiry"? It is not only students but also professors and administrators who (mistakenly) relegate emotional expression in the classroom to the negatively "feminized" act of therapy, confined and contained behind closed doors in the controlled environment of the fifty-minute hour—or trivialized as "softcore" and insufficiently intellectual in nature. The challenge is to use emotions both performatively and pedagogically to deepen the learning experience itself. This allows the students to become invested in the material beyond the duration of the semester and the completion of final exams. To use emotions pedagogically is also to reveal just how political human expression truly is. When Senator Edmund Muskie cried publicly over his forced withdrawal as a 1972 presidential candidate because he had admitted to being treated for depression, he was horrifically chastised in the news. And years later, when Congresswoman Patricia Schroeder also cried in public, she was repeatedly called weak, even after serving as the only woman on the Strategic Armed Forces Committee. Clearly, PDEs, public displays of emotion, are too hot to handle.

Yet it's through our feelings that we know we are alive and engaged, *especially* in the academy. We are not (yet) teaching robots, and neither are we the professors robotic. When we are, it shows in the disinterest reflected back to us. I intentionally create a space for students—men and women, tennis players and basketball stars—to cry in my Women's Studies classes. Students feel free to laugh loudly, boisterously, and so do I. Laughter it seems is socially and academically acceptable: it signals approval. Usually it's a response, a recognition, or an appreciation that the professor just said something entertaining. Students also applaud, and they get angry. Anger and grief, however, are taboo in traditional classrooms: save the pain for later, the rage for the weight room, and take the sorrow to someone who's professionally paid to listen.

For the professor committed to emotions as a pedagogical tool, the expression of anger in the feminist classroom is the most difficult to navigate. Anger, in this particularized environment, has three relevant dimensions: that of the students toward their professor, the students' anger with each other; and finally, the least examined, the anger of the professor toward the students. Given that the material covered and/or the way the material is covered in the feminist classroom often contradicts the standard hegemonic views consistent with "the dominant paradigm," students react strongly by verbally contesting, challenging, and publicly expressing anger toward the professor. This often happens to me when I suggest to the students in 5A that women are perfectly capable of being excellent firefighters. The problem, I suggest, is not that they are not strong enough to carry hoses or tear down walls, but rather that the equipment necessary for these lifesaving tasks is not designed for women's bodies. I point out the ways women's bodies are actually quite strong and remind the class that there was a time when left-handed people couldn't be dentists and were forced to learn how to be right-handed.

In this context, I am asking the students to look at the larger picture, the macro structure at work in society. This type of questioning makes the students angry at and frustrated by the professor. There is a process of reorientation that occurs when firmly held beliefs are challenged. When we start to look at gender roles in the classroom, the students' anger is especially strong. Each student is forced to look at himself or herself, their personal relationships, and families. It is easier for them to be angry at the "messenger" than at either the message itself or the system that enforces the message—in this case, traditional gender roles. A professor has to expect and embrace her students' anger without letting the anger become a controlling force in the learning and without becoming defensive herself.

The next step in the process is to allow the students the space to exchange ideas and feelings—anger—with each other. Since neither suppression of disagreement nor unanimity of opinion is the goal, the students must be free to argue publicly among themselves. This leads to some students becoming angry with their friends in the middle of the class. I have had students who stop talking to each other for parts of the semester, until a new topic is introduced. When this happens, I address outright the function of anger when contradictory ideas are exposed by the people we care about. I point out that anger is only the starting point in the exchange of differing opinions, not the resolution.

Finally, I have had to admit the existence of my own anger toward the students. I am still somewhat surprised when I find myself, at the end of the day, angry with the whole class, a group of students, or one or two in particular. (The actual incidents triggering my anger are irrelevant.) When this happens, I begin by asking myself the same questions

I ask the students when they tell me that they're angry with me. On occasion, I have chosen to address the class directly, not to yell or take out my anger on them, but to discuss the fact that I am angry and to articulate the reasons why. This strategy has been the most effective; my vulnerability is once again exposed, and my humanness affirmed. I am not just another professor pulling rank, misusing her power to put the students down. It is in the public articulation of the anger that yet another transformation in the classroom occurs. For in the affirmation of the full expression of their own anger, the students and the professor—who is also seen when angry—are no longer on opposite sides. Rather, a solid pedagogical bond is created.

Anger in the classroom can be used to expand the flow of ideas, while contracting and suppressing anger only creates more anger. And unexpressed anger (in the classroom) leads to rage and disempowered, silent students. In the performance of feminist teaching, the full expression of feelings makes the show real and fully realized, pedagogically. Without feelings, there is no passion; without passion there is no appetite to learn. Ultimately, the expression of feelings allows the professor to connect with her students and the students with each other on a human level.

Enter Lee Strasberg, a.k.a. the feminist professor as performance artist and emotional acrobat, who recognizes when the pedagogical highwire is so cerebrally taut that it strangles—when a little emotional slack would help a lot. Lee Strasberg (1901–1982) was a disciple of Constantine Stanislavski, the Russian actor and director who revolutionized traditional Russian theater. The goal of this new method, brought to the States by Strasberg, was to engage the whole person on stage, not just from the neck up, used to memorizing line after line. Not to play, but to perform the actions required of the character. Both men believed that "appearance on stage is not the beginning but a continuation of the given circumstances that have previously taken place." This is how I approach the classroom, as an ongoing series of *realized* events in which I too am an ongoing participant. Teaching is similar to Strasberg's performance strategies and requires not only intellectual knowledge but emotional experience. The Strasberg combination (of intellectual knowledge plus the full expression of feelings) creates the theatrical atmosphere I have come to call "performing teaching in the feminist classroom."

Curiously, both Strasberg's method and the actors he trained (including Marlon Brando, Anne Bancroft, Sidney Poitier, Maureen Stapleton, and Dustin Hoffman) were criticized for being out of control and undisciplined. And yet, these actors and their "undisciplined" method permanently and powerfully altered the course of the American stage. It is the Method (as it is officially called) that encourages the "madness" to emerge in the classroom. The Strasberg method stimulates emotional and intellectual concentration while igniting the imagination. This kind of engagement not only contradicts but threatens the order of the traditional classroom, where the mind, particularly the mind of the professor, has always mattered most. Feelings positively and pedagogically direct where a class is headed.

One of the videos that I show in 5A is *Skin Deep*, which is about an ethnically diverse group of undergraduate students who participate in a weekend retreat on race relations. The students come from campuses all across the country. Until now, race discussions in 5A have been largely intellectual and uninformed—and frustrating for many of the students of color. Most of the White students have a distorted view of racism and are emotionally detached from the day-to-day realities of White skin privilege in the United States. I show *Skin Deep* because it is about their college peers; in a sense the students see themselves portrayed and so they can (and do) personally identify. In the video, discussions move beyond a White-Black binary; questions about Jewish identity are covered, as are the differences between Korean, Chinese, Japanese, and other Asian ethnicities. The students in the video are shown adamantly disagreeing, visibly distressed, and on a few occasions laughing, but the mood throughout the three-day retreat is tense and highly charged.

Sitting in the dark as the credits roll, I hear my own students crying; when the lights come on, the mood has shifted dramatically: women are holding hands, the guys are shifting in their seats and sniffling loudly. In the classroom, it seems, crying in the dark is permissible. No one person male or female can be identified and later humiliated. It is as if the whole class cries together; no one is stigmatized and degradingly feminized. Just like in the socially acceptable province of a movie theater, where public displays of emotion are properly "admissible," when the lights go out in the classroom the academic rules proscribing public emotional expression change. The atmosphere of the movie house is so successfully re-created in Lown Auditorium that the students don't even realize they have begun to cry in public. After the showing of *Skin Deep* the discussion on race is no longer purely intellectual or detached. Something has happened to the students' critical thinking about race; they have become engaged emotionally, they have begun to respond to the issues with their whole person(s), not just their minds. It is another moment of transformation in the performance of feminist pedagogy.

Toward the end of every semester in 5A I arrange for a student panel. Students can volunteer, and I also select those in the class who would offer a lot but who might not volunteer on their own. The point of the panel is to illustrate a basic tenet of 1960s feminism, that "the personal is political." I want the students to connect the micro of their daily lives with all the macro issues that we've studied so far. Both the panelists and the spectators are apprehensive about the project. One year I asked Ramon, a Latino student who was a baseball player in the minor leagues waiting to be upgraded to the majors, to be on the panel. He was a senior, had never taken a Women's Studies class before, and was also the first member of his family to go to college and the only player on his team to go on with his education after high school.

Ramon had reluctantly taken 5A at the insistent urging of his girlfriend Katie. He started class one week late because the baseball season wasn't over until the second week in September. I wasn't happy, but I wanted as many men in the class as possible so I grudgingly signed his add/drop form. All semester I watched Ramon Perez, whose body posture went from relaxed to tense to undivided attention. He went from rushing in five minutes late to arriving a few minutes earlier each week. In the beginning of the semester I had to ask him to turn his minor league baseball cap around (I ask all my students, male and female) so that I could see his face when he spoke. Over the next few weeks, as he moved his seat progressively from the back of the room to smack in the middle of the front row, I noticed that he simultaneously voluntarily turned his cap around, exposing a full, handsome face, with deep-set brown eyes. We were communicating and connecting. He had to be on the panel; I knew it, although I had no idea what he would say.

I gave the panelists three questions to address and told them to prepare by writing down their thoughts. "This is serious," I added. Each person had ten minutes to speak to the class; all comments from their peers would be held until the end. Every semester, I refined the questions. *Pick out one of the multiple lenses we've studied, race, class, gender, or sex(uality), and discuss how it relates to your own life; tell us one thing about yourself that represents how the "personal is political" ; and ask the class a question based on your own synthesis of the issues we've studied.* Each panelist had a partner to discuss the questions with privately, and the panel itself was required to meet together once as a whole group, without me, just to talk and hang out—to connect. They would be rehearsing without officially rehearsing.

I never know how the panel will go, but I know it will be powerful and dramatic and synthesize the semester in an unforgettable way. It is a peak performance moment; the students sense it. The day of the panel they enter the class unusually solemn, without saying a word. Everyone is on time, even the swimmers who rush to Lown with wet hair from clear across campus. At first I was surprised how seriously the entire class took the panel before the participants even began to speak. But then it made sense. It was feminist theory unfolding live, the pedagogy in practice, right before their eyes. They, the students, were teaching each other; their professor was now a vulnerable participating spectator, one of them. Once again the classroom was decentered as the genie came swooshing confidently out of her green bottle. I switched places with Ramon, taking his now favorite front-row dead-center seat. I liked my new location; it felt good to sit with the crowd.

Ramon spoke third. He was clearly nervous, and would have been more comfortable dressed in a uniform, warming up behind a pitcher's mound, surrounded by swelling grandstands. He was popular with the students; everybody on campus knew or wanted to know Ramon Perez. He was a star on the Brandeis baseball team, but in class he was just one of the few "cool jocks" who wasn't afraid to take 5A. He started by saying that he had handwritten an entire speech, but that he had, at the last minute, decided against reading it. He wanted to talk and began immediately.

"You don't know how hard it is," he looked at me, before turning his full gaze directly on his classmates, "being in the minor leagues, a baseball player from the Bronx headed for the majors with your whole neighborhood counting on you, and a student in 5A." As he spoke, the lines in Ramon's face grew tense. The rage in his voice built slowly. "The guys on the team call me fag and think I'm losing all my muscle, going soft on them. My family thinks I'm wasting my education taking this course. At first, I thought so too." As he continued, there wasn't a sound in the room. "But things started to change around the time we watched that movie about the girl with the beard and then that race flick, *Skin Deep*, and that Native guy was crying. I couldn't get my mind off him. After that I started to see things differently. The jokes in the dugout weren't all that funny anymore. I can't explain." He looked harder into the faces of the other students. "I know you know what I'm talking about. Now, I don't know what to do, except that I know I don't want to go back to the way I was before 5A. But I'm a ballplayer. That's who I was raised to be." Toward the end, Ramon had started crying almost imperceptibly, but by the time he reached the last few sentences, he had stopped trying to pretend that he wasn't upset. I looked around, the whole room was crying. Ramon wiped his eyes with his hand and continued.

"I'm not the same person as I was two and a half months ago. And to tell you the truth, even though it's much harder and not exactly that much fun, I'm glad." That was it. Ramon crumpled up the handwritten speech he didn't use. From his seat on the panel he lobbed it effortlessly into the wastebasket.

We couldn't move or say a word when he finished. Ramon seemed somewhat oblivious to the reaction his talk had created in the classroom. Right before the whole Intro to Women's Studies class, a heterosexual male student had merged his mind and body, spirit and soul; the entire class, myself included, was brought closer to our whole selves because Ramon wasn't afraid to bring his feelings with him, instead of checking them at the door of Lown Auditorium before entering. This is the so-called "undisciplined" nature of the Strasberg method playing center stage, live and unrehearsed. Although the moment he spoke *and* cried together may have been personally therapeutic, Ramon was not "in therapy" when describing his personal transformation. It was obvious to everyone who heard him that day that what had happened was a form of praxis, that the theory and the practice of the feminist pedagogy had successfully merged. Ramon was not the only student to ever cry on a panel in 5A. Yet his performance was one of the most dramatic: the pedagogy of the performance flowed freely from student to student without professorial intervention or interference, and at the same time Ramon was completely supported by his classmates and the professor.

Equally significant about Ramon's experience in 5A were the added dimensions of his race, ethnicity, and class background. Ramon is Puerto Rican, and the specific cultural mores for men in his Latino community are even more rigidly delineated than for those of his White Anglo counterparts. The range of acceptable male behavior is extremely limited. Machismo reigns supreme. Athletic prowess guarantees icon status. The students understood that Ramon was talking about the contradictory reality of loyalty to his tribe while simultaneously letting in the reality of a newfound loyalty to himself. One that differed in terms of acceptable male behavior. He risked the brotherhood that came with his working-class roots to take a Women's Studies course, and was basking in his own powerful rebirth.

The summer I was writing this book I asked a male student his response to 5A as a whole. We had been e-mailing back and forth as I do with many of my students, and spontaneously I decided to find out his impressions of the course in retrospect. The specific questions I posed Daniel are included in his response, which I quote verbatim (I have edited only for spelling):

> *Hi Daniel J! I am doing some writing on "5A" and would love it, if you could help me out. That is, email me, your reflections on last year's class, the highs and lows. What are your thoughts on that class now. If you could just riff on these questions, and include any spontaneous ideas that pop out, I would greatly appreciate it—the sooner the better. Thanks JLF*

Sorry it's taken me a little while to respond—I was just in Venice, CA for a few days, and could not find a computer anywhere there to e-mail from. Anyway, as for spontaneous reactions to "5A," well first of all, I think that one thing strikes me more than anything else: Usually after a class at Brandeis, people will leave and discuss class—what was discussed/lectured, comments on the readings or the teacher, etc. However "5A" is the one class I've ever taken where people leave class and talk about how they were actually moved—how class had changed their outlook on life.

People leave "5A" and talk about how they FEEL, and how the class affected them as individuals. As a politics major, I've taken many classes that affect how I view things, or that alter certain perspectives on specific issues. I've had classes that make me think of the world in a different context, and that have given me a greater understanding of how the world works. But there is no class besides "5A" which has ever changed ME, which has ever altered how I view MYSELF. Only "5A" has affected how I deal with others, how I think about others, and equally important, how I deal with myself and how I think about myself. From other classes, I have learned. From "5A," I have grown.

Daniel's appreciation of "the feeling" aspect of 5A, while affirming, is also profoundly moving to me. Although I knew that Daniel enjoyed the class, I did not have any idea what he would say in response to my questions. The fact that a male student spoke about the significance of feeling in the process of learning is really about the transformative potential of feminist pedagogy regarding traditional gender roles—and that's not something I take for granted as I teach.

I do not want to elevate either Daniel's or Ramon's response to 5A because they are men. But I do want to point out that when given the chance to have their feelings respected, both men took full and complete advantage of the opportunity. Additionally, Daniel valued his personal growth in 5A, something that is most often traditionally devalued in the academy.

Curious as to what other students might say about their experiences in 5A, I asked Rachel, when she e-mailed me this past summer. Below I quote the most relevant of her responses to the discussion so far (editing only for spelling):

> How am I different after "5A"? For one, I am angrier. From someone who has been in the class this may sound bad, but it is true. It's not passive anger anymore, though, which is why the anger is good. It's anger that inspires me to speak up or try to change things. It is anger that allows me to acknowledge inequalities—to not buy a product because of its offensive advertising, for example, to not attend a movie that exploits women or glorifies violence, things like that.

What's significant about Rachel's reaction is that she specifically mentions anger—her own. And she discusses it as a powerful new tool in her life. She has moved, in her own words, from passive to active, from silence to sound. Her whole person is emerging, and 5A contributed to this process. It is obvious that factual learning alone would not have brought forth Daniel's, Rachel's, or Ramon's responses. Rachel goes on in her e-mail, adding:

> You asked about my different understanding about the difficult class we had. First I have to say that we didn't have "the" difficult class, we had quite a few difficult classes. I don't mean that in a negative way however. It is important to have "difficult" classes and not just academically difficult, but emotionally difficult. Emotionally difficult classes are something I have missed in my education until I took "5A." I needed something that really made me think and this class did. For the first time in a long while I was a part of a class that made me constantly think and apply what I learned and thought about both inside but even more outside of the classroom.

These insightful words are from a twenty-year-old woman. I was surprised at the depth of her understanding of the pedagogy itself. And even more impressed with her ability to so clearly articulate the power of integrating emotions into learning. Gratifying though Rachel's words are, the issue for me is recognizing the fact that students know when something is or is not working in the classroom. And they don't pretend to be engaged and interested if they aren't.

Lest it appear that the integration of feelings within the learning process is limited only to introductory Women's Studies classes such as 5A, I want to discuss an incident in my advanced seminar on Blacks and Jews. We were discussing the difficult question of who was involved in the Atlantic slave trade, and the extent of the involvement of some Southern Jews. I had divided the seminar of twenty-three students into small groups. This is not a random division; it is pedagogically intentional—that is, I want students who don't normally talk to each other to do so. I always give the students specific questions to address and have them write for ten minutes before breaking up into small groups. I do this writing-intensive exercise because it "levels the playing field" for the entire class, allowing each student the time and space to think on her or his own, without the interference of other people's ideas. Once in the group, the students read out loud their responses. Then they talk. I do not know what goes on in any one particular group. I remain on the outside, not eavesdropping even a little.

In this class, I asked the students to consider why some Southern Jews might have participated in the slave trade and what did that mean, if anything, for Black-Jewish relations today. After the groups met, the floor was open for class discussion. First, though, each group was asked to synthesize their ideas and present them. I noticed that one student, a Jewish woman, was upset, but I had no idea why. When members of her group spoke, Sylvia went last. She was visibly disturbed.

"I didn't cause the slave trade," she whispered. "I feel like I'm being blamed personally for Jewish involvment; I feel so bad, I don't even know how to express what it is I'm trying to say." Sylvia couldn't look at anyone in the room. The other members of her group, two African-American students, Tony and Monique, just kept shaking their heads while she spoke.

Monique responded first: "Nobody's blaming anybody, I don't understand why you're getting so upset."

Tony added, "We're not accusing you personally." I looked at Sylvia, who was nodding in agreement, as though she understood that no one thought the slave trade was her fault.

"Pick a partner," I said, this time letting the students choose whomever they wanted. Sylvia and Tony chose each other, which continues to amaze me even now. Why should I be amazed that these two students would choose to work with each other? I understand my reaction to be a trivialization of just how effective allowing emotions into the feminist classroom can be. Once Sylvia could express her own fears publicly and see that no one was in reality rejecting or blaming her, she was able to move forward. That I didn't panic the moment she started crying, or suppress the discussion, difficult as it was, is important. For any transformation to occur, I had to be able to tolerate the rising tension in the classroom. And so did the other students, who in their role as spectators performed an equally important function. They held out the possibility that everyone in Sylvia's group could be heard, and that no one would choose a side or humiliate another student. I asked the students to meet with their partners during the coming week to continue discussing the questions and assigned readings. Finally, they were required to write a two- to three-page response paper to the issues.

After class, I was left with my own discomfort, wondering what had so "dislodged" me, a highly skilled professor. I do teach to incite imaginations and to ignite emotions, and that was just what occurred. Why, then, was I so upset? I "should" feel good, pleased at how well things were going, but I didn't. That night, I realized that as a Jew I felt personally vulnerable and concerned on two levels for the students themselves. For the African-American students, it was important for me that I not shy away from exposing whatever was problematic or racist in past and present Jewish behavior. For my Jewish-American students, my concern was that they not feel attacked. I felt protective of every member of the class and worked passionately to create an environment that allowed us to look deeply at how our two peoples had been historically pitted against each other. What I did not realize until halfway through the course was how I would personally deal with my own vulnerability. In 5A, when lesbian topics are discussed, I know ahead of time that I need to proceed with extra intent and address what is relevant about my own reaction to the material. So, too, I learned in Blacks and Jews that I had to address publicly where I got "triggered," modeling for the students that we are not dealing only on the theoretical plane.

I came back the next week and talked about my own reactions to the last class: my feelings. I then took questions from the students, as I often do. As I had hoped, we were able to move to the next place in the discussion with a far greater insight into the issues concerning Blacks and Jews in the United States. In her final response paper, excerpted here, Sylvia wrote about how her experience in last week's class was a breakthrough for her personally, and that she "got it."

> I walked into the classroom the first day and immediately noticed a huge difference [from 5A]: the chairs were positioned in a circle, not the familiar lecture style I had grown accustomed to the semester before. My heart started racing. The intimacy and honesty of the class frightened me. In "5A" there were so many students that, even with Professor Felman's "involuntary volunteer" policy, I felt safe within the crowd. Now essentially on my own, my discomfort was obvious. From the very first discussion I felt as if I were walking on hot coals, capable of hurting everyone around me with one wrong word. After the first class I remember e-mailing Professor Felman because I was so uncomfortable with the language and so afraid to voice my honest opinions. As each week progressed, my confidence and profound understanding evolved until *finally* I felt comfortable with the learning process and could constructively contribute to the

class. It was not a positive experience which sparked this epiphany however, but rather a class in which I felt extremely angry, frustrated, and upset after a small group discussion. The course had been taking a toll on my emotions, exhausting me and affecting my life outside of class, and I didn't even realize it. I stopped eating, got sick, even gave up writing questions on the readings I loved so much, simply because it was too much for me to deal with every single day.

I believe this course has been incredibly difficult for me because it has changed me so thoroughly. I started out as an emotional, tentative, passive student afraid of opening my mouth in class. Now I realize how much I have learned this semester, what a broadened perspective I have developed, and how much confidence I have gained. "5A" started breaking down the binaries for me, but this class has taken those introductory concepts and applied them to one of the most important, most difficult misunderstood institutions in American society: cross-cultural relations. Blacks and Jews seemed unlikely enemies and unlikely allies as well. Being able to search below the surface of this perception has been an emotional hardship, but overall a phenomenal growth experience.

Although Sylvia had shown us her fears, and I in turn had shown the class mine, equally significant is the fact that the African-American students were free to express their anger publicly and be listened to with respect. At the end of the semester, students echoed Sylvia's final comments, saying to me that this was the hardest class they had ever taken—not just the material, but the emotional investment they felt each week as we worked to uncover the layers of mistrust and coexistence between our different ethnic groups.

Whenever I get scared in the classroom, I call up the image stored in my head since childhood of a long, thin-necked, wide-bottomed green bottle and its resident genie. Only now, the genie has no gender. I accept the sacred responsibility of pulling out the cork, for myself and all my students. Feelings in the feminist classroom are no longer the sole province of the women; neither are the men in class without feelings of their own waiting and ready to be expressed. Together we explore this fertile but too often neglected pedagogical terrain. Together we do not go gently into the classroom. Entering Lown Auditorium, I look over my shoulder and feel Lee Strasberg smiling, as he sees minds and bodies, spirits and souls, already hard at work. We nod at each other as I begin. Engaging the whole student body is surely one of a professor's most revolutionary acts.

ACT II

Opening Night

GI Joe in the Last Row

Performing Masculinities

MASCULINITY: *virility, maleness, potency, manhood, muscularity, manliness, toughness, sexiness*
VIRILE: *manly, vibrant, strong, masculine, forceful, vigorous, vital, robust, male*
POTENT: *powerful, mighty, puissant, strong*
MANHOOD: *legal age, adulthood, voting age, majority, middle age, prime of life, man's estate*
MUSCULAR: *robust, vigorous, well-built, athletic, sturdy, powerful, brawny, lithe, agile*
MANLY: *brave, virile*
SEXINESS: *masculinity, maleness, potency, muscularity, manliness, toughness, virility*
—*Microsoft Word 97 Thesaurus*

Performing Masculinities: To Be Virile
manly, vibrant, strong, masculine, forceful, vigorous, vital, robust, male

"I need an add signature," he always says on the first day of class.

"Great," I say out loud. While rapidly scribbling *Felman* on the add form, I tell myself, *WOW, another man for Intro to Women's Studies!*

In the beginning, not a single question asked, I let in every man who wants to register for 5A, no matter how full the class already is. And it's always full, more than sixty-five students.

WOMANHOOD: gentleness, softness, femininity,
femaleness, sensitivity, kindness

The messages on my voice-mail start as soon as preregistration closes, almost six months before the next semester even begins. She always leaves one of the following:

> Professor Felman, you don't know me, but I have tried to register for your 5A course and I got closed out again. Please, tell me whatever I have to do to get in.

> Professor Felman, I really want to take your Intro course. I heard it's sooooo good but I had a late registration time. I'm going to study abroad next year and this is my last chance . . . please.

> Professor Felman, I'm a really good friend of Amara's [or Autumn's, Pegah's, or Miriam's . . .] and she told me to tell you that, so you'd let me in 5A.

In these situations I ask every female student why she wants to take the Intro to Women's Studies course, and whether or not she is a senior. Occasionally, I will take two or three more women if they have serious and/or sincere-sounding reasons. I also note the different requests by gender styles: the men assume they can get in, and the women assume I'll say no, and that they have to beg, beg, beg until I say yes.

For years I automatically let in any guy who wanted to take one of my Women's Studies courses.

Thankfully, I don't do this particular kind of "reverse affirmative action" anymore. Too many of the men are not academically qualified and/or they end up trying, albeit unsuccessfully, to monopolize the class. However, I am chagrined at my previous unconditional benevolence toward the men. Especially because I am keenly aware of the much publicized negative statistics—*that White, presumably heterosexual, male students are still favored, called on first and most often (by both male and female professors), no matter how many or how few of them there are in the class.* I have always had at least one or two male students in my Women's Studies classes. Over the years, I have become a participant-observer, creating a mental ethnography of the men: the performance of their masculinities during class time, and after class visiting in my office. I observe, too, their multifaceted relationship(s) to me, a strong, outspoken, radical feminist and *female subject* who is in a position of institutional authority, and my ever-changing, fluid relationship(s) with each one of them.

MANHOOD: legal age, adulthood, voting age,
majority, middle age, prime of life, man's estate

Several years ago two men requested my signature the first day of Feminism for the Year 2000 and Beyond, an advanced seminar with Intro to Women's Studies as a prerequisite. Neither Alex nor Jonothan had taken a single Women's Studies course before, although both men considered themselves left of center politically. Feminist theory—until now—was completely new territory for them.

While I knew beforehand that I was going to sign the add forms, I proceeded to ask why they wanted to take the course.

"I heard you were a great teacher," Alex, a prelaw major, said, "and I wanted to see for myself."

"I'm curious, " Jonothan admitted, "I don't really know much, if anything, about feminism."

Still eager to "diversify" the classroom, I ignored my "macho radar," which had gone off immediately, and let them both in. The fact that both men (and myself) were Jews would prove eminently significant in all our future gender negotiations, even though I would not understand how (or why) for several months.

Feeling defensive during the break on the first day, I told Alex I was a lawyer and assured him we would be looking at gender bias in the law. He nodded. As for Jonothan—a Peace and Conflict Studies major—my insecurity was more intimate, centered intricately around my femaleness: *Would he see me as an attractive, smart woman, and not one of those "ugly, man-hating, academically politically correct, rigid bull dykes"?* I was flabbergasted by the excruciatingly painful self-realization that, after twenty years of successful teaching, the presence of White, presumably heterosexual men in the classroom could still unnerve and decenter my strong sense of self-worth. And call into question the breadth of my scholarship as well as the quality of my vast artistic accomplishments.

With Alex, the decentering was clearly about power; or more specifically, my fear of being publicly interrogated (challenged) in front of the other students. (That I *assumed* I had to "puff-up" the course so it would appear "legally" credible to this prelaw senior now makes me smile.) Jonothan posed a much subtler but no less insidious problem for me. Privileging the information that he was a Peace and Conflict Studies major, I assumed he was a "nice" but uninformed guy. I did notice, however, that a particular sense of myself as not being "fully female" was drastically heightened by having Jonothan as a student. Usually, I am confident in the classroom, aware of my own privilege, status, and authority: I especially enjoy being a woman in charge. But it was precisely the "woman" part that felt so "unfemale" and "unfeminine" all of a sudden.

Discussing the impact of male students in our classes, my feminist colleagues often comment how they feel as though their authority is questioned continually due to the fact of their femaleness. Unfortunately (and tragically), most of our male students are negotiating for the first time a woman's institutional authority in ways previously unknown to them; that is, according to the rules of the academy, *a woman who is obviously in charge* of her own course(s). As the professor, she becomes publicly anointed and is (for the time being) the university-sanctioned expert on the subject matter under study. For these men, many of whom are new to Women's Studies, the powerful, passionate presence of a strong, vocal, intelligent feminist professor was not part of their expectations when they registered for the course. Many of the men sense that the professor—she—represents not just a different model, but an entire paradigm shift not only within the classroom itself, but also in terms of their own future relationships to women.

The mere presence of this confident female "role model" seems to create a contemporaneous space for the female students themselves to assume greater voice and agency in the same class. Thus, male students—without any conscious planning on their part—now find themselves immersed in an environment that challenges and simultaneously subverts the omnipresent misogyny indigenous to the familiar traditional academic learning environment. The male students, then, experience a "temporary" loss of personal power that can last for days, weeks, or the entire semester. The amount of this particular "loss of power," otherwise known as masculinity, depends on just how deep the impact this counternormative classroom experience turns out to be, as well as the student's—his—ability to navigate previously unfamiliar, feminist, and womanist terrain.

My male, heterosexual students of color, specifically African-American men, seem not to share "the White man's" fear of me as a strong, outspoken feminist professor. In fact, the opposite appears to be true. That is, my power is welcomed and responded to with enthusiasm. Why this is so is related to the historically powerful and positive figure of "the Black female matriarch" of Black culture—I am not a complete unknown or "foreign" experience to my African-American male students. On the contrary, I am reassuring politically and emotionally; I have not been completely co-opted by the dominant system as I have maintained my strong, distinct voice and agency, so there exists between us a space for bonding collectively as "outsiders" that does not occur for me with White male students.

SEXINESS: *masculinity, maleness, potency, muscularity, manliness, toughness, virility*

As for the impact of the men on the professor herself, I want to look at the mind-body split (an utterly conventional gendered response) that I often experience in the initial presence of certain male students. In "Femme 2000" I understood that Alex threatened my mental prowess, but Jonothan appeared to call into question the totality of my femaleness. I began to see how Jonothan's particular rejection of all things violent, including the use of physical force to settle any global or domestic conflict, impacted directly on the performance *and* reception of his academic masculinity. In choosing a nontraditional major with a Theater Arts minor, Jonothan was choosing not to conform, except in his public admission that he was heterosexual. Here was an American-born Jew who unlike Alex had rejected the upwardly mobile, middle-class Jewish male mandate to succeed in a "hostile" gentile world. Although his family was troubled by his seeming lack of competitive drive to succeed, Jonothan wasn't. In the post-Holocaust, Diasporic lexicon of maleness, Jonothan was boldly refusing to perform his assigned (and ethnically influenced) macho, materialist role. There would be no estate waiting for he who had not earned his large pile of gold bricks.

If Jonothan was not going to perform appropriately "masculine" and Jewish, what would happen to his manhood and adult status in the tribe? Furthermore, what did his very unmasculine major (and minor) mean vis-à-vis the performance of my femininity and the existence of my own womanhood? Synthesizing the issues, I saw that to be truly Jewish and female, I needed Jonothan *not* to perform as poor, defeated Willy Loman in *Death of a Salesman*. But rather, for the stability and preservation of my (Jewish) femininity, I urgently required Jonothan to perform as my Every(successful, super-Jewish)man. Left without a mirror to see my "opposite" ethnically gendered self reflected back, I could only become (in my psychically wounded imagination) Philip Roth's overbearing Jewish mother who ball-busted her beautiful Bar Mitzvah baby into a heterosexual *feygalah* who refused to compete in the cutthroat macho-driven marketplace. Hence, whenever I looked over at Jonothan, I became acutely gender-disoriented. Where was the *all-American*, high-powered, squash-playing, globetrotting *man* in the soft, gentle *Jew* who sat before me? The maintenance of my reconfigured, radical womanhood had become exceedingly vulnerable to the mere presence of a nontraditionally gendered Jewish man in my feminist classroom. (For more on Jewish men and gender, see Daniel Boyarin's *Unheroic Conduct*.) Ironically, Jonothan's reconfigured location away from traditional American Jewish manhood served not to liberate, but to inhibit my now reified tribal and academic femininity.

It's not that the presence of female students never disrupts my equilibrium in the classroom; rather, I don't feel personally threatened by the women. I have learned instead to sympathetically identify with their repeated challenges to my authority, and to interpret their behavior as politically motivated, based on their own extremely complicated and ambivalent responses to the traditionally rigid and contradictory gender training that we unfortunately have somewhat in common. (For a full discussion of women in the classroom see chapter 5, "Performing Femininities.") I have noticed, however, that the presence of a strong, powerful female professor seems to give the women permission to cross over and transgress their own highly gendered barriers. That is, some women can (and do) begin to perform "macho" themselves, becoming traditionally masculine and aggressive whenever they feel too threatened by me, their ambiguously feminine and Jewish, Davidian woman professor. They remind me of Jeanne Kirkpatrick, who was allowed to represent the United States at the UN; or of prime ministers Margaret Thatcher and Golda Meir, who were both frequently accused of being far too masculine and not nearly feminine enough. These three female world leaders, at various times throughout their long public-service careers, felt the need to publicly denounce feminism and fervently proclaim themselves to be proudly "antifeminist" women. Hence, with my own female students, I understand exactly what's happening and on those occasions I consciously step outside their specifically gendered female distress. With some amusement I wish my own testosterone levels would/could increase, thereby enabling me to meet my now gender-bending female students, performing man-to-man!

We sat in a circle in Femme 2000. For Jonothan, learning in a circle was no big deal; for Alex, it was obvious that the face-to-face seating arrangement, eye contact, and physical proximity in an academic setting were totally unnerving. If he raised his hand to speak, he never looked at anyone directly; instead his eyes focused vaguely upward. For the first five weeks, Alex barely looked up from his notebook, where he assiduously drew pictures for the entire three hours. In fifteen weeks, I never saw Alex take a single note; I worked hard not to personalize his doodling. Smug in the knowledge that he would surely fail law school if he spent all his class time scribbling, I decided not to say a word.

Toward the middle of the term, Alex asked if he could bring his mother to class.

"Why?" I was nonplussed.

"I've been talking to her about all the wicked-cool stuff you bring up and she's really interested." At this point I had to wonder if I had misjudged Alex. Maybe he was sincere in learning about feminism; otherwise, why would he spend so much time talking to his mother about class? I agreed to the request, with trepidation, realizing that I had remained somewhat threatened by Alex's presence and was still suspicious of his motives. In retrospect, many of my negative feelings toward Alex were unresolved projections of my own ambivalence toward unearned White male (and in this specific case, Jewish) power and privilege, including my inability to maintain a full Subject position while in the presence of such "omnipotence."

Toward the end of the semester, Alex admitted to me—in private, face to face, with the door of my office closed tightly—that the minute he walked into the classroom, the very first day: *I knew I was way out of my league.*

Stunned by such a personally vulnerable admission, I asked myself:

How could I have so quickly forgotten that insecurity—emotional and intellectual—is most often reciprocal? Once again, I had to confront those ethnically cultured demons that were designed to distort reality, causing me to feel victimized when no such thing was actually occurring. These demons represent the long-term collective impact of the traditional, American Jewish gender training that occurs in many immigrant and refugee Eastern European families. And now, in the present, those left-over caustic Ashkenazi demons had caused me to automatically elevate Alex and to disempower myself simply because he was a HE and I was a *she*. He was the real *yeshiva bocher*, circumcised and blessed, while I was just masquerading, bereft for life, born without a foreskin to be ritually severed and thereby denied my own personal covenant with G-d, HE.

Looking up from where I sat, Alex had become a big, bad-ass, adult Jewish man, a true patriarch in the biblical sense. To me the teacher, here was Abraham, the first Jew, who went around smashing his father's hand-carved limestone idols in search of a divinely masculine, monotheistic truth. Painfully I wondered if in Alex's mind I had become Sara, she who had "humiliated" him for so many years, by sending him off to her dark-skinned handmaiden Hagar to produce the necessary son. In many cultures, the failure to produce a male offspring is personally devastating for the female partner, and yet it is also viewed as negatively feminizing for her male counterpart. In my psychically overactive imagination, I was sure Alex/Abraham experienced me as the emasculating Matriarch, and himself not so unlike Roth's literary iconoclastic son Portnoy, the motherfucker of all (male) Jews.

And yet, the nonresolution of this historical tension enabled us to encapsulate a kind of mutual respect and intellectual reciprocity that included the contradictory, positive acknowledgment of our strong, often clashing, gendered differences. And it led to the very proud admission on Alex's part that *I am now a convert to feminist pedagogy and even—sort of—enjoy sitting in a circle!*

Alex's presence and traditional White male hegemonic behavior taught me that as a strong, powerful female professor I had to resist the repeated urge to perform in class as his "cute, middle-aged soubrette." I understood, too, that if I was going to maintain a strong sense of myself, I had to subvert the traditional, ethnically feminized position of being just another "nice Jewish girl." It had to be okay for Alex and other male students not to like me. Nor was it my responsibility to affirm the masculinity of my male students (as they became newly vulnerable), by performing the classic "mothering" that so many men (and women) continue to expect from any woman in a position of power. In the end, this analysis and rejection of traditional Jewish gendered roles freed me to be the smart, confident, ebullient *vilde chaye* that I actually am.

The participant-observer in me realized early in the semester that when there are only two men in a Women's Studies class, a classically negative feminine paradigm is acted upon the men by the female students and sometimes by me, the professor. Unbeknownst to them, any two men are assigned iconographic status by being seen as the "masculine representatives" on a more macro level. In this scenario, as one of the only two men in Femme 2000, Alex had been succinctly coded by the women students (and me) as the "bad boy," a position he clearly relished, while Jonothan became the "good guy." Week after week Alex played the role of "grand inquisitor." No matter what the issue was—reproductive rights, affirmative action, or sexual harassment—he interrogated the entire class with gusto. So suave and controlled was his public performance of assimilated Jewish masculinity in the classroom that we were never actually sure what Alex, the person, thought. He was the devil's advocate, the *macro macho bad guy* to Jonothan's developing *profeminist good guy* who never disagreed or challenged the theories presented. After all, Jonothan's "real" masculinity had become diluted, as he was into *conflict resolution* without physical or intellectual force. Systemically, in capitalism, there is limited room at the top. Someone—many—must fail in order for any single individual (read: White and male) to succeed. Thus, in my class (capitalist by default) only one of the men could succeed and thereby qualify as good. In this case, as so often happens, the women and I performed our capitalistic, co-opted femininities to perfection: we successfully pitted the men against each other and they happily, virily complied.

With Alex, the class developed a somewhat antagonistic yet friendly relationship; at the same time, Jonothan was embraced with total delight. He even admitted to me (in private) that he knew he was "The Good Guy" and quite liked his regally anointed position. It seemed, too, that there was no middle ground; the men had to be in constant, albeit nonverbalized, competition with each other for the publicly sanctified, singular position of "THE Feminist Man." At this historic time, within a capitalistic social economy, there simply couldn't be two good, feminist men. In this way, not so coincidentally, the eighteen women students mirrored my own ambivalent feelings toward the presence of the two men in what had previously been our—the girls'—class. In future classes, to transform this dynamic from the beginning or to thwart its development altogether, I use the same "decloaking" tactic that I employ around the subject of race; that is, I name at the outset the situation and then define the potential challenges we as a class will have to navigate together. This intervention on my part has the potential to prevent the performance of masculinities from being automatically relegated or confined to the only two males present. Masculinity, then, as is true with femininity, becomes fluid, constantly changing shape, and in perpetual motion.

Performing Masculinities: To Be Manly
brave, virile

I had never taught Simone de Beauvoir's *The Second Sex* with heterosexual White men in the class and had no idea how their presence would impact the discussion. Often, gay men in Women's Studies classes identify with the negative position women have been traditionally assigned in society, so the study of feminist theory becomes a relief for them rather than the threat it proves to be for many straight men. In preparing to discuss de Beauvoir's theory of woman as "inessential other," I write on the board in Femme 2000: *He is the Subject, he is the Absolute—she is the Other* (*The Second Sex*), and then ask the class to write on the following questions: *What would relationships between men and women look like if both individuals were seen by the other as Subject rather than Object? And what are the implications of a Subject/Subject position for Whites and people of color?* The women start writing immediately, fast and furious. They don't stop writing until I tell them to. Alex and Jonothan look stumped. I wait for the men to catch up with the women and write their thoughts down. Alex scribbles a few words, then stops abruptly. It doesn't look like Jonothan has written anything.

"Let's start," I say.

"I don't understand the question." Jonothan is looking around.

"What do you mean *Subject/Subject?*"

As I think to myself that perhaps in Peace and Conflict Studies, everyone is always an *Object*, Alex quickly raises his hand.

"Yes?" I nod in his direction.

"It's impossible." No one says a word. The women in the class seem poised to strike.

"What's impossible?" I ask, knowing exactly what he's going to say, but I want the other students to hear the words from Alex himself.

"There always has to be an *other*, an *Object*. That's just the way it is."

"What do you mean?" Shoshana blurts out. "Maybe it's impossible for you . . ."

"Okay." I don't want the discussion to turn into a series of personal attacks. "Jonothan, do you understand what we're talking about?"

"I think so." He nods, but I'm not convinced. I wonder why this concept is so hard for Jonothan to comprehend.

An hour later we conclude the discussion, agreeing that systemically, under capitalism, Alex may be right that authentic Subject/Subject relationships are a structural impossibility. Although I am pleased that the analysis did not deteriorate into a list of personal grievances between the male and female students, I am struck by where the class as a whole got stuck. Imaginatively speaking, no one could describe what a Subject/Subject relationship would look like. The implications were clear. On a subconscious level, the men, both conventionally male-gendered Alex and newly feminist masculine Jonothan, automatically saw themselves as Subjects—the indigenous I's—but they neither *would* nor *could* imagine the women they were involved with as Subjects in their own right. The women, on the other hand, suggested that they, and people of color, could achieve a Subject status only temporarily, depending on the situation, but that a permanent, structural, and institutional change was out of the question. Because, as Catherine said, "Absolutely everything in society—including the nuclear family—would have to change."

"Precisely," I added, " and remember the uproar Dan Quayle created about a single, working, White middle-class woman character who Candice Bergen played on *Murphy Brown*, a TV show. The character played by Bergen had had the audacity to become pregnant and have a baby on her own, outside the traditional nuclear family model or even with a male partner. Clearly, Quayle could not tolerate Murphy

Brown/Candice Bergen's solo subjectivity in relation to the institution of motherhood. Or," I told the class, "consider the recent national furor over granting legal status to gay and lesbian couples in long-term partnerships on par with heterosexual marriage. The furor reveals the terror of granting the same subjectivity to committed gay couples as is granted to those who participate in traditional heterosexual marriage. In this case, granting subjectivity to gay marriage would seem to take away from the subjectivity that comes with the privilege of straight marriage."

Performing Masculinities: To Be Potent
powerful, mighty, puissant, strong

From the beginning of Blacks and Jews, Jonothan (and his three other Jewish male cohorts) seemed acutely uncomfortable—the exact opposite of the Jonothan I'd known last semester in Femme 2000. I wasn't sure if it was the close proximity of so many Black students for the first time in his life (six out of nineteen), or if the two self-identified Orthodox Jews in the class had called into question his overtly secular, cultural Jewish identity. As it turned out, Jonothan felt "dethroned," and spent three-quarters of the semester angry with me. Finally, right before the second-to-last class, he made an appointment to come to my office.

He began sheepishly. "So, it's been real hard, being in class and all."

"Oh? Tell me."

"It's not that easy." Jonothan stopped looking at me. Usually we had great eye contact.

"Try." I didn't take my eyes off him. I had absolutely no idea what he was going to say.

"Well, at first, I felt kind of out of place, you know, not like in Femme 2000 where everything was so hip 'n' cool."

He kept talking, faster and faster. "Suddenly, in Blacks and Jews, I wasn't the only cool guy any more—*the* feminist man—and I didn't know what to do. I was just another lost Jewish man, who started to feel invisible. Then, and this is really hard to admit, I was super-jealous of all the Black girls, how close they were—supporting each other and all—and I was convinced that you were favoring them, the Black students, especially the women, over us, you know, the Jews, mostly the men. You were always laughing with the Black girls, like you guys had a private joke going on or something."

I was shocked. This was the last thing I expected to hear from peace-loving Jonothan.

"It got so bad, that when I met with Sam and Michael, I devised a conspiracy to take back the class. The three of us planned to walk into the room and stage a 60s-style sit-in, right in the middle of our circle, with big signs that said *Jewish, Male, and Proud*. We weren't going to say a word, just sit there, until you called on each one of us, by name. But we chickened out. I didn't ask Dan to join us because he always seemed so tough and sure of himself." Two weeks later in his final response paper, Jonothan recorded his own particular process of growing self-awareness:

> I started to withdraw . . . to get scared of all the progress we as a class had made. . . . It was at this juncture that the conspiracy was slowly beginning to brew away in my head. I felt the need to share with others (Whites and Blacks) my thoughts of Professor Felman's contrived circus of a class. I was concerned as to why Black people were running the class, but as I eventually concluded what else could I have expected from the concocted curricula. It became an issue of Black vs. Jewish and I couldn't see it any other way. . . . This was a telltale sign of the adversarial rut I was in. . . . We as Jews were angry because we were not consistently in the spotlight.

As he continued speaking, Jonothan's face flushed from embarrassment. "I wanted to talk to you from the beginning of the semester, but I was afraid to. Now I'm glad I waited because I understand what happened to me as a White, Jewish guy in that class, and to all the other Jewish kids. All of a sudden we had to share the space, so to speak, and we weren't prepared to—especially here at Brandeis, where we're supposed to be the majority, whatever that means. But we had to go through it and blame you for awhile, for everything we felt. Mostly, that you were privileging the Black students by calling on them more often, and that you were always focusing on the Black narrative in particular, while abandoning us, the Jews, at the same time. We got caught in one of those classic good-bad, either-or binaries you keep warning us about."

"Thank you," I said, totally stunned, still absorbing everything. "I'd like to share some of this with the class if that's okay. I think it will help everyone to hear what you went through."

Jonothan nodded his consent. I was struck by his reaction to feeling displaced or even replaced. And how, once under pressure and newly vulnerable, he so easily reverted to classic male behavior, turning the situation into an "us" against "them."

Unknown to Jonothan, strong, aggressive, masculine Dan was having his own problems maintaining a firm, whole sense of self. Writing in his final paper, he discussed how he secretly harbored Jonothan's conflict—that there could only be one winner and all the rest had to be losers.

> I do not know why I was so intent on justifying my feelings about Jews. I also do not know when I first started peeking over the edges of my highly fortified enclosure. Was I so locked in the concept of subject-object relationships that I could not affirm a Black narrative without pushing down a Jewish one? . . . I took this class to make my relationship with Blackness subject-subject. However, in reality . . . I was intent on making it subject-object. And my Jewishness would not play the subject. Unfortunately, I tried to do that by making myself object. By attacking my Jewishness.

Dan's writing revealed the absolute necessity of keeping perpetually intact the persona of public masculinity while revealing his own male vulnerability to a woman (me) only in private. Much like the Olympic swimmer Greg Louganis, who felt he had to keep the "feminine" secret of his homosexuality from the public (read: male) gaze, including the eyes of his fellow teammates, for fear of ridicule. Or grief-stricken Michael Jordan, who chose to mourn in private, taking early retirement from the NBA the year his father was murdered on a deserted road, found slumped over in the front seat of a red Mustang with his wallet and gold watch missing. When Jordan returned to pro basketball from his self-imposed "mourning in private," he played in even more stupendous form—far exceeding his previous near-miraculous playing—for the Chicago Bulls. Meanwhile his teammate Dennis Rodman was constantly derided for showing off in public his "queer" taste for pink feather boas, long white wedding gowns, and dyed red and orange hair. In politics, men remain forced to cry in private, as President Clinton did when his mother died, taking only two days off to mourn her. It is clear that in order for men to perform the full range of their masculinities on the court and in the classroom, the range of what it means to "act" masculine must expand to include those *female* behaviors that are continuously reviled as the soft, weak, and/or girlish aspects of feminity.

Five minutes after Jonothan left my office, there was a knock on the door. "Come in."

Esther walked in unannounced and without an appointment. She started talking as soon as she sat down.

"So how are you, Professor Felman? Working hard, as usual. How do you think Blacks and Jews is going?" In class Esther always refered to herself as *Esther, The Beautiful Queen*, so at that moment I was reminded of Queen Esther in the Purim story, who came to see King Achashvarus to warn him of Hamen's impending threat to the Jews of Persia. Like the good king, I thought everything was copacetic and proceeded to say just that.

"Actually, the class is going well, better than I had even hoped."

Esther was from Ghana and one of the "Black girls" Jonothan referred to. "You think so, really?" Esther, the beautiful queen, stared at me. She was always powerfully direct, consistently raising her hand to speak, much more so than her African-American classmates, who often had to be called on by name before they would speak out. I understood that Esther's West African majority status clearly gave her the confidence to speak her mind. As a class we had addressed the differences in growing up in a Black-majority country like Ghana or Haiti versus growing up in White America as a Black minority, and how that impacted one's public behavior.

"Okay, Esther, what's up, obviously you don't agree with me."

"It's not that. . . . Oh girl, this is too hard, never mind. I just knew I shouldn't have come in here and opened my big mouth."

"Esther."

"Okay, okay." She took a deep breath, pausing to sit up and face me. "We've been talking—the Jews and all . . . they think and I kind of agree with them, that you are paying more attention to us, you know, the Black students, well, the African Americans in the class. We're always talking about the *Black narrative this* and the *Black narrative that* . . . well, what about the Jewish narrative?"

"What about it? And Esther, just who is this *we*?" I knew that was not the question to ask, but I couldn't help myself. I wondered skeptically if Jonothan had instigated this quasi revolt, or if there actually were a lot of students, Blacks and Jews, who felt the same way. I figured Esther might be more sympathetic than some of the other Black students to her Jewish peers' sense of invisibility because she was neither Jewish nor African American. Because she was Ghanaian, she could be emotionally more detached from the subject matter. And yet, ironically, now that she was in the United States, as a woman she began to perform traditional, Western White femininity (object) by feeling like she needed to remedy the situation, to take care of the Jews (subject) and make sure their views were heard. She had truly become Queen Esther.

"I can't say. Don't ask me that." She was adamant. I'd never seen her so uncomfortable.

"Okay, well, let's just talk. Tell me what you really think. How you see the whole situation."

For about twenty-five minutes we went back and forth, looking at the syllabus, checking each topic—slavery, the *Shoah*, anti-Semitism, racism, stereotypes, et al.—the readings and films. It became ridiculously obvious to both Esther and myself, that each week every single issue had been covered from multiple perspectives, not just Jewish and African-American, but also, when appropriate, Afro-Caribbean, African, Latino, Asian, and Anglo. Clearly, trying to quantify how much time, space, and overall attention the Jewish and Black narratives received in class was ultimately unproductive, not to mention absurd. Esther saw for herself that her perception—and those of her classmates—was simply inaccurate when compared to what actually had occurred in class.

Something else was going on. But what?

When we finished our survey, I said, "I'll take care of it."

"What do you mean?"

"Esther, this is critical: you're not the first person who has come to see me about this."

"I'm not?" She sat back, relieved.

"No. But I'll figure out how to discuss this with the class." I needed time to think about the entire issue, in terms of feminist theory, Black and Jewish subjectivities, multiple lens, masculinity, and femininity, capitalism, and the whole question of life in a "Democratic Union."

Performing Masculinities: To Be Muscular
*robust, vigorous, well-built, athletic, sturdy,
powerful, brawny, lithe, agile*

Other students commented in their final response papers on the potentially incendiary tension that had propelled Esther to come to see me, incited by Jonothan's now defused plot to take back the class.

Patricia's reflections were especially eloquent. She was Haitian by birth and had immigrated to the United States when she was six years old.

> When I came into the class, I knew that I would be a subject but I never expected the Jewish students to lose their subjectivity. It was quite a surprise to me to learn that many Jewish students felt like they no longer had voice in the class and that the voices of the Black students dominated. I couldn't understand how they could feel like the class focused more on the Black issues than on the Jewish conflict when I knew that I had learned so much about Jewish life in America.

And Betsy, a proudly identified Jewish woman who taught Hebrew school, belonged to an Israeli dance troupe, and came from a family of Holocaust survivors, but who had had an extremely difficult time for most of the semester, wrote with grace and courage by the end:

> Perhaps the worst part is that I came to class with what I thought was an open mind, and while in some ways it was, . . . but the way that my thinking was closed, tended to prevail. I was so distraught over my misconception that the "Jewish perspective" and the Jewish history—my history—were not presented that I missed the point . . . that is if I'd been secure enough in my faith and my personal story, I would've seen class in a much clearer light . . . and been able to listen to my classmates and identify more closely with the Black narrative in this country, while simultaneously realizing that throughout the semester, we really did learn about the Jewish people and their plight. I would have recognized that I need to see all of the history as my

own . . . to fully appreciate and understand the material. . . . Perhaps the most important thing that I finally learned, however, is that it is not a competition between histories. There is no qualifying and quantifying here.

I had prepared a lesson plan for the next class of Blacks and Jews, but after speaking with both Esther and Jonothan, I decided to improvise, to let the content that had just been presented to me lead me—and the class—to where we needed to go next. I had to trust that I knew how to address the concern that I had been privileging the Black students over the Jewish students and one group's narrative over the other. Despite knowing that the heart of the complaint was unfounded, pedagogically speaking I had an ethical obligation to address it, because the issue had begun to preoccupy the students, impeding their genuine receptivity to the course material. Not surprisingly, the complaint itself revealed the sophistry that is so often part of identity politics. Stepping back, I began to view Jonothan's reaction and subsequent behavior in terms of a classic reassertion of the traditional rules of masculinity. And also to understand what had happened to the Jews in the class as a whole, how their perceptions gradually became distorted the more complex the issues of race, power, and privilege became: *The more they learned as Jews, about racism and the African-American experience, the more they recognized how little they had factually known beforehand; and, when finally exposed to the complexities of being Black in America today, the Jews began to feel smaller, less masculine, and more helplessly feminine, and to misperceive that their own history was being represented as much less significant.* The Jewish students had been forced to step outside the political, macho binary of *whose people suffered most,* and to abandon their own previous identity as "most." They had been covertly requested to give up their unearned politically male privilege, and learn instead to share the space.

I saw my now newly fearful Jewish students, both men *and* women, performing classically masculine as they began aggressively asserting their preeminence and their dominance in the face of an imagined, terrifying threat.

Jewish students often come to Brandeis seeking a haven, longing for the comfort of the tribe. Many of my students are observant (as opposed to Orthodox), which means they keep kosher, actively celebrate all Jewish holidays, and speak moderate to fluent Hebrew. Some came from small Midwestern towns of few Jews, while others grew up in proudly defined Jewish enclaves, desiring only to remain within their safe, contemporary American shtetl life. Either way, for four years, Brandeis becomes their homeland away from home. Like White men who feel personally attacked when confronted by their own sexism, the Jewish students felt besieged. And the Jewish women easily assumed antifeminist male behavior, having been co-opted by the Jewish men, who feel doubly under siege themselves.

The direct consequence of taking a course that simultaneously considers the experiences of both American Blacks and American Jews is that many of the Jewish students—who had for years been immersed in the history of anti-Semitism and the Holocaust—find themselves unprepared emotionally, intellectually, and/or psychically to accept the reality of the Black experience in the United States. However, in learning (perhaps for the first time ever) about the long-term impact on African Americans of slavery, forced segregation, police brutality, federal medical experimentation, forced sterilization, unequal access, and so on, Jewish students are forced to confront the fundamental distortions of lived American racism instead of the glossing-over that had heretofore been their primary experience and understanding.

Although they remained somewhat locked into the binary of *who suffered most*, the Jewish students gradually responded to their recently acquired knowledge of African-American history, through the application of *sympathetic identification* with the marginalized position of their Black classmates. But then they began to act in consort by seeing themselves as the *real*, unacknowledged victims in the class itself. Viewing themselves (in class) as a legitimate, newly injured party, they demanded immediate reparations; which translated as: *We Jews need more attention paid to us and our horrible history.* Metaphorically, the Jewish students were reacting to feeling expelled, forced to convert to another oppressed minority's narrative, or dispersed yet again, this time from their beloved homeland Brandeis. So I had to interpret the psychic pain of my Jewish students through the long-term lens of the Holocaust and its continued impact on the construction of contemporary American Jewish identity.

So as not to isolate the Jewish students or their experience, I put their fearful reactions into a larger context. I emphasized that seeing their reactions in class, most specifically the vulnerability they expressed in direct relation to the development of the Black narrative alongside their own Jewish narrative, was similar to the reaction many White men continue to have to feminism and postcolonial capitalism: *they feel excluded and invisible and thus entitled to the outright claim of reverse discrimination.* Like the male followers of "Iron John" (John Bly), who go off howling into the forest together. Or the men in the Promise Keepers, who meet in gigantic football stadiums from Atlanta to New York to assert their total authority and virile domination, lest they be run out of their "castles" for good. Ever so fiercely, and with great pride, the Jewish students rose up to assert their White, male primacy.

Walking into class exactly one hour after Esther had left my office, I was still not completely sure what I was going to do. I understood that the Jewish students felt that their status was immanently precarious, as White heterosexual men often do when minorities begin to occupy the same space the men are used to occupying and controlling—that is, the center. Hence Jonothan, with confident, outspoken Esther enlisted as the necessary and very feminine "righteous gentile," were sent ahead as avatars of the festering Jewish student unrest. (A question left to answer is whether or not Esther—not unlike the original Queen Esther—was ultimately co-opted—by her uncle Mordechai/Jonothan—into betraying her classmates by coming to speak to me about and for the Jewish students' concerns.)

But to my feminist, pedagogical delight, I had been presented with a new place in my own academic performance that I had not foreseen, a location I have come to call *competing subjectivities.* I had to find a question to put on the board that didn't threaten or attack the Jewish students, but one that would help them to comprehend *how they had come to feel so disempowered in class, dethroned as it were, within the context of their own Jewish majority status.* I wanted the rest of the class, too, to understand that they also were not immune from experiencing similar feelings in different contexts. And, that the reactions of the Jewish students were merely reflective of a complex social system based on White, male, heterosexual, Christian hegemonic subjectivity and domination in a "democracy" called the United States of America. That is, you don't have to be Jewish to feel invisible or excluded; heterosexual Anglo-Saxon men are feeling that a lot lately, most recently in Florida, Texas, California, and Michigan, where anti–affirmative action, "English only," and anti-immigration legislation is appearing on public ballot initiatives and winning.

Another consideration was my position as a radical feminist professor; I couldn't just speak theoretically. I had to give the entire class enough private writing time to actually recognize the personal self in relation to the political theory of competing subjectivities. Then breaking them up into partners to discuss their responses would build in self-confidence in their differing, perhaps competing ideas before opening up the floor to full discussion. But still, I had to find a question that would get the Jewish students to critically examine their own performances in context, without excluding the Black, Latino, Asian, and Anglo students from the same analytical process. We had to go through this together. After all, in some not-so-small way, the assumed, vulnerable subjectivity of the Jewish students mirrored many of the present-day political fights going on outside the academy, such as the changing status of affirmative action and presumed race-based preferences in employment, housing, and education. Clearly, as happens in the larger society, the entire performance of the "masculinity" of the Jewish People in my class had been threatened by the inclusion of another's subjectivity appearing front and center. Not coincidentally, it was the presence of a vibrant group of Black women that so threatened the Jews in class, while the presence of the lone Black man didn't appear to threaten any students, individually or collectively.

I put the following question on the board:

Please define and discuss the concepts listed below in relation to the status of African Americans and American Jews in the United States:

1. *Precarious Subjectivity*
2. *Static Subjectivity*
3. *Fluid Subjectivity*

Usually the students write for eight to ten minutes, but after fifteen they were still writing nonstop. I noticed that Jonothan and Esther were smiling, nodding their heads as they happily theorized on paper. After giving the class longer than usual to compare their ideas with their partners, we began to unravel the difficult challenge of holding complex, competing subjectivities simultaneously. What that meant—differently and the same—for both Blacks and Jews, men and women, week after week on the micro level of our class and on the macro level of the world at large, was, in fact, negotiating the *intersections of the performance of race and gender.*

By the end of the second hour of class, it became acutely obvious what had occurred. Our conclusions were as follows.

The Jewish narrative "feels" so vulnerable; that is, it "appears" to be automatically displaced the instant another's primary narrative—in this case the African-American narrative—is introduced. Asked to simultaneously hold both narratives as primary, without elevating or lowering either equally primary narrative, is often met with an emotional as well as cerebral blockade. It became a cultural necessity for the Jewish students to learn to expand their previously narrow and limited definition of "subject space," to break down their own self-erected blockades. In addition, the Black students had to be willing to see the Jewish students not just as White, but also as Jewish, and to recognize the currency of anti-Semitism in the lives of Jews, past and present. Furthermore, the role of Christianity, a religion that many of the Black students actively practiced, had to be acknowledged as the contradictory reality that it is: both a liberator and an oppressor. Many of the Black students—African, Afro-Caribbean, and African-American—had not wanted to see Christianity, something so significant and positive in their present lives, as responsible for anyone else's objectification and suffering. After all, even though it was the master's religion, Christianity had been transformed by the slaves themselves to create a permanent position of subjectivity. Hence, like the women in Femme 2000 understood, we are always negotiating a subject/object dialectic as we strive to transform ourselves into permanent subjectivity. Furthermore, all of us had to understand the role that capitalism played in perpetuating traditional race and gender stereotypes regarding Blacks and Jews. That is, when Jews (read: Jewish men) succeed, their masculinity is affirmed; when Black men like Clarence Thomas and Ward Connerly succeed, their Whiteness (read: masculinity) is affirmed. However, when Blacks and Jews fail, their femininity is confirmed.

Finally, the pathological, yet still operative model for acting out when feeling vulnerable and/or threatened with the presence of multiple subjectivities is the aggressive reassertion of traditional male dominance and superior subjectivity. In understanding just how much the performance of enculturated masculinities influences the entire world stage, and how very threatened his own masculinity was, Jonothan sent me this e-mail:

Dear Professor Felman,

... Professor Felman ... Jyl Lynn ... you have been an amazing teacher and an amazing friend. When I entered Femme 2000 last year I was scared and I was certainly not a Feminist. I expected nothing more than to be able to learn something about modern day Feminism. Never did I expect that it would be one of the most transformative experiences in my life. The process that I have been privileged enough to be a part of first in Feminism and then in Blacks and Jews defies words. I am a changed man ... in fact I am now a man. Before meeting you I was immature and had relatively little systemic understanding of the world and now the fog has lifted from in front of my eyes. I am able to see the world in a new light. ...

Love, your student and friend,
JONOTHAN

What's important about Jonothan's realization is that he recognized the false premise his masculinity was built on before taking Femme 2000 and Blacks and Jews, and that now he was able to include other subjects, myself, Black men and women, as contributing to the reconfiguring of his own manhood. Thus, by the end of the semester, Jonothan's subjectivity was no longer displaced by the presence of another's equally compelling subjectivity.

Other students, reflecting on their personal subject/object experience, wrote in-depth comments in their final response papers.

From Louisa, the only Argentinian in the class:

The discussion ... about the subject-object and subject-subject relationship really put me in a tense state, because there were some inner conflicts within the class regarding how much emphasis was put on each narrative. Although I am not Black or Jewish, I heard both sides ... and it amazed me to see how I couldn't make the connection that people were feeling threatened and insecure that they weren't being properly represented, because they were used to a subject-object relationship. ... I didn't think that we, Women's Studies students, would be viewing things on a competitive level. ... I was assuming that "us" and "them" frame of thinking ... that ... we wouldn't fall for such a conflict in our class, but again this went to show how even though we were becoming more aware ... of the underlying issues between Blacks and Jews, it didn't mean that we couldn't have unintentionally felt threatened by the other. Luckily for us, however, our wonderful wit and humbleness allowed us to realize that both narratives were being represented and why some [students] were feeling insecure and how we could learn from it.

And from Patricia, who is Afro-Caribbean:

Close relationships with Jewish students outside of the class developed because I was no longer afraid of not being in my comfort zone, surrounded by people who act and in some cases, think like me. I was no longer afraid of my subjectivity being lost to anyone because as a true subject, I have the authority to maintain my subjectivity. . . . I feel like I am so intellectually mature about the conflict between Blacks and Jews.

Finally from Marsha, the American-born daughter of Haitian immigrants (she brought her mother and sister to class the day she spoke about what she had written), comes a difficult and vulnerable admission about her own ongoing struggle to hold multiple subjectivities simultaneously.

For the first time . . . I looked at the Holocaust and attempted to hold it simultaneously with Slavery . . . and debated on the use and ownership of the words "Black Holocaust" . . . and came to believe that words cannot be owned, and they definitely do have power. . . . I came to understand the desire in equating Black suffering to Jews as a necessity for recognition. . . . Black Americans needed a point of reference . . . but I remained torn . . . and did not want to believe that European Jews had a similar experience as Black Americans. . . . I wanted to compare the two, even though I knew it was not necessary. . . . At this point I began to logically understand the fear Jews have of losing their status and power in this country . . . and their fear of having their suffering forgotten and their constant need to protect themselves. I began to understand the Jewish perception of the American Jewish Narrative . . . to see the paradigm of Jews being pitted against Blacks so that the myth of democracy can continue. . . . I finally saw the two competing narratives. But I was not able to accept both, let alone hold both.

All along, I had been concerned that I would lose Marsha, that she would just "drop out" psychologically, while remaining physically present in the room. This was her first Women's Studies class, so in addition to the actual course material, she was also being introduced to feminism and concepts like multiple lens and contradictory realities. When she asked for a sticker to take Femme 2000 the next fall, I knew that Marsha had decided not to give up, that she had accepted the challenge of holding at least two (and possibly more) competing narratives. For her final solo performance, Marsha presented the class, including her visiting mother and sister, with an intimate autobiographical monologue in the rich tradition of Ntozake Shange's *For Colored Girls Who Have Considered Suicide when the Rainbow Is Enuf*:

Black, Haitian, Dominican, Catholic, Minority, Student, Athlete, Female, Friend, Sister, Daughter; these are just some of the titles one can use to define me. However there is one other title that directly connects to each of these which is American. "American" is directly connected to all my characteristics, not only by requirement but by choice as well. I cannot speak of being American without touching these titles listed above because they are all intertwined.

I am Haitian American, a child of immigrant parents, therefore, I often find myself caught in the tensions of my Haitian heritage and my American citizenship. For them, being American is what they have become over time. For me it is what I have been from my moment of birth. Being Haitian or better yet American goes far beyond having citizenship in a particular country. I never actually lived in the culture first hand, but the culture was brought here by my parents, and it became a part of my American culture, which is why I consider myself Haitian American.

I am often characterized as African American because I am Black, but I have a complex about that characterization, which I believe to have come from my upbringing. My parents have done a terrific job in establishing themselves in this country without losing their Haitian identity. As I begin to self-identify as African American, do I lose part of that heritage, do I choose to give in, to surrender and no longer fight to be different.

By the end of the semester, Marsha cogently explicated just how difficult the daily performance of competing subjectivities is in America. Yet on her own, she gallantly chose to accept *that the performance of simultaneous multiple subjectivties, within the self and others, is a lifelong challenge.*

As for me, a female professor, I must remain forever vigilant, neither compromising nor losing my subjectivity in the feminist classroom when faced with traditional masculinities. How to get GI Joe out of the last row, to stop lobbing verbal hand grenades when encountering multiple subjectivities, is a major pedagogical feat. But I continue to teach toward a new developing *feminist masculinity*, in which our male students do not feel in competition with either their powerful female professors or their strong, articulate sister subjects, *las feministas*. We can be together at last, eye to eye, subject to subject.

Damsels in Distress

Performing Femininities

FEMINIZE: weaken, enervate, soften, cripple, emasculate, sissify
WEAKEN: enfeeble, minimize, lessen, lower, reduce, sap, undermine, deplete, debilitate
ENERVATE: devitalize, debilitate, enfeeble, exhaust
CRIPPLE: incapacitate, exhaust, break down, stifle, mutilate, lame, destroy, mangle, paralyze
—Microsoft Word 97 Thesaurus

I. STAGE FRIGHT

Performing Femininities: To Feminize
weaken, enervate, soften, cripple, emasculate, sissify

"What's the difference between *real help* and *imagined help*?" I ask.

I am standing in front of my introductory Women's Studies class, 5A, giving seventy-plus students their first quiz of the semester. Although the answers are not graded, this quiz is not superfluous. It is an academic ritual-cum-performance that I use to dramatic effect to reveal the often concealed biases of my students. Although I ask several questions, I am most interested in how the class responds to feminist theorist Marilyn Frye's discussion (see *The Politics of Reality*) of the concept of *help* in relation to the power dynamics and gender roles of opening and closing doors. Those literal ones—solid oak, steel, or double-sided glass—and those metaphorical doorways that continue to be blocked by decades of accumulated testosterone.

Inevitably, no one in the entire room remembers anything about "doors" or "help" from last week's readings. They breeze right through the other two questions—*Is hair political?* and *What is a hierarchy of oppression?*—but they simply are not prepared to discuss help, however real or imagined. The first time this happens, I am totally unprepared. I had assumed that *hierarchy of oppression* would prove the most difficult idea to grasp. Now, seven years later, I not only prepare for their inability to recall Frye's critical theory, but I also enter the room planning to lead the entire class through a very real performance of *help*, and all "her" accompanying, disturbing, political ramifications. Yet I always stop before my helpful performance has a chance to begin. Standing in my knee-high black leather boots, feet spread slightly apart for balance, I come to a disturbing realization about my female students. In spite of what has been so diligently concealed through years of perfecting the female outward appearance, I have finally become privy to what's painfully stuck on the feminized inside. That they are truly damsels in the midst of a major postmodern, poststructural gendered distress. And that it is this ambivalence about their own femaleness that blocks the ability to negotiate the complexities of Frye's theory. No other question reveals the actual acute state of mind—the mens rea—of my female students more than: *What's the difference between real and imagined help?* for it reveals an inability as adult women to grapple with their deepest longings. Most of these highly educated women continue to want the literal and figurative door opened for them. Whether they need help or not, they often lack the powerful transformative desire to open the door by themselves and/or for themselves.

After years of resisting this unnerving "revelation" I can no longer ignore that a gendered distress—peculiarly female in nature—is present in the classroom. I cannot pretend, as so many of my colleagues do, that the academic atmosphere is completely neutral. Neutrality, as repeatedly illustrated by science, psychology, and the misapplication of the law, is a complete and utter fiction. On the contrary, I have come to understand that this intellectual resistance is the students' way of asking me—their strong, very loud female professor—for help, without having to ask at all. This, too, is part of a learned gendered "helplessness" that the students continue to promote, year after year, until I give a quiz that requires them to engage Frye directly. For my women students do not want to publicly or privately name their distress(es) with regards to their own femaleness. But as a professor utilizing feminist pedagogy, I know that I have to resist the temptation to join the students in their "premodern" helpless position, to take care of them, or to commiserate with their poststructural pain. I know, too, that it is up to me to tell these Brandeis damsels that one day their intellectual and emotional ambivalence will ultimately *kill* their desire—if it hasn't already.

Ambivalence kills desire relates conceptually to whether or not our female students see themselves as having both the necessary voice and the agency to make themselves heard in and out of the classroom. Ambivalence, according to *Roget's Thesaurus* (1941), is the loss of willpower: hesitation, lukewarmness, uncertainty, or infirmity of purpose. This is a mathematical equation with far-reaching psychological implications: *voice plus agency equals the absence of infirmity and the presence of desire,* including the specific desire to transcend those paradigmatic structural barriers that are counterintuitive to one's sense of a wholly realized self, regardless of gender. Whenever a woman is stuck in the perpetual state of a historically gendered, "feminine" hesitancy, access to her voice is impeded, and her ability to act solely on her own behalf—to take agency—is immobilized. The question of voice and agency is not about essentializing the category "woman," or erasing differences of culture and class among women; rather, it is about resisting traditional, patriarchal gendered roles that limit female desire. Period. And in the academy, female desire, in all its many forms, from the highly cerebral to the sublimely sensual, has the potential to transform the classroom from a passively gendered, "feminine," regressive space, to an active and progressive, truly radical, feminist space. In the end, desire itself creates the urgency not merely to react but to act.

Open the damn door, already! I shout silently into the room. *Just open it and walk, crawl if you have to. But open the door yourself!*

In the end, I don't say a single word out loud. We look at each other. Those who long to be helped and me, who has often unwittingly refused the very real help offered to her because she/I did not want to appear helpless. We in the "feminist" part of the academy are left with the nearly insurmountable task: *How to teach our women students not to be afraid to open the door first*. Not to be afraid to simply walk straight up to that huge towering dominant paradigm of masculinity and say, "Move over." Or "Open Sesame." In the end, a woman must have the necessary political desire to open the door for herself if she wants to get inside, outside, or cross to the other side, where her power, passion, and potential will face head on the bone-chilling reality of patriarchy and all its fierce intransigence to women's active agency. What does it take for an undergraduate damsel stuck in the thick of her gendered distress to overcome a collective resistance to move away from that position that is traditionally *feminized*, and to move toward the more challenging *feminist* location; to move from a historical object to a fully realized, contemporary subject? And thereby develop the permanent, infinite desire to continuously open the door for herself? Every semester I try something new as I guide the class toward grasping the profound difference between *real, feminist help* and the so often culturally determined preferred and proffered *imagined, feminized help* that they have come to mistake for genuine, democratic assistance.

Performing Femininities: To Weaken
enfeeble, minimize, lessen, lower, reduce, sap, undermine, deplete, debilitate

In the class Reading and Writing Autobiography we sit in a circle. The classroom is small and our desks are pushed in tight, close to each other. Sometimes I stand and walk around the circle, looking directly into the eyes of a particular student. Or, I sit in the circle, occasionally rising up to sit on the back of my chair, lifting my entire torso up high for dramatic pedagogical effect. I am always intentional, moving from one academic physicality to another in the space of our three-hour seminar. It is important to know when to stand up, when to strut around the academic circle, when to sit back and remain quiet, watching, listening, and continually sensing the movement and pulse of the class. Over the years, I have perfected my theatrical technique, missing very little, if anything, of what occurs audibly or visually in the classroom. Take the ubiquitous undergraduate yawn. I now understand that a yawn means many things, not always fatigue; in fact, most often, students yawn when they are having strong feelings about the material in question. Within the performance context, I have to resist the urge to yawn with them or we would all stop for the intellectual equivalent of an afternoon siesta rather than confront the difficult subject matter before us.

Whenever I open my mouth to speak, I always speak loud enough to be heard. Sometimes the room is so still, the students so engaged, that I need merely whisper a point across. The students nod. I am loud enough even in a whisper that no one has ever had to ask me to speak up. Louder. No one has ever said that when I speak they cannot hear a word I say. People tell me that I have a distinguished voice; that my voice is recognizable; that the sound of my voice is unique. LOUDER. I do not speak to hear the mellifluous sound of my own voice. Whenever I speak it is to communicate, to connect across the frightful difference of "otherness" that sets us so apart from one another. I must know that the listener can hear me without having to strain or read my lips. I must speak strongly from the deep reservoirs of a wholly integrated self. Otherwise, when the words come just from the throat, completely disconnected from the body and without the force of feeling, they lose passion and meaning. And then I am no longer heard. LOUDER. What happens when I can no longer hear myself? When I am not here anymore? *The women students disappear right before my eyes. Floating up, up, and away. Out of their seats, their wispy bodies slip silently through the keyhole. One after another, up and out of the classroom they float effortlessly into the hall. All the women leave. I am left alone, mouth fully open, speaking to a room of empty seats.* This is my fear, if I continue to demand that my students speak to be heard. But this is an essential part of the critical pedagogy that informs and infuses the classrooms we continue to inhabit together. The politics of speaking loud enough to be heard by an entire small circle of students.

Twenty-five years ago, in graduate school, I read for the first time, and never forgot, the words of the poet Muriel Ruckeyser: *"If a woman told the truth about her life, the world would split open."* If my women students tell the truth about their lives, their Brandeis universe will split apart, cracking right down the very center, straight to the core where their authentic voices lay dormant, sleeping for years at a time.

In Autobiography, every semester, they tell me their dreams. Diane wants to be a lawyer, Heather a professor, Yael a cantor, Ellen a political activist, Jasmine an international banker, Patricia a writer, and Esther a doctor.

Our circle is quite small. Whether we want to or not, we see and smell each other. The desks are that close together. I know what Martine, the student sitting next to me, ate for lunch. So when Sarita opens her mouth to speak and no one can hear a word she says, and I have to keep asking her to repeat herself, I know that she has to try awfully hard to speak so softly that no one in our small, smelly circle can hear a word she says. She doesn't seem to care. She doesn't seem to understand the politics of speaking to be heard. From where I sit, our eyes meet. *Speak up, Sarita, so you too won't disappear through the keyhole.* Sometimes, I think Sarita would speak louder and we could hear her better if she only mouthed the words. I use considerable energy asking Sarita to *please repeat, again, what she has to say. Only louder, so that everyone can hear. Louder, please, Sarita. For your sake, not mine. For your own sake, not mine.* If I do not ask Sarita to speak up, no one else will.

I have to beg and plead with the "girls" in the class to speak up. It doesn't matter how small the circle is, five students or fifteen, there are always women who refuse to speak loud enough to be heard. I make allowances for cultural and class differences, take into consideration how ethnicity or class privilege may impact the volume of one's voice. Still, the women speak as if the very sound of their own voice(s) is terrifying. That the sound itself will knock them over for good. Over the years, it's gotten worse, not better. The majority of my female students do not speak loud enough to be heard.

I take a professorial poll (at Brandeis and beyond). I ask around. "Can you hear your female students when they speak?"

"No."

"No?"

"No!"

"Any trouble with the men?"

"No."

We are in agreement, the other faculty and myself, that there is an epidemic of seemingly unknown origin and without an immediate cure going around campus. Microphones won't help the situation. The silence will only amplify, louder and louder, as we strain to hear our women students say they are speaking as loud as they absolutely, possibly can. *It's held in the body,* I want to say. *Your voice. The body. Your body.*

"Really, Professor Felman, I cannot speak any louder."

In defense, my ears seal shut, as I feel myself going deaf. There is nothing left to hear in this room but the decorous sound of my own voice.

The epidemic is so severe that I watch, unable to help, when Sarita's entire body bends over in a spasm of obvious pain. As if the sheer effort of speaking loud enough to be heard ruptures her feminized vertebrae, causing the severe abdominal pain threatening her very life, right before my own extremely feminist eyes.

I think to myself that it is gender-specific and contagious, this weakening of the female vocal chord, crossing at will the boundaries of race, class, and sexuality—but rarely gender. While the male chords remain relaxed, reverberating across the width of the large classroom, clear across the campus and back. So everyone can hear, every single word.

Last semester, one of my best students actually held her throat with her right hand while she apologized for not speaking louder. "I just can't. I have always had a soft voice. From the time I was a little girl." I shudder, imagining the day this bright Jewish woman reaches up to her elegant neck and accidentally strangles herself.

Later, I play a barely audible phone message over and over again: the student with her hand on her throat has dropped the course, due to an unexpected conflict. She is very sorry.

I wonder about the female professor trapped in the elevator at the University of Massachusetts in Amherst. I read about her in the *Hampshire Gazette* in April 1998. The woman spent the night all by herself, alone, curled up in the corner of a cold, dark, empty elevator. When asked why she did not scream out, pound on the door, make any noise at all for the entire duration of her involuntary captivity, the professor replied, "I didn't think anyone could hear me. I just sat down and waited patiently for someone to discover that the elevator was broken." The next morning after the stuck elevator was discovered, the woman was carried out of the building. When the policeman on duty asked for her keys, she handed them over and was driven the two short blocks home. According to the article she was physically unharmed by the whole ordeal.

"So, is that real or imagined help?" I ask my Advanced Feminist Theory class, "and does it matter that the professor could have walked through the doorway herself after spending the night in an elevator? Or whether or not she drove herself home?"

At the end of class, I warn the students not to get stuck alone in a cold, dark elevator overnight. No one will hear you. Then I close my eyes: *Yes, it's true: I understand just how much effort it takes to speak so softly that no one, not even the person sitting next to you, can hear what you have to say, and know how important it is. You have to be very deliberate to speak that softly.* When I open my eyes, everyone is nodding in agreement about all the effort it takes.

Performing Femininities: To Enervate
devitalize, debilitate, enfeeble, exhaust

"How can you call on me, when I don't even raise my hand?" An angry student is in my office.

"How can I not call on you?"

"You know how I hate to speak in public." Rivka wants to be a rabbi. She wants me to write her a superb recommendation for rabbinical school. Rabbis give weekly sermons; they stand on the *bimah* facing the entire congregation to discuss the weekly Torah portion. They officiate at weddings, preside over funerals, bless the children and their parents. I will write Rivka a recommendation for rabbinical school. I will lie about what an exceptional public speaker she is. Discussing the eloquent cadence of her carefully chosen words, I hold out the fervent hope that one day this will not be a lie.

Michael is one of the most thoughtful students I have ever had. He's taking Blacks and Jews this semester and he doesn't often raise his hand to speak. But his writing is stunning. His words on the page are sharp, acerbic. Perceptive. I want the students to hear his comments on Jewish immigration and "passing."

"Michael," I say, the third week of class.

He looks at me and shakes his head. I do not know yet that he will stammer badly whenever he says more than one or two words in a row.

"I'll come back to you." He grimaces. I grimace back.

When I return to Michael, he speaks slowly, thoughtfully, but stammering and staring at me the entire time. There is not a sound in the room as Michael speaks publicly for the first time in three weeks. The students and I listen intently, caught in the spell of our colleague's rich intelligence. I continue to call on Michael, until one day he forgets to shake his head *no*, and offers the class a theory on secondary sources that none of us has thought about before. We reference Michael and his secondary source the rest of the semester.

I know that stammering has historically been read by men as a sign of weakness in other men, stereotypically suggestive of effeminacy or sissified behavior in the office or classroom. And that young boys who stammer are still ridiculed and teased violently by the other boys on the school playground. *What was it like for Michael growing up?* I remind myself that it is imperative that he not sit silently in class for the duration of the semester. I must resist the feminized urge to take care of him when he stammers. We of the feminist academy must continually resist the often unconscious urge to enfeeble or "feminize" our students by not calling on those who fear speaking in public.

Katrina is from Russia. I tell her that my grandfather is Russian, and that my best friend, Dr. Linda Randall, is a specialist in the new Russian economy. *She's fluent; when she comes to speak to the class, you can both speak in Russian.* I also tell her that I have been to St. Petersburg and it is very cold. We laugh. At the end of the semester I invite Katrina to apply for a 5A student teaching assistant position. She shakes her head. "Impossible." She is adamant.

"Why not?"

"Because."

"Because why?" Katrina is smart. A TA-ship would look terrific on her CV. I don't understand her resistance. Besides, her crosscultural application of the feminist theories we studied was remarkable.

"My accent." She looks away for the first time since we started this discussion. "Nobody would understand me. It will be horrible. For everybody."

Exasperated, I shake my head. "Think about it, and get back to me."

Eventually Katrina agrees to be a teaching assistant, but warns me not to call on her to speak publicly. Obviously, I will not obey her wishes, believing instead that she is unconsciously asking me for help. At the end of the semester she says, "Professor Felman, thank you, this was the best experience of my life." She speaks loudly, and with great confidence.

Very often the women students in my classes are embarrassed if they speak English with a strong accent. I know they are upset when I call on them, but it is critical that everyone speaks. I discuss the situation with the entire class. "Some of us have accents and some of us don't know how to listen. It's political," I tell them, "to hear only one kind of

English. The notion of standard English is relative." Then we discuss how many students are bilingual or trilingual, and how many speak only English. Inevitably, the students from outside the United States speak at least two, three, sometimes even four languages.

When the students complain to me that they cannot always understand Katrina, I tell them to listen harder. And I tell Katrina to speak up. Louder, so she can always be heard. Katrina wants to be an international banker; she will have to speak many languages, in many accents.

Each year I notice that there are more students at Brandeis who are either immigrants or refugees to this country. I have students from Cambodia, Vietnam, Laos, Bangladesh, Ukraine, Russia, Ghana, Nigeria, Venezuela, Argentina, Brazil, Haiti, Jamaica, Cape Verde, Montserrat, China, and Japan. Sometimes I cannot say my students' names out loud. I am embarrassed. I overapologize for the ridiculous way I mispronounce a particular student's name. I cannot perform effectively when I cannot say my students' names. At night, I make a list of all the names I cannot say. Then I practice each exquisitely strange-sounding name out loud, until I fall asleep. I imagine gently slipping one beautiful name after another—*Ngazi, Ana Yoselin, Grigorias, Mai, Antje, Amara, Sergei, Hyong, Sayuko*—underneath my soft feather pillow. While I dream, all the letters of the foreign alphabets dance their way into my ears, one by one, whispering, lightly tickling their melodious sounds deep into my eardrums, so that when I wake, I am no longer afraid to call out my students' names. *Madhavi, Tovah, Bat, Touk, Tamara, Ariel, Jasmine, Gavriel, Devika, Kaila.*

One day in Autobiography, we go around the circle, and everyone pronounces his or her name the way it is supposed to be said. The silence that follows this public naming is stunning. We have been mispronouncing each others' names for almost the entire semester. We tell the stories of our names, of all the ways we Anglicize their sounds, making it easier for everyone. We forget the melodious sounds of our birth. *How can I teach my students if I cannot say their names? How can my students learn if they never hear their names?* I know in my heart that this is critical. That (the question of) the accuracy of naming has some of its roots in radical feminism and is grounded in the pedagogy of the self in solo performance. With all the attention I give to the names of all my students, it's as if the names are the subject matter of the courses that I teach. And in a way, it's true. I am teaching names, faces, whole people.

The academy as an institution has always been about the business of naming: who is permitted to name, what gets named and the benefits accruing to those so named, and from whom this vaunted privilege is consciously withheld. Anna Deavere Smith says, "If you say a word often enough, it becomes you." I cannot engage the students at their highest level or mine if I cannot speak their names out loud. This is the pedagogy of the feminist performer/professor in her classroom. She must resist the overwhelming, very Western temptation to obscure the differences between us. I see the pain in Ngozi's eyes when she looks hard at me. "Since I left Nigeria, I don't remember the sound of my own name, so when my mother on occasion calls me by my name, I do not answer. I do not know who she is speaking to. I have long forgotten the sound of I."

"Here's your story," I tell Ngozi, "you must write this." No matter how loudly I say it, I can never pronounce Ngozi's name correctly. (This becomes our secret.) Soon, it is hard for me to look her in the eyes. Soon she says she cannot write. She doesn't understand but she leaves class angry. So angry she *almost* loses her voice.

In the most beautiful script I can write, I dip the sharp point of my pen into a small bottle of jet-black India ink. Then, as though praying, I print the name *Ngozi* on a piece of light pink Japanese rice paper and slip it silently, carefully under my pillow.

Marsha is in my office. Her family is from Haiti. "I never speak in any of my classes, except yours and Professor Williams's." I nod. I have heard this so many times before, from the African, Afro-Caribbean, and African-American students. They speak in Dessima Williams's classes because they feel seen and heard. Dessima is from Granada. "You mean for three years you sat through class after class, never saying a word?"

Marsha nods.

"How can you stand that? Don't you fall asleep?"

"Nobody ever notices. Until you, I never even got called on."

I am in the office of my boss, the chair of Women's Studies. There have been several complaints lodged against me. "Is it true that you call on students, whether they raise their hands or not?"

"Yes, that's right."

She looks surprised. "Isn't that rather aggressive on your part?"

"I don't understand the question. It's part of the pedagogy, particularly feminist. I can't imagine teaching any other way. Otherwise the same students talk all the time. "

"Does a student *have* to speak in your class?" She looks disturbed.

"They can pass, but I eventually come back to them."

"But you don't intimidate your students, do you?"

"I hope not. That would be counterproductive. This is about *voice*. About each student developing his or her voice."

She nods and I understand that we are finished. I am not surprised that there has been so much publicly performed distress about this particular classroom methodology. Nor am I surprised that it is always the women students who complain about being called on to speak. They are performing their many learned *femininities* while I am performing *feminist*.

I tell the students in Autobiography: *Write about a time in your life when you stopped speaking. Using microscopic detail and nonlinear narrative, tell the reader how old you were. And why you became silent. Finally, when, if ever, did you start speaking again?*

When they're finished writing, the students volunteer to read their narratives out loud. I do not have to call on a single student to describe the moment she stopped speaking. Everyone recalls an exact time and place when she lost her voice. These are some of the most powerful narratives they write all semester.

It's after ten when the phone rings on Sunday night. I'm listening to the news and reading student papers. I let the machine pick up: *Professor Felman, this is Autumn. I just got back from the Feminist Expo and I have to talk to you. Now. Please, okay? Call me as soon as you get this message. I don't care what time it is.*

I think back to when Autumn took the Intro to Women's Studies course, and then Autobiography. She cried her way through both semesters. Whenever I called on her to critique her classmates' narratives, she refused. *How can I possibly critique someone else's writing? It's so personal,* she used to say after almost every class.

When I call Autumn back it's almost eleven o'clock. "The Expo was unbelievable! So cool you wouldn't believe it." She's shouting, she's so excited. At the end of the conversation Autumn's voice changes. "I can't believe some of them don't like you. I never met anyone before who didn't like you."

"Who? What are you talking about?"

"The students. Some of the girls I went to the Feminist Expo with, were complaining about how you call on them when they don't raise their hands. They don't want to have to say anything unless they want to. And they don't understand why they can't chew gum in your class." She's really upset.

I don't know exactly what to say. I resist the urge to remind her about how, in feminist pedagogy one of the goals is for the student to develop her own unique voice. And that the issue is personal *and* political, not just academic.

"And they complained about how antifeminist you are because you always make them speak in class."

I am taken aback. I had no idea speaking in class was such a big issue. Slowly, almost imperceptibly, I begin to doubt my commitment to feminist pedagogy. While Autumn continues speaking to me on the other end of the receiver, gradually I become a damsel caught in her own academic distress. I feel myself becoming smaller. I curl up on the sofa remembering Sarita doubled over in pain from the sheer torture of speaking up. Smaller and smaller, I fold my knees up to my chest.

Transformatively, next spring Autumn will be a teaching assistant in Autobiography, where she will regularly critique her classmates' writing. She was adamant: "I absolutely have to do this. I've rearranged my whole schedule just so I can help teach Autobiography."

I continue to call on students, hands up or down. I am always interested in what they have to say, whether or not they understand the material. I love when they think out loud, often coming up with new theories that we can all reference for the rest of the term. Like Michael's secondary source idea, which I tell him he should copyright before it's too late. Or Alicia, who doesn't speak in her other classes, who tells us all in Blacks and Jews that she doesn't feel she has a voice on campus.

"What would it look like, Alicia, if you had a voice here at Brandeis? And how would that impact the rest of your life?" We look at each other. Alicia's head is shaking "no." The class is quiet, respectful. I remember two weeks ago watching her sit silently in class for three hours. She was furious at how the discussion was going, but wouldn't say a word. When I called on her then, she shook her head. I moved on to the next student.

She is shaking her head now. But she is speaking. "I don't know what it would look like to have a voice. I don't know. I have to think about it. It just never occurred to me before."

I understand for the first time that all around me, performing in and out of the classroom, are damsels in distress. The academy is full of damsels routinely performing their highly practiced, supremely nuanced femininities: students and professors who no longer recognize the sound of their own fully realized voice(s).

Performing Femininities: To Cripple
incapacitate, exhaust, break down, stifle, mutilate, lame, destroy, mangle, paralyze

In the spring 2000 semester of Autobiography, over half of the class has spent half a lifetime starving. I am not talking about students who come from Rwanda or Ethiopia, but about the fact that many of my women students, across class and race, have basically stopped eating; they actually prefer not to eat at all.

"I never felt as good as when I stopped eating," Trish tells the class. "That was the happiest time of my life." Several students nod in agreement. A few look on in horror. I look away.

In Advanced Feminist Theory it is no different. I hand out low-fat granola bars at the beginning of class because I don't want to hear the collective growl of stomachs as soon as I begin discussing Sheri Ortner's nature/nurture theories. And in 5A, midsemester, I receive a letter marked *Confidential*. One of my best students, Stephanie, is admitted to the hospital for acute anorexia. She never comes back to class. I hear from Stephanie only once, after the first week she's left school. She calls me for the 5A weekly writing assignment. "Just eat, please," I tell her. One month later I dream that Stephanie dies in her sleep with her mouth open waiting to be fed.

The next year Lisa leaves Brandeis after spring break. Before she disappears for good, she spends a long time in my office telling me how much fat women scare her and make her sick. "I knows this is like your very basic 'politically incorrect' position," she says, "especially on account of me being a lesbian and all." Then she asks, "But what do you think, Professor Felman, how do you feel about all those fat girls in your classes?" I don't say a word.

Becky almost faints in class because she hasn't eaten all day. Elisa tells me how she eats only sugar-free Jell-O, bright red cherry, three times a day. And Aviva has to run out of class every fifteen minutes because her intestines are permanently inflamed due to years of self-starvation. For the first time, the sensitive, straight feminist men and their muscular gay brothers begin to write about their own starving feminized conditions. About how in their rejection of the traditional masculine prototype they have, unwittingly, adopted the stereotypically feminine behavior of self-starvation. This is the final act. All the women will be dead. They do not understand that, in the end, they will have also starved their minds back into the historically passive position of objectification that we fought so hard to overthrow. There will simply be nothing left of the regressive femininities for the women to perform, because there will be nothing left of the women themselves. Twenty-five years after the founding of Women's Studies, we are all mainstreaming. Having once been rejected and now accepted, we stream down the main, dominant paradigm that for years denied us the space to perform fully female. I ask myself, *What are the implications of continuing to teach students who are voluntarily(?) starving themselves?* This is a perpetual disappearing act in the media-proclaimed, *Time*-magazined "postfeminist" age.

After three years of teaching Women's Studies courses to women who starve themselves, I begin to weigh myself three, then four times a day. Unconsciously I internalize the hunger of my aching students. *I suddenly feel enormous as I imagine my breasts shooting out to a size forty EEE cup in the middle of a lecture on female firefighters. Overnight my body explodes from a six petite to a sixteen. No one says a word as I take up more and more space, filling all the empty seats of all the absent women students. I begin to eat until I become too big, too loud, too smart for my own Jewish female good. I cannot stop eating, not even for a minute. Who will save all the young starving women who drop out of school because they can no longer concentrate?* It is hard to stop the nightmare once it starts, flashing the academic feminist damsel in acute gendered distress. *What happened to the theory I am supposed to be discussing in this book?* All of *this* is "the theory."

The praxis is the proof that I am caught in the middle of a very live performance with a script that has an opaque yet tragic resolution.

Outside the classroom, I stare at the other Women's Studies professors; we are silent coconspirators. There is the one who, month after month, year after year, brings only carrot sticks to lunch at all the faculty meetings. She eats them raw, chewing loudly, one short orange carrot after another, until the plastic bag hidden in her lap is empty. She recycles, slipping the baggie into her purse. Spread around the seminar table at all our meetings are the Diet Cokes; small containers of plain, fat-free Dannon yogurt; plus the Tupperware bowls full of lettuce. I cannot remember the last time I saw a female colleague eat a real lunch. At the faculty club we fill our plates with salad. The sign requests in small block letters that we take a clean plate on our return trip. We are free to eat as much as we want. No one touches the freshly baked bread on the cutting board at the end of the mountains of green leaves. We reach instead for the Saltines. The faculty club is always low on Saltines.

I take the slices of turkey one at a time off the fresh sourdough roll, and throw the bread away as I have seen hundreds of my students do. I roll each slice of white meat into a small turkey cylinder and then eagerly bite off a piece. *How can starving women teach starving women?* Chewing slowly, I take as long as I possibly can to eat three slices of thinly cut kosher turkey breast. *What is there left to teach but bare bones, and hollow chest cavities?* I swallow hard, finishing the last bite. *What if we just stopped teaching, refused to carry on until our women students started to eat regular meals again, three times a day? Every day. No more sugar-free cherry Jell-O for breakfast.* I do not know how to teach the starving female subject so she will not disappear.

I hear your professorial concerns: "Why single out anorexia? Our students have many issues—sexual abuse, self-mutilation, depression. . . ." I understand. Yet there is something different when it comes to food and gender. Something about those extremely bright, extraordinarily talented female students who can survive only by starving themselves. As the years go by they get smaller and thinner, thinner and smaller, until we too are infected. Freshman, sophomore, junior year, by the time Miriam graduates summa cum laude, she is too weak to walk up to the dais and accept her award. Instead, she is rolled up the platform in a wheelchair; this is the imagined help she has always craved. And I am home weighing myself, counting the Peanut M&Ms as I put them in my mouth one at a time. When did the theory (of anorexia) become more important than the practice (of self-eradication)? How did those of us who risk our lives to reach our students become seen by our academic sisters as raging, misguided activists rather than the radical, creative feminist scholars that we are?

So the truth, finally, is that we in Women's Studies are not supposed to talk about our lives anymore. And neither are our students. There is no one to tell about all the starving females sitting in my classroom year after year. We used to believe that *the personal is the political*, and that there was no separation between the classroom and the street. Today, the personal is viewed as too political, too far beyond the scholarly pale of the settlement. So the accusations have begun to hurl back and forth, from one Women's Studies professor to another across the promotion track: *She is not a real scholar. Her work is not academic. She assigns all the right books without the right assignments.* Campus to campus, the chorus is the same: *Her syllabi are bogus. She is not one of us. She can never be one of us. We cannot ever let her in. She lets the students talk and write about their lives. Too personal. Too therapeutic. She politicizes the classroom. We need real, bona-fide scholars.* Twenty-five years after the fall of Saigon and the monumental push for women's equality, the institutional and systemic evisceration of women's voices is more insidious than ever. Now, we are barely seen and even more rarely heard.

Today, the fully alive, feminist academic performer is far too threatening; all the daring damsels—students and professors—are commanded to keep our desires private, securely locked up deep inside. The only control the women have is to starve themselves in the hope that one day, before it is too late, someone will notice what has happened to them in the feminist classroom. And that the feminist classroom itself has almost disappeared. Someone has to notice, before it is too late, that all the girls have stopped talking. Stopped eating. That there is nothing left to say out loud.

There is nowhere to say "I" because the feminist classroom is no more. This performance is over. Against the full force of my desire, I may have to join all the others who were forced out before me. All those stunningly brave and brilliant academic female Amazons who spun magic, intellectual, priceless silver cerebral threads into the thick web of our beloved classrooms. We knew we were casting powerful, mind-altering spells.

Walking around the campus months later, I see the ghosts of students and faculty past, women fleeing through the keyholes, up, up, and away. Closing my eyes, I pray for the courage to stay.

II. The Play

Performing Feminisms

I bring the female body in to thaw. From the frigid cold of the sacrosanct ivory tower, the women students enter shivering. Front and center, we stand, facing each other, methodically undressing the years of our constricting education. Until we stand naked but lucid, truly, for the first time. I invite the women to be fully in their bodies, to be seen and heard and listened to with all due respect. I bring the female body as subject into the classroom. And I begin with myself. Because I know that if they can embrace me, a *vilde chaye*, a wild beast, then there is no limit to their own (self) acceptance. They will recognize in themselves the first-person "I" that is usually a third-person "she." The "I" that has always been the feminine object to the subject of the standard pronoun "he." This then is the challenge of performing feminisms. To bring the female body "I" fully into the classroom means to resist the continual evisceration through silence and self-starvation of the female subject. Only through this introduction of the unambivalent female body, in all her largesse, can the destruction wrought on the women begin to heal. To embody these ideas is extremely dangerous. It is to assume the risk of the pariah, and permanent expulsion from the beloved academic tribe. But tribal rites and rituals must not go unchallenged. Unexamined tribal loyalty will never set the women students free. Bringing the female subject—in all her magnificent colors—from the margin to the center is the only answer. In the end, the bare-breasted body, with her many threatening, sensuous, and erotic orifices thoroughly exposed, must speak.

In Blacks and Jews the students bring in the body whole, performing feminisms and fully feminist in front of each other. For their final exam the students intentionally turn their presentations into transformative, truly miraculous performances that utilize the body to inform and incite their audience, the class. I am amazed that they have figured out this essential performative piece by themselves. Through watching me while simultaneously participating, the class understands that the body must be present too, active and engaged in the learning process. The body moves the mind as the mind moves the body. The feminist body, embodied as man or woman, when present and alive, electrifies the pedagogical space. And causes a current of radical intellectual sparking to surge through the entire academy, disrupting previously passively rendered, albeit highly elevated, intellectual spaces. Thus the feminist body performing feminisms threatens the very heartbeat of the traditional, patriarchal academy.

After viewing the Bill T. Jones video on how the dance *Still/Here* was created, the students took charge of the material they were to present as their final "exam." Later, upon reading their response papers to the Jones video, and answering the question: *How can art be a tool for political transformation?*, I understood immediately how each group, without any prior consultation with me or with each other, decided to perform the theories they were charged with representing.

The first group in Blacks and Jews—Patricia, Amanda, Tovah, and Marsha—stood together in a circle looking out at us, their elbows pressed in, touching each other side by side, their backs facing the center of their small circle. They began by reading out loud simultaneously, their voices rising in anger, one above the other, louder, louder as they competed for air space. But the power of their words were totally indistinguishable, lost in the nonstop babble of talking all at the same time. The women told their stories: growing up in Haiti and immigrating to the United States; being raised isolated, in an Orthodox Jewish community; a self-loathing atheist, the daughter of a Catholic mother and a Jewish father; and an Afro-Caribbean American who has begun to feel more African-American and less Haitian. We couldn't decipher any single story, because they all spoke at once. When the performers finished, they sat down, faced each other, and dialogued about what had just happened: *about how they had all been competing for the same turf; that only one of them could have suffered the most; and that there simply was not enough space for multiple subjects to occupy concurrently.*

Then almost imperceptibly they traded narratives right before our eyes. Patricia from Haiti became Tovah the Orthodox Jew, her voice plaintive as she described not understanding diversity and the world at large. Patricia as Tovah talked about the terror of assimilation and her fear of isolation. Then Tovah became Patricia, who talked about not being fully seen while being seen *only* as *Black*. On and on the women moved in and out of each other's narratives, performing the ethnically gendered body and bringing the female voice(s) as subject(s) fully active and engaged into the classroom. We watched in awe, and were transformed as the performers so transformed themselves. The group had been assigned Horace Kallen's article on *pluralism* and they were asked to analyze the differences (according to Kallen) between *multiculturalism* and *pluralism*. Through the unprecedented use of their bodies they taught the class the meaning of coexistence without a competition of fears. They embraced fluid subjectivities, as the body was made to hold multiple, competing race and gender narratives simultaneously.

Another group, all Ashkenazi Jews, were to discuss and deconstruct icons of Black and Jewish masculinity and femininity in the United States. Sartorial in nature, the performance began with the way they entered the classroom already in character—a Black afro and a miniskirt; a yarmulka and tallis; baggy pants with unlaced high-tops; designer jeans with a Gap tank top—and the names they assumed: *Ari, the Yeshiva student, Duane from the 'hood, Moneesha the sistah,* and *Shira the assimilated Jewess.* Boldly they crossed the barriers of race and gender: White Jewish students performing as African Americans; men performing as women, and vice versa. They acted out all the stereotypes we had studied and then, in an instant, flipped the negative icons over, turning the images into completely realized, whole human beings. The point of view was clear, undistorted, and magnetic. We laughed at ourselves and with them. The risk they took had succeeded beyond their wildest imagination. As a class we were beginning to physically embody all that we had learned this semester. Slowly we moved out of the stasis of unmoveable, seemingly immutable White male, Western European, mono-subjectivity. We became bigger, larger than life, as each group performed.

The final group was charged with deconstructing the films of Spike Lee and analyzing his representations of Black and Jewish identity. This group of four women chose to act out selected scenes from the movies they had watched, with a voice-over analyzing each ethnic stereotype Lee employed. They spoofed their own clichéd "archetypes" as portrayed in the films *Do the Right Thing, Crooklyn,* and *Mo' Better Blues.* For their final act, they had written a narrative not based on hackneyed conventions of Blackness or Jewishness, but the scene they hoped Spike Lee would film one day. They transformed the destructive stereotypical images they had seen into truly visionary personas, what they have always longed to see portrayed on the screen. This was the finest pedagogical moment of that year. I sat on the floor with the other students, enthralled by and proud of what was occurring in this Brandeis classroom. *Where did these students come from? How did they get the courage to perform the passionate whole body and the body wholly passionate? What had transpired in terms of race and gender, Blacks and Jews, men and women, that could so transform them?*

The students had taught themselves and each other through the spectacle of the body and all its potent desires. Willfully, they let go of their ambivalence, the suffocating fear of offending, and all their own minute and debilitating insecurities regarding race and gender. And it was not just a single group; every one performed, presenting a different question in a new and creative way. As I watched them give up their collective fear of drowning in generations of racism and anti-Semitism, I could not doubt the efficacy of my own so often institutionally contested, feminist pedagogy. Even if no one else in the academy validated our performance in Blacks and Jews, we as a class had understood that the dominant academic paradigm was fundamentally suspect. We refused acceptance while accepting the peril of ostracism implicit in that refusal. We chose instead to cross the river Jordan together in body and mind, loud, energized, and totally feminist. Not a single one of us was left behind on the dry, parched, and decaying land to survive only marginally, as an object of hate or ridicule.

In their final commentaries each member of the class discussed the impact of Bill T. Jones's visionary pedagogy on their own lives:

Theater provides me with the opportunity to be another person. The ability to shed the walls of the self on a physical and emotional level has truly transformed the way I look at the world. —Jonothan

There were two exercises . . . which I found amazing. The first was the interpreting of one's life on paper with simple lines and then walking and explaining that life. I found this . . . particularly powerful because it showed me how an individual can, in mere movements relive her or his life, make sense of that life, and truly understand that life. . . . Watching Bill T. Jones walk his own life was the definition of this exercise. —Gardy

Jones's dance makes you feel the emotions and feelings and not just seeing someone suffering or hearing about it, but really feeling the suffering. It showed me how important art is. We forget how powerful dance and performing and other ways of expressing yourself can be. It is the closest a person can understand another person's suffering without having gone through it themselves. . . . The thing about being the performer yourself, is that you not only see and hear, but also feel the story of another person. That is powerful. I guess art can be a tool for political transformation by being an agent. —Jewelle

Moving is liberating, it shows one's confidence and control, and the body as a source of tension and major energy. That is why Bill uses body movement to do the job, the job he loves to do, which is "to evoke the spirit of survival." The ability to evoke the spirit of survival was used literally for the group and metaphorically for the people of the planet. The only way to get the human race to care for each other is to evoke the spirit of survival. —Esther

Today we leave all damsels in distress—male and female—behind. Together, my students and I carry each other over the complex, raging currents of academe, boldly refusing to take the vastly calmer, easier, and far slower circulating mainstreams. Like African-American dancer Bill T. Jones, we swim with the current of unknown waters and no longer fear the multihued feminist body, whole and wholly present in our classrooms.

A Classroom Named Desire

Academic Bodies in Motion

Walking into the large lecture hall for the first time to take my first Women's Studies class, I heard a loud voice directing the students not to sit in the last four rows. It sounded more like a bark or a growl. The speaker was a short woman with very short brown hair. I was surprised she didn't have a megaphone, because her voice carried so far. She kept moving as she spoke, waving her arms and sort of stomping around the front of the room. But it was the red lips on such a small woman, glistening as she spoke, that caught my attention. For weeks afterwards, I was mesmerized. It was the lips, all that red smeared across that particular mouth—my professor's, that I couldn't stop staring at. I didn't know radical lesbian feminists wore lipstick, especially not that particular shade of red. Besides, I can't remember ever seeing bright red lipstick on a single professor. Before now, I barely remember even noticing the color of lipstick on any female professor. Even though I was put off by her voice, I have to admit it was the bright red lipstick that kept me from dropping the course. —Christopher

I was shocked. But don't know why I should have been. It was mid-December and classes were over. I was sitting in bed with a glass of burgundy—red—merlot, sucking room-temperature-warm, milk chocolate Cadbury squares slowly, one at a time, until fully melted, while reading Christopher's end-of-the-semester comments on his 5A experience. At first I was offended, then angry, and finally I just started laughing very hard out loud and couldn't stop. So someone had finally "noticed." Or decided to publicly admit noticing, my bright red lips.

Eros
god of love

I am in search of a scrupulously honest portrayal and discussion of *the power of the erotic*, and all "her" various corporal and cerebral forms, in the undergraduate classroom. I want to explore the words of the poet Audre Lorde when she says in *Sister/Outsider*: "*The erotic is the nurturer or nursemaid of all our deepest knowledge*." And then to articulate just how this *erotic nursemaid* operates in my own undergraduate classroom. I have always wanted to read about the erotics of the peak pedagogical experience. By this, I do not mean teacher-student seduction or coital engagement of any sort between two so differently situated individuals. That would be a broader betrayal of maximum proportion. (For an elaborate, informative, controversial discussion of teacher-student sexual involvement, read Jane Gallop's *Feminist Accused of Sexual Harassment* and view David Mamet's vexing movie *Oleanna* on the same topic.) So I mean to interrogate on these very pages the barely explored, misunderstood, furtive, nonverbalized, and untapped erotic potential of the classroom, including all the inherent woes and wonders embedded within this explosive, ever-so-hot topic.

In preparing my analysis I queried (via e-mail) former students who had graduated and current student teaching assistants who were no longer my students. The first response came from Michael and Jane, two of the most intelligent, perceptive students I have ever had. Both happen to be White and self-identified heterosexuals, which will later prove to be significant to this particular discussion. Although they did not yet understand the dynamics, I had observed Michael and Jane involved in a charged, passionately erotic, intellectual (as opposed to purely sexual) relationship of their own. So I e-mailed them the following:

> I am working on the chapter about the erotic in the classroom, based on the writing of Audre Lorde, the African-American poet. She has a book "Sister/Outsider" in which she talks about the power of the erotic. I am very interested in picking your brains about how you experience the classroom, mine and others': Is it an erotic exchange/experience or rather un-erotic? What, if any, ideas come to (either of) you?

Jane wrote back immediately: "Neither Michael nor I are familiar with the erotic in the classroom—frankly we're not sure what it means. But if you'd explain a bit, we'd be happy to think about it/discuss with you."

From Autumn and Dan, two other former students who are also White (but not a couple like Michael and Jane), I received separate but almost identical responses. It seems that no one from my intentionally selected control group knew what on earth I was asking about. Only from one former student, Maureen, did I get anything close to a real "riff" on the subject. However, Maureen's response was more classically located, focusing on the sexual politics of the classroom, rather than, as I had asked, the erotics. She did what most people do, that is, conflate sex and erotics, tightly merging the two, so that there is little room for anything to happen inbetween outright sexual involvement and nothing at all:

> I think you are asking about the relationship between students and Professors/T.A. type figures. Fortunately Brandeis isn't one of those places where teachers/T.A. and students hook-up. . . . There are two ways that . . . students view their professors sexually—whether as completely and totally sexless or as 100% HOT and everyone wants to get with them. I've never heard of a middle ground.

Admittedly, it feels risky just asking my students about eroticism and education. For within my written request lies the unstated fact that I am acknowledging that, in conjunction with the exchange of knowledge in the classroom, the erotic does indeed exist. At the beginning of this inquiry, I feared that my request might be misinterpreted as the inappropriate initiation of a sexual invitation. I didn't want any confusion, however slight. That's why I picked (former) students who are particularly sophisticated intellectually as well as emotionally mature. But writing (for the first time) my own thoughts on "pedagogical erotics," and having the courage to include the responses of former students, feels dangerous as well as professionally threatening (being the untenured, popular, yet controversial professor that I am). It's as though I have crossed illegally yet another border and will be rounded up shortly by the academic border patrol, dressed in their heavy black robes, waving their tassels in the air as they vigorously, repeatedly shake their heads into one gigantic, adamant, orgasmic *No! You are not going to go there. We will block your entrance if you continue to advance.* Roger Simon, in his essay "Face to Face with Alterity: Postmodern Jewish Identity and the Eros of Pedagogy," discusses his own vulnerability (although he is a heterosexual, White, tenured full professor) in writing for his first time about the eros of working with graduate students:

> Reactions of colleagues . . . elicited a variety of cautions and objections to introducing the notion of desire and erotics into a discussion of pedagogy. . . . Others thought it dangerous to discuss desires because to do so introduces a terminology that might, given a restricted reading, too easily be misconstrued as providing a possible excuse for sexual assault or harassment.

To open a discussion/dialogue about classroom erotics, *not* erotica, in the age of the post–Thomas/Hill hearings and the general public's corresponding heightened awareness of sexual harassment feels portentous and slippery. Like walking across the pond of thin academic ice that will surely crack, plunging the taboo breaker far below to the bone-chilling world of Hades the minute she steps, too sure-footed, on the smooth, opaque surface of the grand old institution. But I'm doing it anyway.

Eros
energy

So why didn't my "best and brightest" have a clue as to what I was asking? Were they in categorical denial? Or were they just being White and heterosexual? Or did they simply, as Jane said, not understand the question, but would be glad to discuss it with me, with a little more explanation.

I don't know what they think I meant by "erotics"; perhaps they had confused it with "semiotics" of the classroom. Or couldn't they—and I find this hardly plausible, but admittedly possible—comprehend why a lesbian, and a professor at that, would ask *them* (her students) about *sex*.

Graduate students and other professors had equally quixotic responses to the same question. Such as, "No, I would never get involved, you know, that way with an undergraduate." Or, "Not anymore, not after the Thomas/Hill debacle." Or, "Maybe with a graduate student or professor who wasn't my professor or graduate student."

No one, but no one, except for a few gay colleagues, even remotely considered the question beyond the larger, less-standardized, traditionally male, institutional form: that is, the very real existence of eros outside the dominant, Western, White, straight, hetero (read: male) paradigm of *sex*. My gay and bisexual peers knew instantly that I was talking about that *suppressed but delectable, charged, and potent pedagogical moment* that occurs *when intellectual and emotional passion spark in tandem, igniting the perpetually dormant eros of the classroom.* My gay colleagues understood implicitly that I was not talking about intercourse or physical penetration of any kind. But rather a deep intellectual penetration that, when experienced, becomes physical because it has so viscerally entered the body and not just the brain alone. So why didn't my White heterosexual colleagues get it? Or why wouldn't they admit to getting it? Partly because the historical parameters of White, Western heterosexuality have been so narrowly defined and interpreted that the sex act—coitus—has permanently, institutionally overwhelmed the erotic in the narrow birth canal of a highly limited mainstream imagination, leaving any viable distinction between the two an utter impossibility. Or/and as Roger Simon suggests, professors are too afraid to publicly acknowledge—even on the graduate level—that teaching in and of itself is fiercely erotic.

In many communities of color, and/or contemporaneously queer cultures, the erotic has always had an autonomous life of its own, outside the hegemony of straight White sex. For those living on the rich borderlands of future frontiers, the erotic is always present, yet navigated from within one's closet and/or outside the strictures of conventional, racist heterosexuality. Accordingly, for those on the margins, the notions of sexuality, gender, and sex have had to be expanded for the sake of sanity and sheer physical survival, rather than constricted and narrowed into acceptable, middle-class, married, monogamous missionary positions. That would be mimicry; and those who live merely to mimic another's assumed normalcy have all but swallowed whole their autonomous, amorous erotic potential.

As for the classroom, I am talking about bringing the unfragmented body, the actual physical corpus, as opposed to a mere "body of work," out of the privacy of the bedroom and into the public forum of the classroom. There is fuel here to be used and accelerated in epistemological pursuit if only we can stop being in denial or so afraid of the power of the erotic to propel us forward into unknown galaxies. Whether used, abused, or untouched, the ever-present erotic is extremely potent, even more so in the classroom than in the public sphere.

Why? Because the classroom is a highly charged yet contained space operating within a constrained time period. There is a built-in limit—the end of the hour, the end of the week, and then the semester itself is over. So the space is boundaried and bordered by an external—predictable— structure. And if the professor is doing her job well—that is, passionately igniting the students (and vice versa) and herself by the material—the sparks will surely fly. For the erotic is always an exchange, requiring a live audience to receive and respond before any heat is generated. How and what to do with them when the sparks start shimmering midair, hovering between student and teacher, among the students themselves, all the while embracing the entire class in an intellectual inferno, is the quest of this hot and bothered inquiry.

But first the academic scene must be appropriately set and the actors, in the most generic of terms, "theoretically" staged. Certain specifics have to be acknowledged within the performative set itself, such as the perceived gender, sexuality, and overall physical aesthetics of the professor by the students and him/herself. I have lectured or taught at more than twenty-five different universities in the last twenty-odd years. Yet it's always the same in terms of sartorial splendor or lack thereof. Where "dressing" is concerned, White, most often married, men inevitably dress down as is institutionally sanctioned for their gender. By "down" I mean, for left-leaning profs, bona fide faded '60s Levis with a rumpled, plain light blue or yellow 100% cotton shirt; or slightly baggy and mistakenly (only on occasion) unzipped brown corduroys plus an off-white shirt. While plain classic navy or black suits—tie sans coat jacket except for lunch in the faculty club—if one is part of the administration and/or more to the right. There is very little variance and almost no middle ground among men of such esteemed letters, although beards and moustaches swing back and forth, left or right, Republican or Democrat, American Studies, Politics, English, or Sociology. For White, seemingly straight men, the scene hardly ever changes. The costumes and set remain the same year after year, no matter that the actor standing behind the huge oak podium changes every semester.

For us women, the "girl brains," it's an altogether different situation. Those anonymous souls who determine unspoken academic vestment standards have divided us into a minimum of three distinct categories concerning the question of our beauty. Most of these female professorial categories are exclusively White and always reflect the extreme structural racism and misogyny located in society at large. (Female and male academics of color have been generously assigned their own specific categories and will be discussed next.) There is the "All Brain but No Body" female full professor. She's been around for years. Tall, short, fat, thin, she can't "do" hair, wears no makeup, and has no looks worth mentioning. Painfully, and irretrievably so, her brain long ago was severed from her body in hopes that she could permanently secure the job she so coveted and rightly deserved. This brain may or may not be heterosexual, married, lesbian, butch, or high, high femme in the abstract; but the consensus among both faculty genders is that *she* is not attractive, no matter how smart she may be. She is perfectly safe because she threatens no one—neither her female peers nor her students male or female. She is Mother Earth to us all, and we eagerly respond, as the hungry, starving children that we are.

For women, the academy rarely tolerates brains and beauty in the same body without suspicion. It has always been an unwritten albeit understood sacred codification in the faculty handbook. Beautiful, intelligent female academicians continue to raise eyebrows for all the wrong reasons. Brains and beauty have a permanent credibility gap in and out of the university (à la Marilyn Monroe, Dolly Parton, or Mae West). And in the academy, any credibility gap is downright deadly.

Then there is the "Novice," the newly minted assistant professor, right out of graduate school, who has great potential: with a little more confidence and different hair, she could be a real knockout. But the exhausting "publish or perish" requirement eventually saps all her erotic energy while she seeks tenure and a pregnant womb at the same time. It seems big wombs and big brains are fatiguing, consuming all her beauty in the strain of the imperatively gendered female academic performance.

Finally, there is, as always, the "Matron," who is warm, fuzzy, cuddly, and nice: knit one, purl two, bulky wool sweaters and black rubber boots in the winter. Smart, sedate, and satisfactorily without sex, she is allowed to exist undisturbed. I have noticed that on White men, winter rubbers are viewed as sensible protection from the harsh elements, while on women, for some reason, they are thought to look ridiculous. Maybe it's the hose, those thin, skin-toned nylons and knee-length skirts that just don't go well together when combined with a pair of practical, dull, black rubbers on our academic matrons.

Most faculty of color at predominately White and/or private universities continue to remain at a distinct disadvantage when it comes to academic excellence through appearance. For them, the scholastic stakes have always been higher and the wardrobe requirements far less flexible, especially for African, African-American, and Caribbean men and women. (See the film *Shattering the Silence* or the work of bell hooks, Gloria Anzaldúa, Cherríe Moraga, and Paula Gunn Allen for more detailed discussions.) Most of the men wear dark suits with a tie readily available; for the women it's more complicated. Dressing up may also act as a shield of armor, protecting faculty of color from the many negative institutional stereotypes floating around the campus. My close colleague Dr. Linda Randall, an expert on the Russian economy at the University of Rhode Island, who happens to be strikingly beautiful *and* the only Black woman in her department (Business and Management), repeatedly talks about how she is perceived. "It's as if I have no gender, neither male nor female, but rather a genderless, sexless, inexplicably high-functioning brain." Although she and her "sistah" colleagues always dress up, she says it doesn't matter what they wear; the fact of their femaleness within the academy is continuously rendered invisible or simply ignored. This contemporary genderless, sexless stereotype of female African-American academics is rooted in a version of the large, asexual, Black plantation Mama. (See the original Aunt Jemima's broad, eternally smiling face on her yellow box of pancake mix.) She is always holding the Mistress's tiny White infant in her arms, while the precious child suckles away for hours at "Mama's" smooth, Black breast.

I have noticed that my own students of color, especially African and African-American or Caribbean females, regularly dress up for class, to a far greater degree than their White peers. Although this observation may seem reductively racist, after much discussion with other colleagues of color, I think not. I have simply never had a student of color, middle class or not, male or female, wear torn or ripped blue jeans to any of my classes. (Which doesn't mean that they don't do it elsewhere.) In a country that has yet to come to terms with its racist history, the question of the politics of classroom garb is not hard to understand. Politically, the majority can always afford to dress down—or any way they please, for that matter—without any fear of repercussions or "disgracing the race." Although it may sound like a generalization or even a bit essentialized, when White students make up the majority on a campus, they do not, *or so it appears*, feel the need to dress up for class. It's "simply" the privilege of their position. Contrary to their African-American peers, they are seen as representative of no one. While many White women still feel the overwhelming need to be reed-thin, what they wear has definitely become secondary to the coveted "size two, petite" that they crave. (See chapter 5 for further analysis.)

Finally, within the academic hierarchy of gendered aesthetic stereotypes, there are those of us who don't fit. Anywhere. We have spent long hours disproving the oh-so-prudish gender and destructive race biases. That is, we are articulate, smart, some of us brilliant, and attractive by a multiple of diverse cultural, ethnic, or queer standards. We are the loud, flamboyant ones. You see us coming and certainly know when we've arrived (heads are turning). We may be feminist men, nuns teaching at religious or secular institutions, gay men of color, or "good-looking" femmes who know how to dress, "do" hair, and smear bright red lipstick all across our thick, sweet lips. We are the campus conundrums, be we masculine, feminine, or somewhere in between, that no one—male or female, homo or hetero—can quite figure out. Where do we belong on this slippery academic sartorial spectrum? What accounts for our total savoir faire in the Beauty-*and*-Brains department? The truth is that most of us campus "riddles" have consciously chosen the huge risk of maintaining the power of our erotic, and thus never enter the classroom (or anywhere else) without it. Eros becomes our North Star; we follow her eternal light so we won't get lost along the way.

Remember we are merely setting the stage, acknowledging that before class even begins, there is an aesthetic exchange going on between all academic bodies in motion. (There is no such thing as neutral—aesthetic or intellectual—space, especially in the academy.) In that free-flowing aesthetic lay the unfocused and unexplored erotics of the intellectual hour(s) to come. Contextually speaking, appearance has the potential only to enhance the erotics embedded in the epistemological exchange, while not being at all determinative of the erotics themselves. A hairless nun dressed in traditional hood and habit can be exceptionally erotic when in the midst of lecturing; as can a plain, black-suited, unruly-bearded rabbi waving his hands in rapture over a particular Talmudic *parsha*. Ultimately, it's the performance—not the appearance—of the subject that matters.

The erotics of the classroom is somewhat like turning the lights on inside the entire corpus, causing a warm current of intellectual erotic energy to burn passionately among all those who are present and engaged. This is not about pornographic, offensive, or inappropriate pedagogy. For those undergraduate students and professors remaining caught inside the familiar but far more dense, thick, patriarchal, cerebral fog, there is no warm glow of intellectual eroticism surrounding them. This specific eroticism, when severely misunderstood as it so often is, frightens students, teachers, and administrators: it renders the assumed safe space of the classroom (including the "guilty" professor) as now dangerously precarious—unsafe for all future learning. In contradiction of this unwarranted, naïve fear, I encourage (much like Jane Gallop describes) conscious, active erotic awareness within the classroom, so that this untapped energy source can be used to further the learning experience. Set the zealous, lustful ever-so fervent, brilliant nursemaid free!

I began with clothes, because they bear the primary classist burdens of representation, repositioning, and response. (See the work of Marjorie Garber, Judith Butler, and John Berger for more discussion.) The difference between a chocolate-brown, soft, Italian leather blazer, and a big, bulky, warm, Scandinavian wooly sweater is enormous. I know: I've tried both. And the difference in impact—in how I am read, heard, and responded to—is miles apart. The leather-jacket look reaches as far as the last row of the auditorium, while the bulky sweater makes it to the second, maybe the third row, depending on how bright the colors and the students are. How we see and are seen contributes to the erotic potential of the classroom. And yet, the erotic is never dependent on nor solely manifested by appearance alone, as the media and marketplace would have us all believe.

What is most misunderstood, however, is that intellectual eros is about the conscious art of passionate, intimately experienced, energized discourse. It does not rely in any significant way on the aesthetic appearance of the one who initiates the discourse. For female professors, who as women are used to constant evaluation based historically (and solely) on our appearance, this is critical. The striking scent of our own eros can profoundly impact how powerful (or not) we feel in the classroom. The erotics of teaching mean using the entire body from head to toe, within the pedagogical moment. For women faculty especially, this can be liberating, as we no longer have to cut off our bodies for the sake of preserving our brains. Our bodies and our passions—intellectual, emotional, corporeal—contribute to the excellence of our teaching. In this scenario, the classroom becomes an ideal albeit usually unrealized (or suppressed) site of gendered erotic potential.

Look at traditional academic seating arrangements. Row after parallel row in long rectangular lecture halls, with a centrally focused, front-and-center podium for the professor alone. The view for everyone but the teacher is reduced to hats, heads, and yarmulkas (if one teaches at Brandeis). All eyes are either closed or focused vaguely forward on the professor, who is usually coolly staring down at her or his notes. In this scene, the professorial body that supports and feeds the brain is all but absent, obliterated entirely by the large podium. Although the professor meets the class head to head, alas this is no real tete-à-tete. The body as sensuously whole is fragmented, cut off from the brain, and the possibility of an erotically fluid discourse is rendered nonexistent. The smaller rectangular or square classroom with a squared-seating arrangement offers more warmth, but lots of heads and hats just as in the large lecture hall. Personally, I prefer the circle: see and be seen. Constantly. Intimately. No one can hide behind the back of a single head in a circle. Students know it's different too, as Louisa commented in my class on Blacks and Jews: "Sitting in a group of twenty-five people in a neat little circle made me uncomfortable. This was not like my Spanish class that I was taking to go to Spain nor was it like my two Psychology classes that I was taking because it filled the requirements for the major." In Louisa's situation, it is the intimacy and eye contact, which the circle provides, that make up her frightening observations, and contribute to the expressed vulnerability.

But the circle offers still more. It holds the erotic energy and prevents it from oozing and leaking out at the ends, as it always does in the square formation. And often, the square acts to obfuscate and disrupt any erotic mental fluidity from developing. For this reason, I have always disliked unmovable, bolted-to-the-floor desks. So in any large lecture hall that I am assigned to teach in, I design classroom exercises where the students literally have to turn around, front, back, right, and left, and look directly at each other face to face while engaging in the material. With great care and intent, I create the space for intellectual intimacy. Inevitably, when I change the square in Schiffman Hall to a circle I receive an e-mail within twenty-four hours from the administration, reprimanding me for moving the furniture and not putting it back in the standard, de rigeur professorial-preferred square when class is over. It's as if the circle itself has the grand potential to threaten the cohesion and "natural" order of the institution. I want to know who decided that students learn better, and teachers teach better, in a square? Where is the erotic energy in that?!

Eros in Abstentia
fear and self-loathing

The year is 1991. I am alone upstairs sitting upright in my bed, riveted to the small black-and-white TV for the third day in a row. Anita Hill is "on trial" by the U.S. Senate for exposing Bush's Supreme Court nominee Clarence Thomas's pornographic penchant for the sight of a woman's pubic hair on the open "mouth" of a very particular red and metallic-silver, recyclable can of Coca-Cola. The more I watch the more addicted I become. When it's over I too am victimized by this national spectacle, a performance so facetiously democratic that I feel myself getting physically ill. Scene after surreal scene unfolds as patriotic narratives do, ferociously eviscerating while purporting to uphold the very principles that this country was founded on: "Liberty and Justice for All." In the end, I am burning up, consumed with rage at the violent metaphors contained within this true-life drama.

First there is the unseemly public disclosure of private cultural performances: a Black woman, herself an attorney, has the audacity to accuse a Black man, of (supposedly) U.S. Supreme Court worthiness, of sexually harassing her. Feverishly exploited by the media, the "Black Community's" response to Hill's *j'accuse* was ostracism from her beloved tribe. Her expulsion was immediate and appeared, in the beginning, to be unanimous. Publicly blamed (like Alice Walker when she created the character "Mister" in *The Color Purple*), Hill became the "real" harasser, as Thomas claimed on national TV to be the ultimate victim of a high-tech lynching. But there was a counternarrative that spoke to me on a visceral level: *a narrative that revealed America's near-total preoccupation with race and sex*. (For more on this see the work of Angela Davis and Nell Irving Painter.) This was the "sex" of the African-American male and his historically asexual stereotyped Black Mama/Aunt Jemima, as opposed to the other media-driven and publicly reinforced stereotype of the oversexed and exotic Black female. Once again, African Americans were performing the true story of America.

"Patriotic" White men like Thomas Jefferson, Franklin D. Roosevelt, Dwight D. Eisenhower, John F. Kennedy, Lyndon Baines Johnson, Henry Hyde, Newt Gingrich, Bob Packwood, Gary Hart, and Bill Clinton, just to name a few, have always been too scared to tell the truth when it comes to race and the delicate intricacies of their own private sex lives.

Metaphorically speaking but also quite literally, Anita Hill was giving America the chance this country had secretly longed for: the opportunity for redemption. The redemption of the Master's creation of the Black male slave and his voracious appetite for all things sexual (a projection of the narcissistic Master himself). I watched redemption American-style unfold before my eyes, like the Stars and Stripes unfurled in the midst of a headstrong wind. One after another, the grief-stricken senators lined up in their consensus: from Arlen Specter to the reluctant chair(man) of the mock judicial interrogation, Joseph Biden. (Only Edward Kennedy remained openly befuddled.) In their eyes, here was an honest-to-god-fearing Black man that this time had truly—savagely—and finally been wrongly accused. Justice was demanded.

But what of Anita Hill—and what was the impact of her narrative for teachers? (And what does this have to do with the erotics of the classroom? Patience, please.) I remember vividly the full-page ad in the *New York Times*, paid for and "signed" by prominent outspoken Black women feminists from bell hooks to Patricia Williams to Toni

Morrison, all in support of Anita Hill and against sexual harassment of any kind in any community. Name after impressive female name shouted across the page. No, the "Black Community" was not monolithic after all. But it didn't matter. Redemption American-style was already swiftly on its way. Word leaked out over the AP wires that Thomas and his wife, Virginia, knelt at their bedside to pray the night before his "high-tech lynching" was to occur.

Watching it hour after spectacular hour had a freezing, nearly numbing, paralyzing effect on me that didn't pedagogically reveal itself in full force until I walked back into the classroom months later. *Sexual harassment* as a cause célèbre and as a redefined state and federal cause of action had now reached the mainstream, albeit distorted and deranged in all its newly codified definitions. Although the "Black Man" had been officially redeemed by his White "Massa," the Black woman once again had to pay the price for her brother "Uncle Tom's" hallowed freedom. Walking into the classroom as an out lesbian professor had never been easy, but in 1991, after the Thomas/Hill hearings, it felt nearly impossible.

Previously in the public acknowledgement of my sexual orientation, I had by default and unintentionally sexualized the "always neutral" classroom. For me and others similarly situated, the homoerotic presence *in itself* sexed the learning site. I didn't have to do a single thing but stand there with my feet on the ground. The effect of the hearings was that I too became an Anita Hill, as if on trial for harassing my students with the fact of my sexual orientation but without any concrete sexual or erotic practice. Unconsciously I began to teach from the head up. *Look but don't touch*. Contrary to my own Jewish culture that had always included large physical, public gesticulations of the arms and the hands, plus my own performative erotic artistic self, I now kept my arms glued to my queerly Hebraic, female sides. I rarely paraded back and forth in front of my students. Leather was out, big bulky sweaters that completely concealed the female body were in. It was as if my body had absorbed by osmosis the near-total antierotic toxicity of the Thomas/Hill hearings.

Over the next several semesters, faculty and student handbooks were aggressively rewritten and legally revised (although often in constitutionally unsupportable ways). They spelled out in no uncertain terms that all student-teacher amorous relations—however consensual—were inappropriate. Professors (not the students) would be subject to the strictest of censures including but not limited to permanent removal from the campus. In this new academic lingua franca, the word *amorous* had become dangerously vague, so broad in definition as to be applied to almost any kind of human behavior and, most significantly, no longer confined to the nonconsensual sex act alone. (See Jane Gallop on the negative consequences of the new sexual harassment definitions and in particular their impact on feminist professors.)

Before the hearings I had been careful to monitor any physicality, which included limiting the performance of sexuality (as opposed to sexual preference) in the classroom. That meant I didn't fully bring the passionate essence of me into my teaching or pedagogical practice. I taught instead in small, safe erotic doses and unleashed the whole essence of my selfhood, body and mind, on less controversial stages. As a consequence, I was far less effective than the true-to-life (and self) engaging, and unfragmented, erotically feminist professor that I actually am.

Now I became paralyzingly vigilant, monitoring every verbal and physical movement that might possibly be mistaken as sexual innuendo. Politically (that is, heterosexistly), I understood that I and other gay colleagues around the country had always been judged by a much stricter sexual harassment scale because of our publicly acknowledged identities, not our behavior. But with these newly revised, frighteningly broad standards, I became even more circumspect about erotics in the teaching environment. I no longer looked deeply into the eyes of students. I lectured with much less intensity than I was accustomed to. I was careful never to touch a single student, male or female, however in need of comfort he or she might appear to be. Platonic kissing, hugging, or even offering a hand to shake goodbye at the end of the semester was off limits. I became all brain and no brawn. Was I overreacting? I don't think so; having previously been reprimanded for saying the word *lesbian* too often in class had signaled to me that I could never be vigilant enough.

I was miserable. Confined to a totally constricted pedagogical physicality, I could barely move, let alone teach. *This can't be the way it's supposed to be,* I told myself as I began withdrawing all verbal and emotional support even from those students who were openly gay or who were in the process of coming out. *This is not natural. I can't teach like this.* I was completely cut off from all things physical as well as the art of passionate erotic discourse that is so fulfilling. The pain was acute, not only mental, but running throughout my entire body. Unwittingly, I had begun to change my previously spectacular pedagogical wardrobe. Now I wore only muted colors, black pants, and more black pants. I bought them in every shade I could find—from charcoal to midnight. And rarely, if ever, did I remove my blazer, for fear of removing my essential armor and thereby exposing the evil amour underneath. I was bland, doing penance for all past erotic performances, and mundanely pedestrian in every sense. During this period I was teaching at the University of Massachusetts in Amherst, and one of my students wrote the following on her anonymous evaluation: *Why does Felman always wear black? Week after week, that's all she ever wore. It's so boring, will somebody take her shopping, please!* Closed off from my erotic energy, my pedagogy began to resemble the old-boys style, rigid, contrived, and in the familiar rhythm of the classic solo lecture. I had successfully morphed myself into just another asexual talking head, predictable, repetitive, and above institutional reproach in the classroom.

Responding to my initial inquiry on the erotics of the classroom, Maureen discussed the particular vulnerability of gay faculty. Because she was in high school during the Thomas/Hill hearings and the oppressive Republican family values campaign spearheaded by Dan Quayle, I was surprised and pleased with her answer:

> I once read this essay . . . which I fully believe, that Gay and Lesbian faculty have so much more scrutiny placed upon them. First of all, since GLBT faculty are out of the norm, their sexuality is of huge issue. There is something overtly sexual about taking a stance on your sexuality versus just having it assumed. People really don't think about straight, but do think about queer. Plus, everyone loves a scandal, especially when it is out of the norm. . . .
>
> There is at any school, a deep analysis of friendships between queer students and faculty, while the queer students and faculty do the same analysis so as not to give anyone any question about the relationship. It is all deeply imbedded and burdening. This essay also talked about how college is when a large amount of people come out, so students in a confusing position tend to crush on strong queer role models . . . and that is why you see a lot of first/second years crushing on . . . the most out faculty, such as yourself. Or they take the complete

opposite stance and won't align with queer faculty, since they do not want uneducated people to overanalyze the relationship or cause jeopardy.

It was both reassuring and disturbing to read what Maureen had to say. Yet it is necessary to acknowledge that our students (gay or straight) discuss among themselves the entire erotic range of the classroom—much more so than we the faculty ever do. On an intuitive level, students experience those professors who are passionately engaged in the material as erotic. However, they do not yet have a language to describe this particular experience because their vocabulary has been structurally confined by compulsory heterosexuality, which (as previously discussed) perpetually compresses sex and the erotics into (hetero) sexual intercourse.

In a later e-mail Maureen concurred with me; she wondered if this near-total lack of eros in the course of a lifetime is specific to her generation.

> Sex, love, and eros, in my generation has been mass-marketed, homogenzied, and essentialized into simply het sex. The notion of love/lust for the many beautiful things in life seems nonexistent. I just assumed it was a generational thing that 15- to 26-year-olds are very essentialist in their relationship to love, eros, and sex in the world. Was your generation, at this age, in love with ideas and life itself. Because if yes, my generation is deeply in trouble.

My response was that eros is not confined generationally to the past, but rather that the dominant cultural hegemony of penis-vagina penetration is enforced and exaggerated by the marketplace and the media.

Additionally, I had earlier asked Maureen to discuss, from a student's perspective, what was it about myself or any other teacher that created an aura of eros. She responded:

> I still don't know if the crushes are personally or more politically oriented—for instance, are they in lust with you or what you represent. . . . I don't think that the eros around your aura would be affected if you weren't an out lesbian. We all know you are an extremely sexual and intellectual being. But maybe again, it would affect the perception of the queer kids at Brandeis. I don't know.

While I am pleased that students notice the aura of eros around me, I must add that this is not a scent only I carry with me into the classroom. The eros of my courses is atmospheric. That is, it's like the harmonic conversation of birds in the woods calling to one another at dawn. There is a back-and-forth, an exchange of ideas, which I may initiate by asking the class to ponder a certain idea, but the resulting eros is a human dialogic. The eros surrounding me in the classroom exists because my passion is received unconditionally. As I receive in turn the energized, stimulating enthusiasm of my students, I am challenged to go to the next level of discourse as are they. The manifestations of the erotic aura of eros would be with me whether I was an out lesbian or not, but only if I had an unambivalent relationship to both my brain and my body.

Desire in the classroom is as a moving vehicle, traveling constantly on green lights, blinking yellows, or right-turn-on-reds, but never coming to a total four-way stop. Fluid access to the heat of the matter(s) in question, not identity or appearance, is central to maintaining the power of the erotic in the classroom. I remember Barbra Streisand's directorial debut with the Issac Bashevis Singer story of Yentl. Within the intense, isolated environment of the Eastern European yeshivot, young men were infused with the erotic as they argued with each other, back and forth, day after day, all day except Shabbat, certain weekly Torah *parshas* and the accompanying great rabbinical *Responsas* of the Mishna and Gemora. Watching *Yentl* over and over again, I remembered my adolescent longing for the atmosphere of the yeshiva, where young minds were constantly on fire, ignited by those other young minds seated nearby on hard wooden benches. As a young Jewish girl preparing for her Bat Mitzvah, I could imagine no environment except a convent where I might have a similarly erotic experience. Today as a professor, I am completely aware of the erotic potential of the classroom, long before I ever walk into the room. For the erotic and I have finally become inseparable.

Eros
electrifying, stimulating, life-giving, vitalizing

Three years after Hill/Thomas I was teaching at Brandeis and ever so slowly my behavior began to change. I don't know exactly why. Out of nowhere, in the middle of discussing sexuality, I slipped. That is, I began to cry, in public, while describing to the class that I had stopped being fully myself in the classroom, because I didn't ever want to be accused of being sexually or physically inappropriate with a student. Surprising myself as much if not more than the class, I nevertheless continued. *I had to be extremely careful*, I told the hushed room, *not to touch, hug, or look too long or hard at any one particular student. Lest anyone—student or innocuous observer—interpret my behavior as a form of sexual harassment.* I added that the fact of my out lesbianism only made matters worse. In closing I said, *I am under, as are all gay faculty, stricter scrutiny than my straight peers.* Then, in typical feminist pedagogical strategy, I brought my spontaneous, personal disclosure back to the original subject of the class—sexuality. I asked everyone to think about the consequences of what I had just described. I wanted to know: *How had both the act of my admission and the content itself impacted the classroom, and their own learning process? And what if anything did this disclosure have to do with sexuality?*

Hours later, I realized that this surprise disclosure was the beginning of the way back. I had, without any planning, brought the feminist body, my corpus delicti, back into the sexual, forbidden zone of the academy. There was no turning back. I began to wear purple again. And burnt red, fire orange, sun-drenched yellow, sea-green turquoise, and royal blue. Lovingly I draped myself in long, flowing, hand-woven Indian silk scarves. This was a public, pedagogical self under reconstruction. I wore huge dangling earrings in every imaginable shape, added another piercing to my right ear and cut my hair shorter than it had ever been. Once I even dyed it red! My new costuming was not meant to be flirtatious or rhetorical. I was communicating a self-acceptance to my students that I had been suppressing. Finally I smothered my lips with a hot new shade of red and even polished my toenails later that spring. But most important, I began to talk in class about the erotic as the authentic "nursemaid of all our deepest knowledge" (Audre Lorde). Looking directly at my students, and once assured of their eye contact, I galloped across the room telling class after feminist class that *ambivalence—that is, the emotional inability to make concrete decisions— is not sexy and that it will kill all intellectual desire.* Afterwards we spent the next several sessions discussing how *ambivalence politically not just personally negates voice and agency, but also cuts off the power of the erotic contained within the entire corpus.*

On the last day of class of that semester, Amara walked up to me and said loud enough for everybody to hear, "Can I give you a hug goodbye? Just a small one. I want to thank you, for everything, especially that time you talked about yourself." I was caught off guard. But before I could explicitly refuse, my arms gathered Amara in a warm embrace. "Thank you," I whispered as we parted. I could feel then the asexual, antierotic repressive curse that had been haunting me break for good. A new spell was cast as one student after another, male and female, lined up for a goodbye hug from me, their radical, lesbian, feminist Jewish professor. This was astounding. In twenty years of teaching, no matter how much I cared about my students, I had never done anything like this before! But now, I was too busy hugging to be afraid. At some point, we all started to cry. Vital, life-giving erotic energy had been returned to our classroom, initiated this time by the students themselves—and their professor had reciprocated. We knew it was a public, political, and intimate healing, full of all the sacredness of an authentic peak religious experience.

In retrospect, I see that my students responded to me with total integrity and that my personal disclosure was both necessary and appropriate, in order for us to reach the erotic height of our own learning potential. Unbeknownst to them—beginning with Amara—my students had given me their blessing. The blessing I had so longed for: to be *as I am* not just *who I am* in the classroom. I had never imagined the remote possibility that my Introduction to Women's Studies class would bring the body, theirs and mine—student and teacher, as it should be—back inside, out of the bone-chillingly cold rhetoric of compulsory heterosexuality and banished eroticism. Finally, without enormous trepidation, I could now take future classes into my arms, not just in the privacy of my imagination, but mentally and, yes, physically. With much joy, I could again touch the erotic in my students and myself as I taught.

Eros
lustful, amorous, hot-tempered, invigorating

In describing four instances of the complex range of desires in which faculty eroticize students Roger Simon mentions several that mirror my own experiences. One of them

> appears when my teaching is structured by my desire for an intellectual partner; particularly if the institution I work in provides little

opportunity for the gratifications possible in collegiality. The form of desire acknowledges my pleasure in intellection . . . a partner in pedagogy who is prepared to take me seriously and provide a sense of engagement, one who will construct with me the sensuousness of the academic dance.

[In another] instance my teaching may be structured by desire for solidarity, for a partner in whom I can see how my work might continue to inform and be informed by something beyond the boundaries of my own work.

Although Simon confines his observations to dissertation students specifically, it is a relief to read another professor who unabashedly acknowledges, welcomes, and cultivates the active existence of eros within his pedagogical practice. Sadly, outside the work of Jane Gallop, in book after book on feminist pedagogy I have found little or nothing that discusses the power of the hot-tempered and invigorating erotic in the classroom.

The most erotic classroom experience I have ever had was in Reading and Writing Autobiography when I assigned my memoir, *Cravings*. The students were to read and discuss the book in small groups before writing their own critique of the narrative, its tone and style. We would spend half of the three-hour seminar discussing their reactions. This was the first time that I had ever assigned my own book for such a full-bodied workout. Previously, I had made several stories from my short story collection, *Hot Chicken Wings*, required reading as a way of breaking down the barriers between theory and literary arts, and across academic disciplines. Although the particular stories were relevant to topics that were part of the class, I was never satisfied that I had used the stories to their full erotic potential.

I had waited until after midsemester so that the class would have acquired the necessary critical tools and confidence to deconstruct their teacher's writing, and to form their own opinions of the work itself. Also, by then they would have been intimately engaged in the actual process of autobiography, having worked on their own narratives for the previous ten weeks. By reading positive and negative reviews of *Cravings* to the class before we began our discussion, I hoped to prepare the class to proceed uncensored, without fear of repercussion or reprimand of any kind if they didn't simply rave about the work under their consideration.

I was not invested in whether or not the class "loved" the book. Rather, I was eager to sit back and listen, wanting nothing more than to hear them discuss the success or failure of the narrative structure. Based on the passionate authority of their own writing experience, I believed they were more than ready to engage the professor (me) directly. While I felt myself get nervous as soon as someone brought up the short staccato, one-word sentences that permeated the text, I never stopped the discussion by imposing the power of my position. Instead, I took notes, as they did all semester as we discussed each other's work. What follows here are some of their written comments, which in their own way represent the power of the erotic as potent pedagogical exchange—*the dialectic in hot pursuit of the erotic dialogic.* In their critiques the students speak in strong, unique voices. The confidence of each writer glides across the page, while infusing everyone with a keen sense of literary authority unavailable to the students before taking this class.

> The sentence structure of *Cravings* . . . is the most striking aspect of its style. While I applaud telling the story in one's own voice and stretching conventional (white heteropatriarchal) notions of what writing is, I find the short sentences frustrating. . . . The shortness makes the sentences abrupt to read, and because sentence after sentence is short, the power of the short sentences diminishes. In some instances, an abrupt sentence has power, while in others, I have trouble understanding why two or three weren't combined into one. Perhaps this sheds some light on my own . . . writing style: I have been writing in a way which I feel expresses myself (long rambling sentences, lots of feeling statements and few capitals), and while this style may be true to me, it may also be somewhat elusive to a reader who does not me know well. —Eliza

> The non-linear narrative worked very well for this story . . . the writing style was fantastic. The small broken up sentences really gave a different feel to the book. Like it was truly a unique part of the author's story. I cannot remember reading any other book written in similar style. —Susan

> At times her use of family to tell the story somewhat eclipsed the focus. . . . Using the device of family, Professor Felman was able to

avoid certain topics. I felt that some important areas in her own life were not given enough attention (that is told, and not shown), specifically her lesbianism. . . .

The most interesting experience in reading *Cravings* was the privilege of reading the autobiography of a professor. I am so interested in how the experiences of our other classes would be if all of our professors required that their autobiography be read. It creates a sense of equality that I find very refreshing, but which I think many professors would be afraid to attempt. —Rebecca

For me, the professor, this was by far one of the most satisfying experiences I have ever had in a classroom. Two critical elements were present that made the experience simultaneously erotic and conventionally transgressive. The first is that I saw and experienced the essence of my teaching reflected back to me: engaged, critical thinking outside the classic binaries of good/bad, right/wrong, authority/novice, mentor/mentee. And what makes it transgressive is that the work in question was the professor's—my own. Not a theoretical text per se, but a creative nonfiction narrative—a memoir of my life was under strict scrutiny. The power in the classroom shifted dramatically; I was no longer (to the students) the sole repository of knowledge, which in this class meant how to read, write, and deconstruct an autobiography. This hierarchy was interrupted and redirected as soon as *Cravings* was introduced as part of the course requirements, rather than as one of the optional books that were supplemental to the syllabus for those students who wanted "more." Listening to and later reading their comments was completely revitalizing—a truely zestful learning experience. I got to experience each student's application of the theories we had been learning all semester. And they got to speak and write from the authority of their own learning experience. The ingredient present most specifically was: *the intellectual reciprocity necessary for a peak pedagogical erotic experience to realize its full potential.*

Eros Live
positively redux

If we have been successful in engaging the power of the erotic in the undergraduate classroom, we must remember that this erotic, experienced so viscerally between student and teacher, does not die at the end of the semester. Perhaps this is what is most frightening. For a long time I avoided any conscious awareness that the erotic relationships I so intentionally engaged in the classroom had come to have a complete life of their own. A life that continues to include me the professor, while at the same time extending beyond the institutional walls within which it was nursed so sensuously into existence. Beginning in kindergarten and continuing on through graduate school, the erotic that was lovingly ignited by our teachers specifically for us, their students, never ends. I know. For all those treasured nursemaids, my beloved professors, men and women, who fearlessly dared set fire to the intellectual erotic sparks within me, whom I honor by taking them with me every time I walk into a new classroom.

So I end this chapter carrying on the passionate pedagogical practice of the erotic. For the first time, I have invited previous students to visit me in the cottage where I spend my summers writing and where most of this book was written. I will conclude my retreat by preparing a feast for my passionate pedagogical partners, including Maureen and Autumn. We will build a huge bonfire at the beach as the sun goes down. Against the pounding waves as the tide comes in, we will feed all the burning embers. I know full well that a fire not tended properly becomes too hot and quickly becomes out of control. But we will watch over this fire together, talking and eating by the lusty flames. For we have come to share the sacred responsibility of the power of the erotic that burns forever between teacher and student, student and teacher.

Stage Notes

A Midsemester's
Day Dream

PUCK: *The hard rubber disk which ice hockey play-*
ers try to drive with their sticks into the opponents'
goal. To blow up, swell, whence pout, pucker. A mis-
chievous sprite or elf (see William Shakespeare).
    —*Webster's New World Dictionary, 2nd Ed.*

i don't know what to
wear on the first day of Harmonies and Tensions, a course on Blacks and
Jews. This is a specific question of cultural authenticity as well as one of
academic performativity. I ask myself: What image do I want to present, to the Jews in the class, to the African Americans, and for what purpose? What exactly must I signify the first day? I have asked myself
these questions before, in preparation for other classes such as
Introduction to Women's Studies or Reading and Writing Autobiography. The challenge is precisely that I recognize the ethnographic
and sociological power of the sartorial medium and its impact on my
audience. The signification of "the dress" matters, impacting how what
I say is ultimately received and interpreted. It becomes a trope, and one
of the many theatrical ways I choose to communicate in the classroom.
No matter what I actually decide to wear, I always wear a scarf around
my neck, tossed intentionally, dramatically, over my left shoulder.

I add a small gold *chai* hanging from a thin braided chain at the base of my neck. The Hebrew letters "chet" and "yod" communicate a sense of cultural and ethnic pride (albeit not necessarily religious) to all the students in the room. Whether or not they know that the *chai* means "life," I am saying publicly that I am a Jew teaching this particular course. (For more on "teaching as a Jew" and "a Jew teaching," see Roger Simon.) In fact, midway through Blacks and Jews, Perry, an African-American student, asks me the meaning of my necklace.

"For four years, I've seen Jews at Brandeis wear that charm and I knew it had to do with something Jewish, but I didn't know what. And I never felt comfortable enough to ask."

In this exchange, the *chai* was an express—rather than implied—signifier, opening an important, authentic cultural dialogue. At the moment of engagement, Perry and I were no longer just professor and student. The *chai* had become an agent of discourse as well as a form of positive cultural currency. And, we decided that there was no cultural "Black" equivalent. That much of what originally had signified as Black—dreads, braids, rap, and so on—had already been commodified by a White middle-class marketplace and so the meaning and intent of the culturally Black signifiers had changed in the process.

At this point in the class, Rebecca spoke up about the significance of the Mogen David, the Star of David, that she always wore around her neck. She told the class how, depending on the context—whether or not she felt safe as a Jew—she tucks her Jewish star inside her clothes; or as many students do at Brandeis, she "tucks" it out. On campus, she is surrounded by Jews and wants to communicate clearly her membership in the tribe. This led to an analysis about voluntary and involuntary visibility and the option of invisibility that Jews have, and all the ensuing privileges that accrue when one appears to "blend in." The Mogen David as active "tribal" symbol led the class to an in-depth discussion of the fact that overt identification for Jews in the United States remains ambiguous; that is, non-Orthodox Jews in public can choose to assimilate and are then culturally "Whited out." African Americans have no choice about being identified as Black. I added the personal detail that I never "hid" my *chai* because I actually wanted people to ask me about it! So, referenced for the rest of the semester, a decorative piece of ethnic jewelry worn by the professor became a permanent part of the pedagogy, which opened previously closed yet potent learning sites for both professor and students.

Decoded, the rest of my outfit communicates the fluidity of performance as pedagogy. The scarf is handwoven silk, fibers of red, black, and white in a repetitive geometric design. I am not unaware that the silk scarf could be mistaken for an authentic African weave or a contemporary tallis, a Jewish prayer shawl, depending on the cultural location of the viewer. At the beginning of each semester, the fact that I am lesbian remains invisible to those students who have not had a course with me before. And now that multiple ear piercings coupled with extremely short hair are fashionable and no longer absolute signifiers for gay women, this part of my identity remains intentionally ambiguous. The prop of style can thus be used to conceal whatever the professor is not yet ready to reveal. In the course on Blacks and Jews, I want to gradually work "the ambiguity of identity" (mine included) into the course material itself.

Seize the Moment
Il faut vivre dans l'instant!

I enter Schwartz room 211 with a confident, academic flourish, sprinkled generously with a queerly female verve and strong Hebraic panache. Swinging my right arm into the air while wrapping my scarf around my left shoulder, I choose my opening lines with care. "Why is this class different from all other classes? And why is this subject historically more often important to Jews than to Blacks?" I walk up and down, back and forth, circling the horseshoe arrangement of students and desks. I watch for body postures and eye contact to shift. Then I take off my dark chocolate, soft Italian leather blazer and say, "For five minutes write your thoughts on the questions I just asked."

I am at this moment a woman playing the *role* of professor, using the power of the destabilized postmodern feminist Trans Vestite (as opposed to transvestite) to teach difficult material and to reach out across difference. Cross-dressing or "vestment crossing" in an academic context allows me to pedagogically cross channels, boundaries, subjects, and cultures. I intend my classroom appearance to be as fluid as the discussion of the day, reflecting both the anxieties and assurances of what I plan to convey. It is the trickster Puck who not only comes to class with me but—in actuality—is me.

For I have begun to understand that the "I" of the me who enters

Blacks and Jews, is and is not the same "I" of the me who enters Reading and Writing Autobiography or any other course that I teach. This means that within the language of *pedagogy as postmodern performance*, the roles the professor performs are fluid in and of themselves, and in constant flux, depending on the environment and the subject under discussion. In Blacks and Jews, I am a public and self-publicizing Jew; that is, my persona in class is ethnically specific by personal design. In terms of my own subjectivity and as the one who teaches the course, it is understood—by the students and myself—before I enter the classroom that the professor is performing "Jewish" in this particular course. However, in Autobiography, the me that is the I who enters the room is as "literary auteur." The subject position from which I teach is no longer primarily based on the fact of my Jewishness, but rather it is based on the fact that I have written several books, most important in this context *Cravings*, a memoir. So I am now in that specific pedagogical moment (and in contrast with other pedagogical moments) imbued performatively with the identity of creator/writer. It is in this reconfigured location from which Puck the professor performs the act of teaching how to read and write autobiography.

In the introductory Women's Studies course, I am clearly read as lesbian, no matter how my vestments are construed or constructed. Here, my homosexual persona is more a reflection of the students' perception of *just who would teach this kind of course to begin with*; combined with their actual ignorance of the subject matter itself, rather than any one identity that I might choose to perform. That is, in the minds of students, men and women, Women's Studies (still) equals Dyke Studies, which is very different from Queer Studies. Based on this publicly traded "insider" information, I often play with their lesbian misconceptions and reliance on outmoded, offensive gay stereotypes, as I did last semester.

I wore a smooth black silk pants suit with a light blue, sleeveless camisole top underneath; and short, geometric, silver post earrings rather than my usual two-inch, brightly colored, dangling ones. Although I received many compliments on my suit I knew that I was still performing "academic dyke, soft butch" in the students' perceptions. So, I decided to perform a "gender fuck" without saying a word. The next week I wore my first ever ankle-length, velvet-smooth, light cranberry scooped-neck dress with long, elegant tight-fitting sleeves and matching French silk floral-patterned nylons. I stepped out from behind the podium that I never use in chiseled black heels with spaghetti-thin straps crossing each foot and a small faux-diamond clasp at the ankle bone. Pausing for the moment's full effect, I knew my shoes were magical, meant to change the very nature of my firm pedagogical gait. Standing perfectly still, my eyes closed for no more than a second, I arched my torso and stretched out my arms, ready to dance a most sensuous tango encircled in the graceful arms of an equally regal, but genderedly vague, partner. The impact was swift and remarkable. The class literally stopped. Then they began, a chorus of loud voices: *Professor Felman, you look soooooo good. Sooooo beautiful. I like you in a dress. How come you never wear dresses?* Although Puck was having a blast, I was not so sanguine. In a week, my performance had changed from soft butch, a kind of feminine masculinity (read: lesbian) to the recognizable, culturally sanctioned and determined more feminine appearance (read: female). Hence, dressed in long flowing cranberry velvet, I now upheld most of the students' traditionally rigid gender assumptions. But I wanted to challenge those very assumptions that in the present were applauding my highly feminized female performance. In this way, through the act of puckering up, I publicly conferred upon myself the necessary subjectivity concerning gender fluidity and sexual orientation to teach this particular course, Introduction to Women's Studies.

In my advanced feminist theory seminar the facts of my Jewish and lesbian identities receded into the background, as I now embodied the theory itself; that is, the I who is me was now seen and saw herself as the "Radical Feminist Theorist." Once again the location of my academic subjectivity changed. The trickster Puck can be fully engaged in the classroom if one understands the power the professor possesses to become, to embody, the subject of the course itself. Only then, in reality, has the pedagogical moment truly been seized. The subject lives through the professor when she plays true to the character Puck. Thus the students can never predict what I will wear or do, nor how I will costume myself from class to class. And, most important, who exactly it is that I am when I stand in front of them. For if I am the same subject in every class, then I am actually not performing in the present at all. I am merely a form of theatrical arbitrage, the past revisited in the present for the benefit of future performances. Tomorrow's classes become predictable if not identical because past ones remain the same, semester to semester, year after year. There is simply no academic "return," for the value of the course continues to lessen the more repetitive the professor and her lessons become.

Students sense whether or not the professor is fully engaged or to what degree she is disengaged from both the subject and her own corresponding subjectivity as professor; and they react with interest or disinterest accordingly. In this way, our students mirror our own performance, all its magnificent strengths and glaring weaknesses. So if we can understand our deep personal relationship to the subject(s) that we teach *while* we are teaching, and thereby allow Puck to roam free, we can tap the full magnetic power of our pedagogical ability. Where nothing is forever rote, because nothing is predictable when the trickster breathes fresh life into our classrooms.

Slowly the students too begin to pucker up, swell, and change their own appearances from week to week. For whenever Puck is present in the classroom, the fever she generates is contagious and spreads like wildfire. In the sizzling academic heat, students acquire new, more fluid, and previously suppressed subjectivities as the semester develops. Body postures change, facial expressions become unpredictable, until I do not know who will wear what and how what they wear will impact what they have to say. When the magic of the performance is fully in progress, I can no longer surmise who exactly is whom. That is, which students will assume the positions of leading roles, and who will be the best supporting actors/actresses. Many professors find this kind of student fluidity disarming; they too seek emotional order, familiarity, and intellectual repetition in the classroom. It makes teaching so much easier and far less exhausting if we can predict ahead of time who the students are and how they will react to the course material.

So without any further delay: *Il faut vivre dans l'instant!*

The Student Puck(ers)

Once I permitted a student to take two of my courses in the same semester, although I had severe reservations about the heavy workload, writing assignments, and sheer emotional and intellectual intensity of both courses. But Nicki begged me, repeatedly arguing that as a senior this was her "last chance." So in the spring of 2000, she was a student in both Reading and Writing Autobiography, which met on Tuesdays for three hours, and on Wednesdays she was in Blacks and Jews for another three hours. Ironically both courses met in the same classroom. But that is where all similarities between Nicki and myself stopped. As the weeks went by, I began to think of Nicki as two separate and distinct people who were in two of my classes in the same semester and who happened to have identical names. The "two" women themselves couldn't have been more different from each other.

In Autobiography Nicki wrote about her close, nearly symbiotic relationship with her mother and hardly ever brought up or wrote about her identity as an African-American woman; while in Blacks and Jews almost all she talked about was being an "Angry Black Woman." On Tuesdays, she had one persona, a daughter entwined with her mother. On Wednesdays, she had another one: Black female activist. Never did the two personas mix. Each subject tapped different selves of Nicki and she presented herself accordingly. Her performances in my classes were fluid rather than incompatible or fragmented. I had little or no intellectual or emotional vertigo experiencing the two Nickis. Perhaps it was because my own performance reflected back a similar fluidity, as I too was much more the academic activist in Blacks and Jews, while being the literary and performance artist in Autobiography. From Nicki I learned never to impose a rigid or fixed identity on a student.

So, caveat emptor: let the professor beware; it is the student who shows the teacher who she is, and who she becomes. From that semester on, I follow the student's lead as she confirms again that it is the content that ultimately determines the form.

Ruthie, on the other hand, proved to be an unexpected challenge. She had taken both the introductory Women's Studies course and the Advanced Feminist Theory seminar; and by her own account had had an intellectual and emotional life-transforming experience each time. I knew she loved my classroom methodology, the intimacy between students that develops and the strong teacher-student bond so central to my work. I assumed we would have an equally powerful (if not more so) experience in the upcoming Blacks and Jews. I was wrong. The first sign was that she was significantly late for class three weeks in a row. Each time, she offered a seemingly bona fide explanation. But her theatrical entrances caused disruption in the epistemic flow of the classroom, and we had to stop while someone explained to her what she had missed.

Word came to me through her close friend that she was unhappy, that the course was nothing like what she'd expected. *There were no weekly epiphanies.* Around the same time, I noticed that Ruthie didn't seem to be as engaged as the other students. So diffident was her behavior that she became to me a completely different student than the Ruthie who had been my student in two earlier semesters. She and I met in my office and discussed the situation. She kept saying, "I don't get it. What's the big deal about Black and Jews? This is nothing like your other courses." We were having opposite experiences. From my point of view, I had never taught better nor been more excited about the level of intellectual rigor among the students. But as I listened closer to Ruthie, it became clear that some part of the course material was deeply upsetting to her, even frightening on a personal level.

Our previously stimulating rapport continued to deteriorate. I simply couldn't reach Ruthie. I asked for help from my teaching assistants, but they too were stumped, and disgruntled by their own interactions with her. This was the first time in many years of teaching that communication and connection had so totally broken down between myself, a student, and her relationship to the course itself. Or so it appeared for the first eleven weeks.

Toward the end of the semester, with only three classes left, Ruthie's behavior shifted dramatically. She came on time, and participated with genuine enthusiasm, and finally she began to speak about her experience: *I just couldn't deal with what I was learning about Jewish identity—assimilation—in the Diaspora. It was too painful; and I didn't understand the Black narrative for the longest time.* She even admitted that she had seriously considered dropping the course. It was a painful and public lesson that teachers have to resist the urge to typecast and slot students who are well known to them from previous courses. We cannot assume and thereby expect our students to behave in familiar, predictable ways in courses with significantly different content and/or presentation.

Ruthie's situation was not at all similar to that of the two Nickis. While Nicki was engaged and excited about both Blacks and Jews and Reading and Writing Autobiography, Ruthie clearly was unhappy her third semester with me. The pedagogical challenge she posed became clear: *How do I respond to a student whose behavior changes drastically from one class to another, moving from positive to increasingly negative?* My encounter with Ruthie involved a process of rigorous self-scrutiny that continued for some time: *Is there any intervention that could have changed the direction she was headed, to prevent the rupture in our connection?* No. With some students rupture is both inevitable and an essential part of growth and transformation. Frustratingly, Ruthie and I never reconnected completely. I disappointed her in ways large and small; but she may not know that she too disappointed me. What to do with a professor's unexpected personal disappointment in a student becomes a very private academic angst. For Ruthie and myself, I needed to fall from the academic pedestal on which she had so grandly placed me. I can live with that. Yet the lack of true resolution and reconnection still aches.

Finally, there was Dan, who changed his behavior and appearance so drastically midsemester in Blacks and Jews that I honestly didn't recognize him.

I was walking across campus one day when coming toward me was Mr. Clean-Cut-All-American-Preppy-Republican, neatly dressed, smoothly shaven, and hair perfected into the appropriate short style, parted on the right.

"Professor Felman."

I stopped in front of Goldfarb Library.

"Professor Felman!" I knew the voice but not the person who stood before me.

This was my third semester with Dan. Most recently he had been a student teaching assistant in the introductory Women's Studies class. During the past two years, his appearance and behavior changed little. Dan had always had shoulder-length hair, sometimes a beard, sometimes not; he wore loose-fitting clothes hippie-style and was extremely self-assured and laid-back. But the man who stood before me, calling out my name, looked like former Vice President Quayle's son.

"Dan?" I said.

"Yeah, it's me."

"What happened?" I asked.

"I don't know. I got tired—wanted a change," he said.

It took weeks for the old Dan and the newly reconstructed Dan to blend together in my imagination. In truth, I had been concerned about him all semester. His work, much like Ruthie's, was not up to the high level that I had been accustomed to from him. It turns out, he was confronting for the first time an enormous amount of internalized anti-Semitism and self-loathing as a Jew, which was reflected in his somewhat antagonistic class behavior, and which he later movingly wrote about.

However, Dan's sartorial transformation provoked in me a series of disturbing and complex reactions. As his professor—one who embraces and teaches fluidity both as theory and praxis—I was unexpectedly unnerved by the "loss" of the old, familiar Dan. I had unwittingly become used to Dan's hippie persona as a signifier for his politically left-of-center thinking. Now his appearance and his ideology existed in sharp contrast to each other. And I didn't know how to respond. Here before me was my own theory on asymmetry writ large and in life. The question became how to reconcile the conflicting messages I received each time I looked and listened to Dan. This was a wonderful pedagogical challenge. For I had made the mistake that so many others do: I had equated appearance with a person(a), thereby creating a false sense of symmetry in my mind. I had to consciously watch myself so that I treated the "new" Dan (whose appearance brought out enormous ambivalence in me) the same way I had always treated the old, familiar (read: more likeable) Dan. Clearly we as teachers are far more affected by the puckering up of our students and their appearances than we ever like to admit!

I don't know what exactly motivated Dan's revised persona, but I do know that he experienced a profound awakening of himself as a Jew. Perhaps he felt the unconscious need to physically embody his transformation. But his physical metamorphosis reminds me of Bob Dylan and Franz Kafka, who belong to a long list of brilliantly ambivalent, soul-searing Jews who went through numerous physical embodiments (on the literary page and in real life) before feeling at home in their own bodies.

It is the unrealized Trans Vestite within our psyches who holds our multiplicities and pushes against the institutionalized binaries of culture and gender. Once the Trans Vestite is released into the classroom, a new sensibility emerges, one that suggests counterpoint and a unique, compatible incongruity. That is, one that validates those complex contradictions located within a single individual without splitting the self into halves, thirds, or quarters or magnifying the fears that so often accompany the contradictions. The role of the Trans Vestite is to suggest the multiplicities of race, gender, sexuality, and class as contained (and constructed) in one corpus; thus it is particularly potent in a class like Blacks and Jews. (See Marjorie Garber on the history of "Sumptuary Laws" in *Vested Interests*, and Siobhan B. Somerville's *Queering the Color Line*.) The performance of the Trans Vestite in the feminist classroom opens the intellectual space while liberating traditional pedagogical structures for both the students and the professor. As I watched the students relax into the difficult material of Blacks and Jews, this "liberation" was manifested not only in their behavior but also in the very vestments they chose to wear to class.

Renate, an African-American woman whose father is a minister, was always dressed up, impeccably put together, even though every week she rushed in five minutes late from swimming. As the course progressed, so did Renate, who one day ventured into the room with her wet head wrapped in a bright, multicolored towel, and her dress clothes conspicuously replaced with gray sweatpants and matching shirt. As Renate walked into the room athletically garbed, turban-headed, and exaggerating every step she took, the entire class (me included) erupted, laughing out loud. The once serious and adroit Renate had (intentionally?) created the perfect affect/effect to release the building tension in the course. By "Trans Vesting" herself, she completely destabilized who we as a class perceived her to be. And she knew intuitively that she had the power to do this. Her outstanding performance led to a lengthy discussion on the assumptions (some) White people make about (some) Black people.

Eileen, on the other hand, wanted to communicate a different message. She was an Orthodox Jew who always wore a yarmulka, which was interpreted on campus by some Jews and non-Jews as a sign of rigidity rather than a level of religious observance. To communicate her ideas and mediate her mistaken public persona, Eileen wore clothing in cultural contradiction with the skullcap on her head. She regularly dressed hippie-style, in long colorful paisley-printed skirts and matching blouses, and spoke often in class about her predicament of being the very unorthodox Orthodox Jewish woman she really was. Once she wore pants on campus and told the class that the negative reactions she received from the Orthodox Jewish students amazed her; incredulously, they told her she didn't look "Jewish" anymore. The ostracization was too much, and Eileen quickly returned to her long paisley-printed skirts.

As Blacks and Jews developed, many of the women students' personas began to reflect the complex race, class, and gender theories we were studying in class. Maureen, the only non-Jew, non-Black student in the class, began dying her dark brown hair bright orange midway through the semester, and wearing a huge, thick metal chain with a large, heavy square lock at her neck. She never discussed her vestment accessories with the class. But I knew it was important to Maureen, who often spoke of growing up poor, not to be invisible in the visually charged room of Blacks and Jews.

Seemingly much more role-restricted (in terms of gender and race), the men in Blacks and Jews played with their appearances far less than the women. Usually it was only the ubiquitous baseball cap—worn by both Black and White male students—that was used repeatedly to signify interest or disinterest, depending on whether or not the brim was face forward or turned around. However, in both Autobiography and Introduction to Women's Studies male students experimented with appearance much more often, painting their fingernails in bright colors, dyeing their hair, and adding various body piercings. Contrary to the stereotypical view, these male students were most often heterosexual rather than homosexual.

For those students who felt most threatened by the course material (in any of my classes), a stable, nonfluctuating appearance added to their personal safety level. Week after week, the type of clothing they wore did not change. And I knew they preferred that my own persona remain performatively "neutral." Physical stability was necessary if they were to remain open to negotiating the challenging and fluid terrain of race, class, gender, and sexuality throughout the semester.

The pull to bring the feminist Trans Vestite into the classroom is ultimately the recognition of the necessity for boundary crossing within a rigid, highly structured, fixed academic environment. This recognition includes the equally imperative introduction of uncertainty around gender and race conventions, and the lack of predictability accompanying these embodiments. I have spoken to other colleagues about the desire to positively destabilize our classrooms through the theater of appearance. In response, an African-American professor talked about wearing dreads to class one week and an Afro wig the next, all the while observing her students' unsettled reactions to her change in hair style—and then working those reactions into her lecture. A Latin American colleague professed her desire to "punk out" in outrageous clothes in her Spanish language classes, so restricted did she feel by Western academic professional dress codes. In the end, she felt her students responded better to her Latin flair and "non-Western" look as they became more engaged in the class.

And a lawyer who teaches ethics spoke of her preference for men's suits rather than the skirt and jacket coordinates she was expected to don. For White male colleagues who want to signify a certain '60s left politic, blue jeans, sneakers or Birkenstocks, long hair, and beards are most often donned as the most effective tropes. The students "get it," without a word. The question the "academic" Trans Vestite poses for the professor is one of degree: To what extent will costuming be employed to further the performativity of the pedagogical *trans* formation?

Multiple Pedagogical (Pur)suits
Professor Puck Performs

I owe a great debt to Shakespeare. He taught me the power of learning from a destabilized site and that people are not always who they appear—nor do they need to be for the story to progress or make complete sense. In *As You Like It*, Rosalind cross-dresses as a man, to teach her suitor Orlando how to woo a woman properly. She is a great teacher: Who better than a woman knows how to woo another like herself? It is from Rosalind dressed in male garb that I learned to woo my students away from fixed positions of gender.

From the great Divine, who cross-dressed as a woman in the movie *Hairspray*, I learned the art and sheer theatricality of total femininity writ large. Blanche DuBois, in Tennessee Williams's *A Streetcar Named Desire* is the most convincing masculine woman I've ever seen. Madonna opened up infinite possibilities and enormous power to me as she repeatedly reconstructed her public self: from virginal Catholic girl to whore to dominatrix, and then literally embodying the "Queen" mother herself by giving birth. Here was a public woman in charge of her body and all its pleasures. Slowly, almost imperceptibly, I understood the meaning behind all that untapped potential residing dormant in my own female self. Madonna was not the only female conjurer: I too could call forth all my other selves, both imagined and those still longing to be imagined. By following the "Queen's" many reconstructed selves, I found another source of pedagogical passion to release into the classroom, as much mental as it was physical.

Similarly, what was so electrifying about Anna Deavere Smith's *Fires in the Mirror*, her one-woman show about Blacks and Jews in Crown Heights, was not the subject matter per se, but that she employed the art of the Trans Vestite to explore culturally embedded notions of race, class, gender, and ethnicity. In her performance she affirms the notions that race and gender are fluid and socially constructed. Live on stage, she moves from character to character, effortlessly transforming herself right in front of the audience from Afro-Caribbean to Orthodox Jew, from the Reverend Al Sharpton to liberal Jewish writer Letty Cottin Pogrebin. It is in the hats she wears, the style of hair, the expressions on her face, her posture, and in the tone of her voice; she floats in and out of masculinity and femininity, from Black to Jew and back again. Watching my students watch Smith's performance on video is to witness their own preconceived ideas of fixed identity slowly dissipate. And when I teach, I too seek to defy categorization. Identity in the postmodern classroom becomes the ultimate floating signifier.

The Disappearing Act

I am *Professor* Dr. Puck, the character who has the ability to transform all the lovers on stage from antagonists to protagonists, from receivers to active agents. This is a fulsome task, for Shakespeare's Puck is full of intellect and a mischievous spirit. To view the professor as a contemporary Puck is to understand that "professor" is not a fixed identity any more or less than is "student." What does it mean that "professor" is not fixed? It means that our knowledge cannot reify.

Not only is the professor Dr. Puck, but it is she who first pushes forward the puck of knowledge, which is then passed from student to student, back and forth, until a goal is scored, underscored, or scorned. This is about letting go, puckering up and out of a particular, institutionally sanctioned "Master" identity.

At the moment of transformation, Puck the character needs to disappear. The students can go on without the professor, if the professing has succeeded. Once the questions are asked and the dialogue begins, my goal—counter to the dominant paradigm—is to push the class toward a place of autonomy and away from their dependence on me as the omnipotent, omniscient one. My work is to let go, so that I can become another participant in the discourse. As Puck, I too am transformed and can move off the podium and into the classroom with my own questions. Sitting with students, the tone in class changes. The locus of the debate moves away from me as the sole, primary authority and toward the students themselves, who take the lead by asking their own questions. This style of active pedagogy creates more space for learning. When the perimeters are expanded to allow infinite possibility, rather than restricted to finite borders, the source of knowledge can be successfully passed from hand to hand.

Puck as Pedagogy

Performing feminist pedagogy is not entertainment. What keeps the drama from becoming purely theatrical is in the mens rea, the intent of the professor, her goals and teaching strategy. Entertainment, although it can be dramatic, is most often a passive form of relaxation, as exemplified by watching a TV sitcom. It does not disrupt, disappoint, or displace the viewer; it does not require undivided attention. Entertainment often assuages and pacifies the audience, whereas feminist performance pedagogy demands full participation and engagement: critical action and reaction is required. Good theater is unsettling, disturbing, and potentially mind-boggling. Students used to being entertained are often confused in an active classroom. They spend the first few weeks disoriented, and some (of my) students even drop the class because it will require too much active participation.

When students tell me that they liked or didn't like a video or an assigned reading, rather than saying how it prodded them to think about an issue differently, I know that their expectations were to be entertained, not to be changed or drawn in emotionally to the material. My response is always the same: "It doesn't matter if you liked or disliked the video, what issues did it raise for you? How was your worldview changed?"

Because the classroom is a stage, I move around, remaining in motion throughout the three-hour seminar block. My exits are as grand as my entrances, although they are on occasion misunderstood as pure theatrics by students who have not worked with me before. If my students find me entertaining, that is in addition to the meaning of the actual performance. But if a professor is *only* entertaining, then he or she is merely performing, rather than performing pedagogy.

Conceptually, the power of the audience too often goes unacknowledged in the classroom. But *audience power* in the academy means that the professor is perpetually engaged in the process of viewing her students and being viewed by them: one is always "on" and on stage. The question then, within the performance of feminist pedagogy, is how to utilize the audience, including the act of being viewed and viewing back, so that all does not turn to farce, empty pretense, total mockery, or boredom.

Audience use or misuse depends on the rotation of the gaze. I do not want to be the center of the gaze for the duration of the class. It is exhausting and counterproductive. Although the narcissistic pull to remain the center of attention is compelling, the dramatic effect of decentering the gaze is far more meaningful in the end. The audience members become actors in their own right. The necessity of audience contribution to the act of learning is validated when the students learn to turn their gaze away from the professor and toward each other. Destabilizing the gaze contributes to the energy in the room by heightening the tension and creating a sense of responsibility in the speaker. Students begin to feel ownership over their classroom experience; their investment in the material changes qualitatively when they realize that their participation matters, and when they know they are seen as well as heard.

Seeing is believing. Throughout the semester the effect of actually seeing the students and being seen by them is powerful. It enhances the learning process as students see themselves and their classmates emerge from the masses into unique actors and actresses, individuals with important ideas to share. Students come to class prepared to speak and to listen. Watching the body language of my students, I can tell if they are engaged or merely entertained. It depends on how they sit. When they literally sit on the edge of their seats, they are acknowledging physically their involvement and commitment to the action unfolding before and within them. The connections students make are real—and fully realized.

The exchange of "living knowledge" as opposed to the rote repetition of historical facts ignites the full person. In this way new bonds and authentic relationships are developed among the students who were previously not intellectually and aesthetically attracted to each other. Within the context of a living, vibrant, shared knowledge students find themselves engaged with their peers outside of their traditional, tightly bordered, self-selected cliques. Unorthodox connections are made between students whose lives are vastly different in terms of race, religious observance, sexual orientation, gender identity, and class background. For it is in the heat of the epistemological exchange that superficial but tenacious human barriers melt away.

I have spoken earlier about the role of guerilla theater in the feminist classroom. Here the "academic guerillas" surface in a call-and-response exchange: student to student, student to teacher, teacher to student. The professor as vestment crosser destabilizes the preconceived notions of her students, who become spectators, active agents in the process of learning. Through the rotation of the gaze, a standard lecture hall or seminar room becomes a theater-in-the-round. Then in a most exquisitely outrageous *coup d'théâtre* the spectators destabilize the professor through an active gaze that demands open recognition and reciprocity. In the guerilla classroom the status quo is not reinforced but rather intentionally un-reinforced. Questions are asked (performed) rather than solutions promulgated. Intellectual assumptions and all preconceived ideas are meant to be reworked. Roles are fluid. Nothing is assured.

To the outsider and uninitiated this performative process looks and feels too theatrical, or possibly manipulative. But to those on the inside, it is the drama of knowledge exploding on the academic stage, with a rhythm and rhyme of its own organic creation. It is a production driven from passionate internal forces as opposed to external politics or procedures. Guerilla theater in the classroom is disturbing by design. Meeting face to face, vulnerable, our preconceptions exposed, there is the disturbing moment of recognition: we are in this epistemological chaos together. Guerilla theater is positively revolting. And nowhere is the art of costuming put to greater effect than when the guerillas are in our midst.

If It's Tuesday,
It Must Be Improv

*IMPROVISE: to foresee, anticipate: 1. To compose, or
simultaneously compose and perform . . . 2. To make,
provide, or do with the tools and materials at hand,
usually to fill an unforeseen and immediate need*
   —Webster's New World Dictionary, 2nd Ed.

My students con-
stantly view me while I am constantly viewing them. I see every yawn,
catnap, and smile, including those few discreet caustic sneers. I see boredom and engagement; and the moment of disengagement when Alicia
in the front row has simply had enough. Like an open book, the students
read my enthusiasm and passion as well as my confusion and frustration
with them. This is how power shifts, professorial power is destabilized,
and the professor made human. The "teaching podium" behind which
the professor's power is located is never a fixed location in the feminist
classroom. Thus I can be repeatedly unnerved if I don't psychologically
plan ahead for the inevitable cosmic classroom shift. The question for me
is how to respond to the act of being viewed. Will I use, misuse, or lose
it? I must use it, to the utmost dramatic effect possible.

It was Visiting Day for Prospective Students on campus, and Brandeis
professors were asked to open our classes. (It was toward the end of my

class on Blacks and Jews.) Usually I don't open the class, but the students were eager to have visitors so I relented. The previous week's assignment had included the video *The Longest Hatred*, about the history of anti-Semitism, which the students watched in pairs outside of class. All semester we had been interrogating the function of "Whiteness" and what it means for Ashkenazi Jews to be viewed as White in the United States. The video on anti-Semitism was assigned to further our discussion. We began, as usual, with my posing a question for the class to think about and then write on for ten minutes. We were considering philosophy professor Laurence Thomas's concept of autonomy and narrative identity (see his *Vessels of Evil*). The students were particularly intrigued with the questions Thomas raised, so I asked them to write on whether or not Jews and Blacks have narrative identity and group autonomy.

But before we could proceed, Renate waved her hand nonstop, while blurting out, "I have something to say and I want to say it now." Her interruption was unexpected. I had no idea what was on her mind, although I knew she had struggled all semester with the concept of Jewish identity as a unique and separate ethnicity from that of Anglo-American. I nodded in her direction.

"I just want to say that I get it now, after that film we had to watch I understand why Jews don't think of themselves as White."

I pretended to faint. I stood up from my seat in the circle and dropped to the carpet. On my way to the floor I said, "I don't believe it, what happened?" Everyone, visitors included, laughed and applauded. The laughs were for me; the applause belonged to Renate. In the moment of performance, she and I were joined, as actress and best supporting actress and vice versa. It was obvious that I didn't really faint, because I got up immediately. Renate continued to address the class, explaining her transformation, and her new, more complex understanding of anti-Semitism.

What was the function of my fainting spell? And how did I come to faint in front of the whole class, six prospective Brandeis students, and one parent? Why did I dramatically act out my response to Renate's sudden disclosure? My response was both intuitive and cognitive. That is, I "composed" and "performed" simultaneously. Responding to an unforeseen and immediate need, I intellectually, theatrically, improvised on the spot. I wanted to maximize the effect of Renate's words on the audience.

To those students who had listened week after week as Renate exhaustively questioned the nature of Jewish identity and whether or not anti-Semitism was a real threat, her impromptu pronouncement was a profound disruption. She was articulating what many of us had been struggling with throughout the course. Her enthusiasm, honesty, and overt desire to share her newfound insights with the class made the learning process especially vibrant as well as fully realized in both the performative and literal senses. When she spoke this time I had chills. So powerful were her words that the Jews in class visibly relaxed, easing into a new place of visibility and political viability. As Renate spoke, we went from being merely White and part of the oppressive majority (in her eyes) to also being Jews, and a distinct ethnic group. In the context of identity, we were seeing and finally being seen at the same exact moment. The immediate impact on the class was the profound manifestation of the power inherent in reciprocal viewing.

I fainted because I had no words—at that moment—to communicate the depth of what had just been said. It was a pedagogical instant of metasignificance, performed entirely for the students' benefit. To the students in the class, the professor's dramatic re/action was a recognition, and a symbolic act of our journey together. A sign that we were operating on both the theoretical and literal planes of human interaction. After all, if one African American (Renate) could understand how Jews could be both White and non-White depending on the context, there was hope that others also would someday understand. That I "fainted" communicated to the visitors that something beyond the ordinary parameters of regular class discussion had occurred. It was also a totally spontaneous reaction. The possibility of the "spontaneous reaction" only existed because enough trust had been established in the preceding months. Before falling prostrate to the floor I didn't stop to worry what the reaction would be in and out of class. I trusted the process and that the students would metaphorically "fall" with me. The students knew too, intuitively, that they were being trusted. I let myself be professor-cum–performance artist, just as Renate let herself engage in the performativity of the classroom—by the way her hand waved back and forth demanding immediate attention, stopping the show before it even began, and turning the academic spotlight on herself.

Renate's act was just as intentional as my own, although the origins of each differed. Renate had entered the classroom with a scripted performance; she knew exactly—having planned beforehand to speak up as soon as class started—what she was doing. I, on the other hand, had not planned to faint. But as I often do, I allowed the content of the moment to inform and determine my actions. Had Renate not raised her hand and said exactly what she said, when she said it, I would not have fainted.

Often I am asked by colleagues, What does it mean to allow "the content to define the form?" How does this idea impact my teaching? And finally, is this a particularly feminist theory? Leading with content has always been my method of choice in the classroom. I know no better way to teach. This means that the particular subject for the day always influences and impacts how I structure the class itself and that there is always room for improvisation. What questions I ask my students and how I ask them are informed by the content, and then by the students' immediate reaction to the material presented. No matter how prepared I am, teaching in the feminist classroom is never formulaic or predictable. In fact, it is the unexpected moment that I seek to reveal to the students and to me, the professor.

The "unexpected moment" is one of the most unrealized pedagogical opportunities in the academy. It is often thwarted by overlecturing, speaking in the face of tension emerging from nervous, uncomfortable students; or consciously avoiding and/or intentionally stifling disruption of any kind. This includes the actual silencing of students who disagree with the ideas presented, and suppressing any potential conflict by structuring the classroom so that almost nothing unpredictable can happen. This restrictive pedagogy comes from the belief that we are teaching solely the subject matter, rather than the actual reality that we are teaching live human beings. Teaching a subject is much more controllable and hierarchical than teaching students. (See Carla Golden, "The Radicalization of a Teacher," in *The Feminist Teacher Anthology*.) While the unexpected moment is regularly repressed and intentionally avoided in the traditional classroom, as a devout feminist educator I teach toward it, knowing that the intellectual and emotional benefits far outweigh the extreme vulnerability and exposure that the educator—standing erect behind a podium—inevitably feels. The applied benefits of the "unexpected moment" include the following opportunities for the professor: the immediate incorporation of new theories arising from the discussion itself, the chance to make previously unrealized connections on the spot, and the development of an emotional rapport with the students based on the seemingly informal exchange that simply does not occur in the traditional lecture-style format. This emotional rapport is important to understand because of the criticism leveled at Women's Studies as a soft discipline. The act of professorial improvisation calls forth in the student a passionate engagement in the material heretofore not experienced in the classroom. It is this cerebral and visceral passion that is so misunderstood, occurring as it does within a feminist learning environment.

Knowing that meanings change over time and that some material in the introductory Women's Studies course is potentially more volatile than other material, I do not expect to teach the same content the same way twice. For instance, since the mid-1990s, the issue of abortion has become increasingly more difficult to teach (due in large part to a polarization of the topic that has occurred in the media whereby the life of the mother is of secondary importance to the "life" of the fetus). In order to be successful in leading a discussion on abortion while presenting the relevant legal questions, I have to let the content lead me. Reminding myself that *form* follows *content*, I find my way not by opening class—as I did in the early '90s—with a short lecture on the history of abortion in the United States because I have learned that most students today "check out" when they hear the word *abortion*. The historical overview will come later, when I know that my audience is with me. One of the key differences in teaching a *subject in academic isolation* versus teaching *students within a human context* is that the professor must take into consideration the impact the material presented may have on the students themselves. Were I merely teaching the academic subject of abortion, I would continue to begin, as I used to, with a brief historical lecture.

In the early '90s the 5A syllabus listed under current issues the topic "Abortion." Today, "Reproductive Rights" replaces the word *abortion*. Why the change? Six years ago the majority of my students were "prochoice" and had even completed internships at local clinics. Back then, students were informed and spoke with great fluency about the absolute necessity of keeping abortion legal. Today students are much more ambivalent and confused, having been repeatedly saturated with the "prolife" agenda to the point where some students believe uncritically that a fetus is a person. (I know some Women's Studies colleagues who don't even address abortion rights anymore because it has simply become too explosive.) But I continue to wrestle with how to present the content, seeking a way into that topic that won't shut out "pro-life" students. I want to challenge them to think structurally about the issue. And to look at the language itself, embedded in the various arguments. I do not want to avoid such an important topic out of fear of class conflict. As I prepare my lesson plan, I intuitively prepare for disruption—and for the possibility that I will have to improvise on the spot, using whatever "tools" are present.

Putting the subject of abortion into the larger question of reproductive rights, I position both myself and the discussion in a mental and emotional zone that the students will not refuse to enter. This is not a facile dance of semantics. I do not want to lose a single student. I want the class to understand that the question of abortion is not just about "the life of the fetus," as the current debate adamantly purports. But rather that it is a much bigger, far more complicated issue than the students themselves could ever have imagined. I want them to make structural connections, outside their emotional and/or religious investment in the topic. I also have to give up wanting to change minds. My goal remains, as always, to teach the students to think critically. Instead of reading out loud the questions to be considered at the beginning of class, I write them on the board ahead of time. This slight change in my usual approach is because abortion as a topic in the feminist classroom has come to require acute pedagogical care. When the students enter the room, the questions for the day are obvious. This creates the space for them to have their internal reactions before they have to think critically. The following questions begin the "Reproductive Rights" class:

1. Should a woman have absolute control over her body?
2. Does the state at any point have a compelling interest in regulating medical procedures?

I tell the students to write for ten minutes.

Last year, as soon as she finished writing, an extremely quiet student who always sat in the back raised her hand. Assuming she wanted to read her response, I smiled at her. In a firm yet tense voice, she addressed the entire room without pausing.

"Last summer I had an abortion, and I just want the class to know this is not some big academic or theoretical discussion that's out there, outside our class." Her words filled the large lecture hall while the whole class stared at me, as if to say, *This is all your fault, you got us into this mess, get us out. NOW.* This time the unexpected moment came in the form of personal disclosure. I knew the students themselves were feeling instantly burdened with this uninvited offering. I was temporarily stopped, momentarily exposed. It's not that I didn't assume some students in 5A had had abortions or knew some one who had, it was that I was caught off guard at the timing of the announcement (before discussion even began) and the demanding tone in the student's voice. *Was she challenging us? Did she want to say more? Did she want to silence those who disagreed with her choice? Was this an unconscious plea for help? Did she need therapy? Why did she want to speak first?* These were the first thoughts I had, all the while meeting the gaze of the class directly, trying to assure them that what had just happened was fine. It *was* fine, wasn't it?

In the moments before I began to improvise, a rising self-doubt crept in. This arose from the knowledge that one of the major criticisms about Women's Studies in general and my Brandeis classes in particular is that the introductory class is too personal and emotionally "like therapy" and therefore not academically rigorous. Every semester several students and a few colleagues render this verdict in their written and oral evaluations of my course. From my colleagues, this sentiment often comes from hearing about incidents of personal disclosure like the one just mentioned, although they have never attended any of my classes in person. (For a further discussion of students' negative oral reporting to other professors on their uneasiness in Women's Studies classes and the impact it has on reappointment questions, see *Where Is Your Body? And Other Essays on Race, Gender, and the Law*, by Mari J. Matsuda.) At this point, if I feed the growing unease, I will intellectually cower, and teach only to allay my critics. This is a pivotal moment: balancing my own integrity in the classroom against the fear and distortion Women's Studies has been subjected to as a discipline.

Looking at the student who spoke, I say calmly, but in a strong voice, "Thank you. Is there anything else you want to add before we continue?" Then, I purposely wait, thinking fast about what to do next. I remind myself that the content defines the form, and I have just been presented with "new" content. What form can efficaciously follow the student's announcement? I improvise on the spot, speaking extempora-neously, trusting that we will, as always, return, albeit circuitously, to the place in my notes that I had stood poised to address.

"What you have just heard is what makes the feminist classroom unique. That a student can feel so connected to the professor and to her peers in a room of seventy-five people that she wants to contribute something most of us would deem too personal for public consumption. In fact, many of us [I always include myself] may be feeling uncom-fortable with the disclosure, fearing that we too may be called upon to volunteer something private. But it is important to remember that this is not a course requirement, and that the function of appropriate per-sonal disclosure can help us connect the theory with the practice, a key feminist tenet. Also, this is a good example of how 'the personal is po-litical,' another feminist theory we have discussed." I paused, checking to see if the class was still with me. There wasn't a sound in the room as all the students looked at me. The woman who had spoken was smiling, nodding her head, as if she herself had begun teaching the class. I con-tinued with my impromptu public address.

"In fact, I know some of you are thinking that this feels and sounds a lot like therapy. But *this* is not therapy. We are not being paid to lis-ten to someone's life story, neither are we being asked to help solve someone's personal problems. What is being asked of us, by the admis-sion from one of our classmates that she had an abortion, is that we not overtheorize the topic. I believe we get scared when our feelings intrude into the academic environment. And when we have feelings, we auto-matically escape to the safety of the concept of 'therapy.'" I finished by asking if there were any questions so far. As there were none, the im-provisational moment ended. I then returned to my lesson plan and the questions up for discussion.

The rest of the class was uneventful until the last ten minutes, when I decided to call on Martin, a soft-spoken young man who never seemed to raise his hand but who always had a thoughtful response when called on. I was sure he was "pro-choice," and thought ending on this note coming from a male student would be a good thing. In retrospect I over-essentialized what I thought Martin would say because I knew he was gay, and therefore assumed he was sympathetic to a more liberal, truly democratic point of view. I couldn't have been more unprepared for this unexpected moment.

"Martin, how do you respond to the question about a woman's right to absolute control over her body?" I walked as I spoke, crossing from one side of the room to the other, gathering energy with each word.

"I don't know. I'm just not sure." He was barely audible.

"Can you say more? What aren't you sure about?" I had stopped promenading in front of the front row, listening intently as I stood still.

"Well, I'm just not sure when life begins. And in my church, we believe that all life, especially the innocent, is worthy of protection." There was nervous shifting going on in the room; a few students coughed loudly; I cleared my throat. It was obvious that I was caught off guard—placed in the challenging throes of the unexpected moment. I looked at the clock: I had five minutes to pull it all together.

Staring out at the entire 5A class, I spoke slowly and with great care. "I understand the dilemma, and how difficult it is. Perhaps if we put the question in a different but related context, it may clarify some of the issues involved. Thinking structurally, does a woman have the right to control her sexuality? Does a man? Or is it up to the state to define and determine legal and illegal sexuality?" I was trying to make the link that the question of abortion is also most definitely related to other questions concerning state regulation of the body. Because I knew that Martin was gay I wanted him to make the connection that the same laws that governed his choice of a consenting homoerotic partner—including what the two of them could do in private—were also the same laws that he was potentially invoking to force a woman to carry an unwanted pregnancy to term. Finally, I said to the class as a whole, "My favorite bumper sticker is helpful here: 'If you're against abortion, don't have one.' Seriously, we have to think micro and macro about the long-term impact of outlawing abortion, and state regulation of the body." We were out of time.

Right afterward I met with the teaching assistants to discuss the class and to plan what they would cover in their individual discussion sections later in the week. One TA was shaking, she was so upset. "You were pretty hard on the church today." She was crying. The rest of the TAs were quiet.

"Say more," I continued, as if class were still going on.

"I don't know, this is a hard topic for me." I was reminded that my teaching assistants, older and more mature than the students, also have strong reactions to the course material. Before the meeting could proceed, we had to talk about abortion more personally. Otherwise their feelings would be in the way, and the TAs would not be effective discussion-leaders in the sections. This is the human content that often makes Women's Studies so contentious both in the classroom and in the academy. No subject ever exists in isolation. By the end of the day, I was exhausted, emotionally and intellectually.

The pedagogy of improvisation is not a breeze, something to substitute when you haven't had the time to prepare properly. On the contrary, good, effective improv only follows good, effective preparation. I am extremely conscientious when it comes to planning my classes by plotting out the entire three hours ahead of time. Every ten to fifteen minutes is diligently blocked out and highlighted in red on a yellow legal pad, listing facts, questions, comments, and a final synthesis. And I do not simply reuse these notes; each semester, the course material is updated and feedback from last year's class and incorporated into the new lesson plan. I never enter a classroom unprepared, because I know what the ultimate consequences will be: boredom and fatigue, high absenteeism, and in the end, lack of engagement by the students and ultimately the teacher. Improvisation is deceptive. It simply looks too easy. As though it truly does require absolutely no intellectual preparation. But without an assiduous command of the material and an ability to synthesize and create on the spot, the improvisation itself becomes merely an irreverent and professionally irresponsible response to the technical demands of teaching. Although some educators are more adept at improvisation than others, it remains a skill with specific techniques to be honed and learned through practice. But without a commitment to feminist pedagogy and performance, there can be no successful improvisation.

Copia Verborum
The Power of Speech

I want to discuss two other improvisational situations because they raise additional questions. The first one concerns the guest appearance of a talented performance artist and playwright at one of the many 5A classes on race. Jenetta Martin and I discussed her performance of African-American characters ahead of time. She was concerned about the impact on the students of the language she uses to portray each one. I tried to reassure her that together she and I could handle whatever came up.

Inviting Jenetta Martin to perform in 5A was another instance of form following content, a departure from my "standard" approach to the section on race. Usually, after the students and I have worked together for several weeks on issues of cultural miscues, dominant paradigms, virtual integration, and White hegemonic models, I ask a close friend, Dr. Linda Randall, to speak to the class on her particular experiences as an African-American woman in the United States. But Dr. Randall was unavailable this year, as were several other academic colleagues of mine.

Previously Jenetta had performed in my Reading and Writing Autobiography class, and as I was always interested in integrating the arts more fully into the Women's Studies curriculum, I invited her to perform relevant autobiographical material for 5A. As a performer myself, I was comfortable and familiar with the semiautobiographical, one-woman monologue style that Jenetta employed. No matter what happened, I thought the exposure of the intersections between race and gender through the theater arts would be a good experience for the class. I knew from personal experience that viewing questions about race through a dramatic presentation was an effective way of discussing a topic that is difficult for many students. In addition, viewing an autobiographical sketch by a professional artist is an excellent way to study racism because the format is so nontraditional that student attention to the material is heightened. *What could be more powerful than a one-woman autobiographical portrayal on being Black, female, and lesbian in America?* I thought.

When introducing Jenetta, I explained to the class what performance art is, and what a terrific experience they were about to have. Then I sat down in the back of the auditorium, ready to enjoy the show myself.

"Before I start, I want to give y'all some background," Jenetta spoke in a long, slow Southern drawl. "I suffer from multiple personality disorder, but I am learning how to integrate all those folks and all their business into one big me." The students turned around, looking for me, as Jenetta discussed her condition. I nodded, totally unprepared for this bit of personal disclosure. I also gripped the arms of my seat, hoping no one could see how tense I was. She continued. "So ya gonna see lots a folks in my show, and they're all me. Any questions?" Then she took a slight bow, arched her back, tilted her head, and stretched her arms out to the crowd and announced in a raspy, Bronx accent, "I'm Ghetto Girl, and I know what y'all thinkin', but it ain't so. It ain't so. I am a hero. Listen here. Y'all think all us niggers alike, but I'm here to dispel the notion that y'seen one nigger y'seen 'em all. This here Ghetto Girrrrrrl, make no mistake. Know what I'm sayin'?"

For the next thirty minutes Jenetta performed an amazingly varied collection of Black characters. Her language ranged from the "N" word to *fuck this shit* and *fuck that shit,* to exquisite poetic renditions of her life as a Black woman in America. The students were enthralled; in the middle of the performance I relaxed somewhat. As the performance came to a close, Jenetta, who had already exhibited a phenomenal dramatic range, portrayed one last character, a male janitor working in the White House. The class was transfixed by her gender fluidity, which appeared effortless and unaided by a costume change or a single prop. The portrayal came entirely through the body itself. When she was done, they didn't know whether to applaud or remain silent. I thought they were in awe, like I was, stunned into silence by the sheer power of Jenetta's artistry. Quickly I realized something else was also going on. When she asked for questions, the usual automatic array of hands did not shoot up, waving back and forth, demanding attention. There was silence. I knew they had questions, but no one spoke. I would have to find out why.

Walking quickly down the aisle to the front of the room, I addressed the students, hugging Jenetta as I joined her "on stage." After weeks of discussing the issues, viewing videos such as *Skin Deep* and *Hidden Faces*, we had reached a gravamen, a critical, essential point in the "argument" called race.

"Check in with the person sitting next to you: What did the performance bring up, what questions were the characters asking?" While the students spoke quietly in pairs, I checked in with Jenetta. We agreed that they might be reacting to the strong language she used, and that they did not know how to respond. But not even the African-American students were raising their hands. I wondered if I had made a miscalculation. Perhaps the students could only handle a traditional, formal lecture on race from another professor, and that what they had just seen went beyond their own boundaries of permissible pedagogy. I was in sympathy, at that moment, with the majority of professors who choose not to take risks in the classroom—the resulting unpredictability is unnerving. Yet, somehow, I held on to the idea that nowhere else were these particular students going to be exposed to a talent such as Jenetta Martin, the wide range of her character portrayals, and the complex questions she was asking about race.

I told the students to write a two-page reaction paper to the performance, thinking that they needed more time to absorb what they had just seen. Often I assign a reaction paper when a topic or video is controversial. Students can think critically and analyze better when they are not emotionally distressed about the subject itself. The reaction papers give them the opportunity to say anything about the topic, uncensored, knowing that the papers aren't graded. And (through their response papers) I, the professor, receive a lot of information that I otherwise might never be privy to, which assists me in planning future classes. Through their papers I found out that the root of the silence came down to the "N" word. Students, Black and White, were dismayed and felt betrayed by Jenetta's use of traditionally offensive language. (She had tried to warn me.) Relevant excerpts of response papers follow. These examples represent the range of sixty-five students' comments.

> What struck me most . . . was Jenetta's use of language. I was not disturbed by her swearing, God knows I say "f-ck" enough that hearing it no longer even draws my attention. As the words have become part of my vocabulary they have lost their meaning, and I know I throw them around so often my mother thinks I have joined the Navy. But it is for that reason exactly that I was so disturbed by Jenetta's use of the word "n-gger." It is my understanding that this word is often used within the Black community to speak about one another, and it . . . was that apsect of her community which she wished to portray. However, I cannot understand why any person would ever choose to use a word which loosely translated means less than human, in their everyday speech. Prof. Felman touched briefly on this topic when she said it was OK for her, as a lesbian, to call herself a dyke. But, again, I must wonder why. These words have no positive connotations, they have been used to oppress and degrade, so how is there anything positive in using it about yourself. Why would anyone want to take back, to own a word with such a history? Because, like swearing, when words are used repeatedly they lose their meaning. But this strikes me as very dangerous. What happens when we forget what "n-gger" means? What happens when it is appropriate for college kids to say it in

everyday conversation, just as "f-ck" is? The thought frightens me. Conversation in discussion section was dominated by people's account of how shocked, put off, embarrassed, and uncomfortable Jenetta's language made them. . . . Just discussing how we felt in relation to Jenetta's language is not enough. We need to take the feelings of discomfort and analyze them. We need to understand why we were shocked and uncomfortable and why we used those feelings to distance ourselves from Jenetta's message.

I was not exactly sure what to make of her performance. While I most certainly found it entertaining and enveloping, I questioned it. Why would she want to perpetuate negative stereotypes that are affiliated with the African-American community?

Ok . . . granted, I was a little perplexed by her performance at first. I felt a sort of relief when it was time to discuss the experience with a partner so that I could gain another's insight. . . . I asked her what she thought of the performance and her answer left me completely dumbfounded. Her reply went . . . "I can't believe she subjected us to that so-called performance. I was totally offended by the vulgar language and subject matter. There wasn't any point to it." When I questioned her in further detail, I found out that she had never actually befriended a Black person. . . . Furthermore she said that she learned enough about racism in school. . . . Unfortunately, the feedback from my discussion group wasn't helpful either . . . everyone gave the same answer. "Well, she was a really great performer. She even quoted Shakespeare." What kind of an answer is that? Did these people learn anything from Ms. Martin? Did they recognize that there was substance to her performance? How many . . . were truly able to listen/look beyond the use of obscenities and recognize her purpose? The language wasn't meant to offend. As discussed in class, language is political. Personal is political. Race and gender are both performances. Language is but part of the performance.

I couldn't help but notice that her characters . . . exemplified the stereotype of Black people. Most noticeable was Ghetto Girl, the brash, loud, demanding hero created out of the various parts of famous Black women. . . . I began to wonder what message Jenetta was trying to present. . . . During our discussion section, one of the students mentioned that, when listening to Jewish comedians poke fun at Jewish stereotypes, she finds it hilarious. However, if a non-Jewish colleague were to try the same thing, she would find it offensive. Maybe Jenetta's motivation was the reverse of that; her presentation was written for a Black audience who find it funny, but we saw it out of context.

While all the papers commented on the talent and skill of the performer, most of the students expressed similar frustration or confusion about Jenetta's language and use of culturally specific Black stereotypes. Many students revealed their lack of familiarity with the genre of performance art and "real" Ebonics, and just as many discussed how they had never seen "Black Theater." Some even said that, if given the chance, they would never choose to see a show like this. The White students' comments also revealed the cultural isolation of many of their lives, a sheltered naïveté and near-total lack of cross-cultural experience. Most welcomed the exposure to such an unusual event, but were made acutely uncomfortable by what they saw.

Through this class and others such as Blacks and Jews, I am continually reminded how important risk-taking is and what an integral part of improvisational pedagogy it is. For what was revealed to me through the risk of Jenetta's performance was that my students, whom I had thought had reached a new level of understanding, were still in need of much more knowledge and comfort with regards to "talking race." While a traditional lecture, the kind that Dr. Randall would have given, would have helped them, it would not have brought such a profound cultural and emotional chasm to the surface. In the weeks that followed I viewed early Richard Pryor and Lenny Bruce tapes, studying their early use of incendiary language, remembering Pryor's early dystopian, explosive taking back of the "N" word. I also spoke with Dr. Randall at length about Jenetta's performance and the students' reactions. Finally, I discussed with the students what I had learned from them, specifically about their own cultural isolation and the importance of risk-taking—confronting directly that which we are afraid to discuss for fear of offending someone. And I included a brief history of Pryor's language and the public outcry that followed his early performances.

I want to discuss one final paper because it raises a painful question for me about my responsibility as an educator. A West African student's response summed up many of the general reactions of the other students of color in the room. I see her questions as a moral dilemma that must be confronted and addressed directly within the academy.

> As I enthusiastically read the book *Why Do All the Black Kids Sit Together in the Cafeteria*, I could not wait to go to class to hear a well-educated, Black, successful, strong, loud, outspoken woman stand in front of the class and in person reiterate the points made in the book. In essence someone coming to disprove all the Black stereotypes.
>
> Jenetta had all the above qualities I was expecting, however her intentions were not to disprove any stereotypes but to perform her life, past, present and future. . . . She made a very important point, which was that, not all Black people are the same. . . . Her purpose was definitely fulfilled because as a Black female I did not identify with any of her acts and neither did any of the other Black students in the class (I asked them). I'm from Ghana, WA, and her act of the African lady was neither a generalization of how immigrants or Africans act. It was a portrayal of the Africans she had known and been around. I thought she was a great performer, who did not become a slave to the dominant culture once again in disproving society's stereotypes.
>
> However I would have preferred for us to have a speaker with whom the class could have had a discussion about the whole race issue. With a class of a large number of White students it would have been a great chance for those who barely know anything about Black people to get informed and vice versa.

Just what is a White professor's specific responsibility to the students of color who sit week after week surrounded by a sea of White faces? At Brandeis, with its majority of Jewish students, I am a de facto role model whether I choose to be or not. I am seen as a strong, proud Jewish feminist who is willing to challenge the traditional Ashkenazi establishment in the Diaspora and in the state of Israel. For the gay students, I am also a model because I am unabashedly and culturally "out." For women students in general who struggle with gender contradictions, feminism, and how to find their own voices, I am also a role model. These are not modelings I have chosen; they were put upon me.

But the question remains, Who am I for all the other students, most especially the students of color? And in this instance, how much does it matter that the one Black speaker to come to 5A this semester happened to be an avant-garde, cutting-edge bolt of black lightning? She was not a staid professor, who looked and sounded like the race theory the students had been reading all semester. Had I failed these particular students? Painful as it was to comprehend their responses, I understood that Jenetta Martin, theater arts queen extraordinaire, was not the role model of choice for these students at this time in their lives. They thought that they and the White students needed a much more mainstream, traditional, and socially acceptable Black role model—which Jenetta most certainly was not.

These questions are not mine alone. They date back to the establishment of cultural studies in the late '60s, and are still debated today in terms of who are appropriate African-American mentors and role models for students. (See Henry Louis Gates Jr. and Manning Marable in the *New York Times*, April 18, 1998.) Should the status quo be upheld or should the edge of academically accepted role models be pushed? And can a radical Jewish lesbian feminist professor do the pushing? As soon as Jenetta began Ghetto Girl, I realized that I had pushed the edge—yet another unpredictable consequence of improvisation and risk-taking.

In the end, what was also revealed to the entire class by Jenetta Martin's visit was the internal, often extremely privatized (as opposed to publicly debated) cultural lacunae between African Americans, Afro-Caribbeans, and Africans. This revelation had the necessary space to occur precisely because I did not take the safe, secure, easy approach to race this year. Instead, when Dr. Randall was not available, I improvised. And what happened was a rich, far more complex public discussion. We talked about what it means to be from a Black majority culture such as Jamaica or Nigeria, where the "N" word has little or no currency; and about the class antagonisms between American Blacks and their immigrant Afro-Caribbean and African contemporaries, who often are far more economically successful in the United States than are African Americans whose families have lived here for centuries. And all the Black students discussed how these issues are never discussed when White folks are in the room.

I was forced to extend my own intellectual reach into questions of race precisely because Jenetta had come to class. In the weeks following her visit, I had to work harder, do more research, and dramatically revise last year's lesson plans before I could use them. I was forced to journey inward and to find my voice in 5A around heretofore unspoken aspects of intraracial and intraculural tensions. Clearly the risks of improvisation are many. There is nothing gratuitous about improvisation. Methodologically speaking, it is rigorous and demanding. For me, it is the only way I know to push myself and my students forward simultaneously. In fact, I am convinced more than ever that we must challenge our colleagues to greater acts of improvisational pedagogy.

The final aspect of improvisation and risk-taking that I want to discuss concerns a fundamental question in Women's Studies: *How much of women's lives from the outside world do we bring into the classroom as a form of textual study?* Versus staying close to the printed and by now classic Women's Studies texts. Is it permissible to incorporate into a course syllabus material from the lives of our students? Or are we venturing into personal disclosure and academically suspect teaching if we ask students to apply the theories studied to their own lives? One of the criticisms levied against my teaching by a member of my evaluating committee at Brandeis is: "She assigns all the right texts, but doesn't use them appropriately, and her assignments are totally inappropriate." This attitude concerns me because it reveals a lack of understanding about the roots and strengths of academic feminism, and what actually occurs in class—including how the personal voice is used to illuminate the text itself.

In Feminism for the Year 2000 and Beyond, an advanced seminar for seniors, there are two books I use that require some amount of written personal disclosure on the part of students. In reading Susan Douglas's *Where the Girls Are*, I ask students to apply her theories of "good/bad girl" to their own lives. I never know what I will get, nor am I concerned with who sees her/himself as "good" or "bad." It is through this act of "improvisational writing" that the students learn to think critically about their own lives, to analyze systemically, and to bring feminist theory out of isolation and integrate it into their daily actions. In contrast, staying too close to the text stifles discussion and intellectual development, and can be monotonous or repetitive. In this case, Douglas's text is merely the point of departure, not *the* point. The good/bad girl papers, always a significant turning point in class, are referenced throughout the semester. What is revealed through the application of the self to the text are the multiplicities inherent in the construction of a good/bad girl. There is more than one definition, and what kind of a "girl" one is, is always influenced by the race, class, and sexuality of the subject. We do not dwell on the specifics in each paper. Rather, in applying the theory to their lives, students actually see both the strengths and fallacies embedded in Douglas's own arguments. In the end, what is illuminated is that these are real questions, confronted by women every day, not merely academic inquiries. This matters to students in the contemporary undergraduate classroom, when so much of what they are studying seems (or is) irrelevant to them.

Three-quarters of the way through Feminism for the Year 2000, the students read *Reviving Ophelia: Saving the Selves of Adolescent Girls*, by Mary Pipher. Each time I have taught this book, which discusses at length the loss of voice and self-esteem in young girls, my approach changed because I always felt the students were too distanced from the text. This year on the day we were to discuss Pipher's conclusions, I decided on the spot to do something different and not to follow my written lesson plan. Instead, I started class by asking the following questions that had repeatedly occurred to me as I read the book for the third time.

1. Was there ever a time in your life when you had vision and lost it?
2. If so, when and why did you lose it?
3. Did you ever regain your vision?
4. How is vision political?

The students wrote for a solid fifteen minutes before breaking into partners to discuss their answers. Then I opened the floor to the class as a whole. One by one we went around the circle until everyone had spoken. Clearly these questions had reached the students. Everyone but Debra enumerated in extraordinary detail whole narratives concerning vision, lost and found. Several students cried describing the loss of their vision in adolescence and the fact that no one had ever asked them these questions before. They remembered the exact moment when their visions had left them. Debra's answer was that she didn't know there was such a thing to have as vision. This added even more fodder for discussion.

What was remarkable about the discussion was that although it didn't appear as if we were discussing Pipher's book, we were, in a much deeper and more thorough way than if we had talked in a linear modality about the individual case histories she presents. To me, with the semester almost over, that approach would have been an intellectually gratuitous exercise. Because I was not afraid to improvise, we arrived at a wholly new and unexpected place. This was terrain both barren and fertile; it was as if we were writing feminist theory as we spoke. No one left class that day unchanged. Students e-mailed me for weeks afterward, continuing the vision discussion in many forms.

I have learned to trust my instincts in the feminist classroom, equally or more than I trust my lesson plans. This means that sometimes I risk both my methods and motives appearing suspect to students and administrators. But I have all the proof I need that this is the way into feminist theory. It is in the strength of the connections that I make with my students and those they make with each other; and the powerful, sustained learning that occurs as a result. Students tell me that "it feels different" in my classroom. And that they can't explain why exactly, but it's there, "that feeling," the minute they walk in. I feel it too. It is the anticipation that comes from knowing that something is about to happen; that the form truly does follow the content, and that none of us—student or professor—will be the same afterward. This is where learning is a whole-body experience and the radical notion that personal disclosure is relevant, integral, and essential to increased knowledge. This is the true power of effective improvisation.

Backers and Flackers
behind the Scenes

CHAOS: the confused unorganized state of primordial matter before the creation of distinct forms; synonyms: *anarchy, lawlessness; a utopian society having no government and made up of individuals who enjoy complete freedom*
PRIMORDIAL MATTER: synonym: *creativity*
PRIMORDIAL: fundamental, primary; synonyms: *initial, original*
  —*Webster's Seventh New Collegiate Dictionary* and *Webster's New Dictionary of Synonyms (1968)*

I. STAGE (F)RIGHT: FLACKERS

Chaos
the confused unorganized state of primordial matter before the creation of distinct forms

"It's an utter mess in here," a colleague says.

"What do you mean?" I ask, looking around the space that is my office in the Women's Studies Program at Brandeis University.

"Really, Jyl Lynn, you should fix this place up." She's shaking her head in dismay.

"Why?" I honestly don't get what the problem is.

"Because, you just should."

"You're kidding, I hate this place, I can't even breathe in here. I wish I had your office in Schiffman."

"That's exactly why you should fix it up; it looks—absolutely feels like you hate it." Lourdes is so visibly disturbed by the state of disarray before her that she continues her harangue unabated for another five minutes. "I just can't believe this is your office, Jyl Lynn. . . . How do you work in here? . . . What do your students think?"

"No one has ever said a word to me." Locking the door on the way out, I come face to face with the montage of politically correct posters I've wallpapered to the door, barely leaving room for my own name and academic title.

Driving home, I can't stop thinking about Lourdes's comments, what exactly they mean, and their implications, if any. Then I realize . . . I lied.

Students *have* commented on my office, I just haven't paid any attention to what they've said—until now. Usually, the wording went something like this:

So, this is Professor Felman's office. Or: *This is it, your office?* Or: *This is not at all what I expected . . .*

I never gave my students' disappointment much attention. My answer to their chagrin at finding me ensconced in such a chaotic office is always the same: *Oh, this place? I can't stand it. I never work here. You should see my office at home, now that's a place I love. It's all windows and quiet, really quiet. That's where I write. And dream.* This seems to satisfy even the most inquisitive student.

And yet, something must be the matter with my office (even though I can't see it). The director of Women's Studies discreetly calls my attention to the "problem" in various magnanimous ways, such as: *This place could use a fresh coat of paint. How about it? Any color you want. Let's call Maintenance now."*

"It would be too much trouble to move everything out," I say, meaning, of course, the ubiquitous piles that accumulate with great regularity during each semester. All around the room are extra copies of course handouts—newspaper articles, book reviews, editorials—laid out, right where I can see them. I actually think better this way; perusing the course material while I wait for students to come for their appointments, my imagination is engaged, planning future lectures or articles that I long to write. Besides, I don't like to file.

One semester, right after Thanksgiving break, I opened my office door to quarters even more cramped than usual. *Something's different in here.* I panicked, ready for a fight if anything, especially my piles, had been disturbed. Then I noticed that a huge, beige, six-drawer file cabinet had been securely placed against the right wall, next to the windowsill. Being short, I could barely reach the top drawer. This bland monster was surreptitiously added to my office as an unexpected, and anonymous, administrative "gift." Outraged, I requested that it be removed immediately. It never was.

The file cabinet is way too heavy, or by now I'd have dragged the big, ugly thing out into the hallway myself. It remains stuck in the corner, forever unused and *un*filed.

In my spare time, I begin to reflect on the meaning of the antiseptic space that is called my "office." I begin by studying the offices of other Brandeis colleagues. No one has to tell me how important *size* is: intellectually, size is everything, the transformation of poured concrete into hard cold blocks of uncracked, cemented power. Corner locations are always preferred because they're L-shaped, larger at the angles. Big picture windows that can open are essential extras for deans and department chairs. And preferably not on the first floor—there's less view from "on high."

I had heard the horror stories: friends in offices without windows or ventilation; stuck in basements or unheated, poorly lit prefab trailers; or worse yet, partnered with the one person in the department who is intensely disliked by everyone. As an assistant professor I was pleased not to have to share an office. But I had no fresh air: the only window was sealed shut. I understood perfectly the "sacrosanct" culture of material intellectual space.

What I didn't comprehend was why anyone would care about the "tidiness quotient" of any particular office. To me, clutter and disarray had always been one of the hallmarks of *creativity in action.* Clearly, no one was keyed in to my personal display of creativity. Except me. *What was it that was so disturbing about my use of space within the elite walls of higher private education? And in the privileged context of scholarship, could it be extrapolated that the meaning and worth of creativity might be perpetually distorted and devalued?* These questions I prepared to engage in all seriousness, while my creative, chaotic office has become (for me) a signifier sine qua non of academic anarchy at its finest.

Anarchy
a utopian society having no government and made up
of individuals who enjoy complete freedom

Complete freedom does seem to be the "problem" in my office—and beyond. I act like a "free agent," rather than a grateful, repressed, Jewish lesbian assistant professor. It's not that I don't intentionally play by the rules; I just have a philosophy that differs substantively from the dominant academic paradigm. For instance, pedagogically speaking, I don't believe in failing any students. If a student fails one of my classes, I have come to believe that the professor—me—is the real failure. If the student is in trouble academically, the end of the semester is far too late for notification. I see it as my ethical and professional responsibility to let him or her know the situation early on. That way, there are choices to be made by the student—to get a tutor or drop the course. Ultimately an F represents a profound mutual failure, not an isolated "student problem." An F suggests a failure to communicate on the most basic human level; the electric current of knowledge that should have flowed unimpaired between student and professor must have been repeatedly severed or thwarted. Thus, neither the professor nor the student did the job required. But this approach contradicts the traditional bell curve of classic academic grading by emphasizing the very primacy of the act of learning rather than the significance of the grade itself.

When I first began teaching, I was told my grades were too low and would discourage students from taking Women's Studies classes. Several years later, I was told they were too high, that I should not give so many As because it makes Women's Studies appear academically "soft," not rigorous enough. For those of us who prefer to de-emphasize grading, we often receive failing grades in the peer review of our own academic excellence. (Of great interest to me is the fact that top-ranked Brown University no longer offers any grades at all for undergraduates. And as of fall 2000 Mt. Holyoke College has decided to make SAT scores optional for the next five years.)

The next problem that I encountered was with my course requirements; some of my peers considered them inadequate and not conducive to serious scholarship. I have never assigned a final term paper and I don't give traditional exams. Initially this does create a chaotic, unpredictable learning environment for those students who rely on fixed criteria so they can plan ahead—from the very first day—precisely how much work is required for an A.

My assigned work consists of weekly response papers to the readings and films; short, three- to five-page papers on a particular question that is discussed in class beforehand; regular, mandatory group meetings outside of class time; and in the seminars, a final performance/presentation. In the large introductory class, 5A, the midterm is a take-home set of questions to be discussed in partners and then written individually. Because I use film as text throughout the semester, for the "final" I show a two-hour feature film (such as *The Ballad of Little Jo*) that is to be deconstructed based on the theories we've studied in class. Students are required to meet in groups before writing their analysis, and they are limited to the length of one exam book, plus a one-page outline, to cover all the issues addressed in the film.

My courses are designed for maximum benefit to the student, to encourage unlimited critical thinking and to engage each individual in active, sustained learning beyond the narrow parameters of accumulative, regurgitative, and reductive quantitative or "manipulated" qualitative analysis.

I am unconcerned with arriving at the "right" answer, stressing thought processes rather than concrete products. I teach toward the *unexpected moment*, when both student and professor are caught together mentally dangling in midair. We become academic acrobats pleased to twist and turn on those intellectually charged high-wires. That's how the classroom becomes a uniquely postmodern, percipient performative space and, as a result, no course is ever exactly the same from semester to semester. The form is fluid, not fixed: human, not robotic. Within this paradigm there is no need to fail a single student, particularly as I have found that final grades become barriers to excellent, original scholarship. My approach to grading neither compromises my pedagogical integrity nor renders the students' classroom experience passive or predictable. I assume from the start that each student will do well, and that my job is to challenge the unexamined space, that cerebral vortex that lies intellectually fallow. Teaching then is as an active agent, encouraging a student's full potential and participation for the entire semester.

Most of the time I am met with as much intellectual verve and curiosity as I put out. Michael describes his first semester with me in Blacks and Jews:

> I like this class so much—it is important—because it is unexpected. I sit down, and I never anticipate what will be said. I do all the readings, and *still*, I never anticipate what will be said. This scares me, too, since now I *know* that I will never "get it" all. No one will (and that doesn't make me feel any better). . . . It is the *why's* that this class deals with, which is so important; it shows me what answering a *why* question actually looks like, rather than providing description.

In the beginning, however, some students are suspicious and balk at many of the unorthodox requirements in my classes. The mandatory group meetings are especially frustrating for some of the heterosexual White men, who often resent the time and energy necessary to work "femininely" *in community*. In his final response paper Sam discusses his impatience when encountering his initial group:

> The biggest change . . . has come from the weekly group meetings. I never liked working in groups. . . . I worked much faster alone . . . and [had] full creative freedom. My past experience [with group projects] . . . from Politics and Sociology . . . led to frustration—wasted time and a final product that did not always make me proud. The group discussions in Prof. Felman's class were different.
>
> This revelation happened during my first group meeting, although . . . I was horrified. While Emerald and Mike were talking about race relations, hate, the Black-American experience and even gay rights, I was worried we were not going to finish an outline. . . . I was noticeably upset, and sat . . . fuming. . . . After expressing my concerns they informed me . . . there was no group paper—only brainstorming! I was . . . confused and then elated. I pondered the benefits of just talking. . . .
>
> Talking to others, freely and openly, and then beginning my writing process was enlightening. . . . Our talks were not centered on getting a finished product done or "Getting the fuck out of here so

I can go to my next meeting/television show/hot date." Rather each discussion was an intelligent exchange of ideas that led to more creativity on my part. . . . This informal structure led to some excellent debates that were the foundation of . . . my papers . . . and afforded me the chance to explore other people's ideas without having the added pressure of turning in a final product. . . . I was more likely to extend a meeting because such a high level of learning was happening.

Process not *product* is foundational to performativity, critical inquiry, and feminist pedagogy. And it is precisely process, like the anarchist mess in my office, that is so often misunderstood. Through the years I have developed a distinct feminist pedagogical style that is utilized by others who share a similar teaching philosophy. I work from the institutionally suspect premise that *the formal act/art of teaching—by itself— is an oral form of unique, performative scholarship.* It is the *form* of my teaching methodology rather than the *function* that has come under academic scrutiny. But what appears as lawless, unrestrained chaos and "mushy" academic anarchy is nothing of the sort. It is a form of living scholarship, and one that originated in a culturally specific context long before the formal building of universities.

I was influenced strongly by my ethnic heritage, which is a tenaciously verbal culture, with a rich oral religious tradition: the active study of the Talmud, Mishna, and Gamara. Orthodox Jews teach and learn in a form of engaged reciprocity. For centuries there has been a complex, completely physical and intellectual immersion into the art and act of intense discourse: question and answer, back and forth, unending and unanswerable, until the spoken word becomes a living, vibrant text and can stand on its own terms. Jews are not the only people who relied on an oral tradition for their erudition; the Romany, African Americans, and Native Americans also come from strong linguistic traditions of orality that have historically, in the patriarchal academy, been undervalued and misunderstood. Early slave narratives were seen as unreliable because the form was "spoken narrative." And medicinal uses of herbs were thought to be unscientific because they were passed unrecorded from one generation to the next (and most often by women). When the Jews codified the oral law, creating a permanent material "text" in the form of the Torah, there was little basis for questioning the reliability of the subject matter by outsiders, who saw us as isomorphic. (See Laurence Thomas's

Vessels of Evil.) As a child I was enamored as well as challenged by this rigorous form of human discourse. Today, as then, it remains intensely satisfying, nourishing my inquisitive intellectual spirit.

So as an adult professor I routinely ask questions for which I do not have a particular answer in mind. Although it takes a few weeks before students believe that I am not looking for one definitive response, eventually they "get it." And that's when we actually begin. Through their responses, students communicate to me and the entire class their own organic, indigenous thought processes, including whatever issues might require more discussion. As their critical thinking skills develop, so does their unharvested intelligence, including the capacity to transgress old, safe, familiar learning patterns. When it becomes obvious to us as a class that we are moving forward together in pursuit of greater understanding of the material, and that no one is left behind, everyone is exhilarated and invigorated. Ultimately, this form of learning is so powerfully experienced that it is contagious. It does, however, suffer from constant (negative) institutional inquiry.

The success of my methodology has led me to imagine two tracks within the academy: a performative track and a publishing track. While both would require ongoing public scholarship, the forms available for the successful accomplishment of each track would differ substantially. I am vitally interested in having teaching perceived, experienced, and evaluated as a necessary, viable, valuable form of contemporary active scholarship. To a performance artist, feminist theorist, and creative writer, the classroom is an intellectual laboratory, where the script is perpetually in progress, regularly revised, and then performed by student and professor alike. "Living research" as pedagogical text is what I seek: in/credible "cerebral theater" dramatically performed in the classroom unrestricted to the formal stage of any one program or department.

Barriers to the creation of a bona fide performance track include the territorial nationalism sustained by those professors who locate their subjective expertise within a single, permanently personalized discipline, where very little or no departmental "border crossing" exists. And those who do intellectually transgress, crossing the heavy, heady borders of any one critical subject, often lose their academic citizenship and all the rights inherent therein. This institutional punitive response is similar to Freud's theory of the narcissism of minor differences: I am so like you/your sister subject that I hate you because you are too similar to what I am/do. And so the academic border crossers are perpetually envied for the risks they take, and thoroughly reviled at the same time.

I nearly experienced this loss of "citizenship" when I designed, at the request of my program director, a new course on Blacks and Jews. It appeared that I had dangerously overstepped the scholastic "nationalistic" border of Women's Studies by several subjects, disciplines, and departments. Once the border patrol took over, the issue became why a course on Blacks and Jews was being taught in the Women's Studies program (Why not?), instead of the quality of the assigned texts, the skill of the instructor, or the amount of student interest in the subject matter. It didn't matter that the School Council of Social Sciences had unanimously—without request for a single revision—accepted the course proposal and syllabus. Or that scholars at other universities who have written or taught on the subject from diverse departments such as Sociology, History, Judaic, and African-American Studies (including John Bracey, Maurianne Adams, Jonathan Reider, and Julius Lester) had offered high praise for the breadth and depth of the syllabus. The "final flaw" was the huge success of the course, which contributed to the acute suspicion that the course was academically misplaced, recreational, therapeutic, and far less intellectually engaging than it should have been.

The fact that my border crossing in this instance was consistently challenged is not unique to me. Within the academy *all* border crosses are suspect. In designing Blacks and Jews as a Women's Studies course, it was as if I had intentionally taken by eminent domain a subject that was not to be removed from the more traditional departments of Judaic or American Studies, History, or even Sociology. That my approach was based on theories central to Women's Studies, including the intersections of race and gender, the application of multiple lens, and competing hierarchies of oppression, was ignored. Territory and borders were in high relief and contention. This reveals a strong bias against interdisciplinary teaching and "transnationalism" regarding subject matter itself. And, such a colonizing, provincially paternalistic, and ultimately antifeminist position can cause the creative, unorthodox but excellent classroom professor the permanent loss of all citizenship rights and privileges within the coveted ivory tower.

The larger question should be one of territorial expansion outside classic academic borders. If the undergraduate classroom is to thrive and not merely survive the invasion of the cyborg classroom, subjects must be taught from different perspectives in different departments and performed pedagogically in multiple styles. A good example of this multiplicity is how the subject of autobiography could be approached in Creative Writing programs compared to how it is taught in Women's Studies. When I teach Reading and Writing Autobiography: Creating an Ethnic, Gendered, Sexual Self, I am interested in the contemporary, constructed, "politicized" self through felt memory, as in Richard Rodriguez's *Hunger of Memory,* Esmeralda Santiago's *When I Was a Puerto Rican,* or Eva Hoffman's *Lost in Translation.* But whenever I teach a class in writing autobiography in a Creative Writing program, in contrast with the more traditional English department, my focus is on the creation of the smaller, more personally poetic and artistically rendered micro narrative rather than the large, grand-scale, politicized macro one. In another example, whenever I use film as text in my classes, I ask students to analyze the narrative line; in a Film Studies course, we would be more concerned with the overall technical structure—lighting, camera work, soundtrack, script progressions—of the film itself. In a Film Studies class the process is primary, versus using film as text in my other courses where the final product as autonomous narrative is key. In the end, whatever the subject, the border crosser—regardless of the academic venue—gets no respect.

Primordial Matter
creativity

"bell hooks talks about moving from the margins to the center. What happens when the margins themselves become mainstream?" I ask the students in my advanced feminist theory class.

"Give us an example, please," someone in the circle says.

"Think about it," I say back. They pout, pretending to be angry whenever I won't tell them the answer.

"Cynthia?"

"Like Women's Studies . . ."

"Say more."

"Well, twenty years ago it was this new, unreal subject that nobody knew anything about, except maybe a few radical dykes—I mean feminists." She blushes.

"And now?" I ask.

"Well, now we have Women's Studies programs and departments and requirements and it's basically just like everything else . . . there's very few universities without Women's Studies something."

"Yes," I tell the class, "it used to be far more *improvisational* [for a full discussion on life as improvisation, see the introduction in Mary Catherine Bateson's *Composing a Life*]. Conceptually and in practice, Women's Studies was far less rigid than it is today. That's part of the consequence of mainstreaming. The institutional acceptance that Women's Studies has achieved after nearly twenty years has come at the high cost of innovation, continued risk-taking, and the loss of the original motivating creativity." I go on to explain that assimilation, in any context, has its consequences, and that the acceptance of Women's Studies into the dominant university paradigm is ultimately a contradiction, even though it has found a home of sorts and is no longer institutionally exiled.

The students nod in agreement. Lisa raises her hand to speak. "Yeah, like now the personal is taboo. Women's Studies classes are more traditional today, and we're not supposed to talk about our own lives and all the ways we're different. What still makes Women's Studies so unlike other academic programs?"

"That leads me," I say, "back to the complex question of whether or not the academy is, in the end, simply antithetical to feminism and Women's Studies, respectively?"

No one says a word as I write on the board the next question for analysis: *What's the structural difference between liberal and radical feminism?*

In their article "Foundations for a Feminist Restructuring of the Academic Disciplines," in *Feminism and Women's Studies in the Academy*, Vivian P. Makosky and Michele A. Paludi discuss the acute structural limitations inherent in institutions of higher learning: "The stereotype is of the academy as a place where new ideas, approaches, and views are welcome. Although educational institutions may be more liberal than society at large, the fact remains that they are strong pressed toward conformity of the status quo operating in the academy."

For professors such as myself, whose major discipline and intellectual preoccupation is Women's Studies, the pedagogical implication of the demand for conformity in the academy is frightening. Feminism itself is only superficially rather than structurally accepted as an essential part of the academy. And Women's Studies by default, as it moves from the margins to the center, develops a subaltern relationship to the larger, colonizing institution, remaining precariously on the border, living at best half in and half outside the colonist's pedagogical paradigm. The question for committed, feminist professors like myself becomes one of integrity: *What are the institutional parameters and how, without committing professional suicide, do I operate within and outside them?* And then: *How can I retain my subjectivity while being located in a discipline that is perpetually suspect, even by its own members?*

The problem is partially one of isolation. My primary affiliation is Women's Studies, while most of my colleagues at Brandeis and at other universities have as their primary affiliation that of a recognized, traditional department, such as History, English, Sociology, Anthropology, or Psychology. In essence, these professors have a structurally embedded and institutionally sanctioned "backbone" so they are free to have an ad hoc relationship with Women's Studies. Since their credibility remains firmly anchored in the status quo, it permits them a kind of acceptable, floating feminist status. But those of us committed to feminist pedagogy are engaged in an ongoing process of transformation in the classroom that is directly counter to the pedagogy of most of our colleagues, and additionally subject to attack by the university as a whole. This inevitably leads to a certain amount of intradepartmental academic distrust; Women's Studies is notorious for its perpetual infighting, pitting sister against sister. Ultimately, we remain suspended in midair, but not the midair of emergent engagement; instead we swing on the dangerous academic high-wire between the classroom, the students we so love, and the institution that pierces the very heart of the work we do. Holding on to my vision in this atmosphere of constant academic confrontation is a profound political challenge, one that is often demoralizing and exhausting.

Hark(ness), the Herald Academics Call

The Harkness plan . . . places students at the center of the learning process and encourages them to learn from one another.—Exeter Academy website, 2000

Ironically, as feminist pedagogy in general and Women's Studies in particular were coming under increasing critical academic scrutiny by women professors who professed to be feminists (see the work of Daphne Patei, Christina Hoff Sommers, and Elizabeth Fox Genovese), there appeared in the *Boston Globe* (February 6, 2000) a feature story on the Harkness method of teaching, used and developed at Exeter Academy, a private, exclusive prep school in New Hampshire. The Harkness method sounds remarkably similar to the principles of feminist pedagogy, relying almost entirely on class discussion led by the students themselves, who have prepared for class by doing the necessary reading ahead of time. The students and the teacher sit in a circle:

> Since the arrival of "Harkness tables" on campus, the principal mode of instruction at Exeter has been discussion around an oval table. The Harkness table is central to both the Exeter classroom and the curriculum. Though teaching and learning look different in different disciplines and at different levels of study, all Exeter teachers and students are committed to an ideal of active, participatory, student-centered learning which values teaching students not just a given course's content but the skills required to become their own and each other's teachers. . . . Learning at Exeter is a cooperative enterprise in which the students and teacher work together as partners. (Exeter Academy website, 2000)

So the content of the class itself, as originating with the students' intellectual preoccupations, leads the form. Like feminist pedagogy, the Harkness method emphasizes connection through the oral process of critical thinking. In the *Globe* article Barbara Eggers, chair of the Exeter Academy History department who also teaches a class on traditional East Asian civilizations, unconsciously states just how related these two pedagogies are: "You kind of look for the students' answers and see where they want to go. . . . Different things can happen with different groups. There is no script." The *Globe* article goes on to discuss that teachers must learn how to "guide students skillfully through a subject." Mentioned too is the fact that those individuals coming from traditional teaching backgrounds have to "learn how not to be the center of the classroom: In Harkness, students are always the center. And a teacher has to ensure the class discussion is balanced with all voices."

It turns out that Exeter Academy is so pleased with the success of its classroom methodology that it is in the process of copyrighting it, and in summer 2000 offered a Humanities seminar on campus to train teachers in the Harkness method. Furthermore, Harkness consultants were made available to university campuses around the country, Brandeis included. The question is unavoidable: Why do those same "backers and flackers"—men and women professors who are the most critical of feminist pedagogy—so quickly embrace the Harkness philosophy and then sign up for a workshop? Not surprisingly, Brandeis University, always interested in innovation, offered its faculty free on-campus training in the Harkness method. In an effort to improve teaching campuswide, we were all encouraged to participate in the seminars in spring 2000. What concerns me is not the unacknowledged similarities in methodology, as neither Harkness devotees nor feminist pedagogues claim that their methods are unique, but rather why feminist pedagogy attracts institutional attack while the Harkness method is now being heralded from Exeter Academy to Brandeis and beyond.

Perhaps the Harkness method has been so lauded because it appears to be politically neutral as compared with feminist pedagogy, which acknowledges from the beginning its commitment to the multiple lenses of race, class, gender, and sexuality, and to including works by women and peoples of color in all course curricula. Or is it that the Harkness method began within the dominant paradigm itself rather than as a reaction to it; and that it was the result of a substantial endowment to Exeter Academy by the oil magnate and philanthropist Edward Harkness, who (in 1930) intended his gift to continue a certain social if not sociological paradigm that included student-centered learning? I would like to think that the word *feminist* is not the sole deterrent to the acceptance of the eponymously named pedagogy. But it is. For just as Women's Studies is undergoing a name change on many a campus to the more inclusive-sounding (and less off-putting) Gender Studies, so the word *feminism* is being replaced more and more with *humanism*, which doesn't threaten any one. "I'm a humanist, not a feminist," is the au courant rallying cry among the "Net generation." The disempowerment of feminism, as a political philosophy as well as a holistic pedagogy, is evident throughout the academy. I remain, however, committed to the goals as well as the vision of feminist pedagogy, and am happy that student-centered learning is being applauded, no matter what it's called.

A Question of Degree

How is academic success evaluated when most—nearly all—of the women students of color, year after year, are encouraged to drop out (and eventually do) of the pre-med track because they aren't doing as well as their White peers? Is the success of the pre-med program calculated on their successful departure? Is "positive" diversity on campus measured only by counting the number of Spanish-speaking short-order cooks in the cafeteria? When a Political Science department still has no women or professors of color in the year 2000, how can success legitimately be measured? What if a university has no full-time African-American female tenured professors (like Harvard Law School until it hired Lani Guinier in 1991)? Clearly, the answer is one of degree. But what degree, and by whose decree?

I find myself teaching in the midst of the contradictory reality that I so often discuss with my students. Neither my skill as a classroom instructor nor my talents as a creative writer have ever been in question. Yet the question of my academic appropriateness arises only in the quantifiable form of my degrees. Like others, I don't seem to have the "right" initials after my name for such a terrific professorial performance. Although I have been teaching at Brandeis for seven years, I never know if my contract will be renewed. The question of my qualifications comes up repeatedly, leaving me on edge. Every fall when the semester begins, I wonder if this will be my last year teaching at Brandeis.

In addition to the standard bachelor of arts degree, I have a masters in English and a terminal degree in my field, a master of Fine Arts in Creative Writing. While in residence at the MFA program (at the University of Massachusetts in Amherst) I was awarded a coveted graduate writing fellowship and won several awards for short stories. Later, I completed a juris doctorate in law, passing the state and federal bar exams. I have published three books (including this one) and numerous articles. Finally, as a performance artist my one-woman autobiographical show, "If Only I'd Been a Kosher Chicken," was aired on C-SPAN's education and arts channel. I have also been interviewed on National Public Radio and the British Broadcasting System arts programs. But we have all heard the stories of the bright, young, beloved-by-students professor who is denied tenure. The campus erupts; the student newspaper cranks out editorials; colleagues send letters of support to the dean, the provost, the chancellor, even the board of trustees—but none of that matters. The teacher is asked to leave.

So much for qualifications. Although my classes are repeatedly ranked in the top fifteen of all the university courses (and year after year I am cited as an "outstanding professor"), the "form" of my degrees is constantly being challenged. This is not unlike many of my colleagues whose doctorates are in education, or those who come from new, non-traditional (hence suspect) disciplines such as Social Justice, Pop Culture, Multicultural Studies, Performance Theory, and Feminist Theory. What I am raising here is the hypocrisy of "the institution" that offers degrees that it doesn't recognize as professionally legitimate in the academy itself, as is evident from their frequent discounting by hiring committees. Any degree that deviates from those that are classically accepted or are from "unacceptable" graduate schools (such as The Union Institute, Antioch, or Goddard College, all of which have some of the most innovative interdisciplinary programs available today) renders the applicant unqualified for most college and university teaching positions. This particular standard of academic evaluation reminds me of the "arbitrary and capricious" standard that is used by courts to evaluate the constitutionality of state and federal laws. For instance, many anti-abortion statutes have been struck down (most recently New Jersey's in state court and Nebraska's in the U.S. Supreme Court) because the breadth and depth of the statute is far too arbitrary in its restrictions, and thus deemed unconstitutionally broad and "capricious" in application. Yet the status quo is continually rewarded, reproduced, and validated in academic hiring decisions.

Real innovation cannot occur if success is to be evaluated on a retro-quantitative standard rather than a context- and content-specific, in-depth, qualitative analysis. Such an analysis does not imply a relaxation or lack of standards, or a relinquishing of baseline academic requirements. In fact, it requires *additional* competencies beyond those basic standards. I am greatly distressed by the contradictions inherent in a system that professes to be concerned with the quality of the erudition of its faculty, including pedagogical ability, but in truth is much more concerned with the quantitative form the erudition arrives on campus with. If there is no space for experimentation or deviation from the traditional forms, in fact, if innovation is not encouraged and supported, we shall all end up reified, locked far away in those isolated ivory towers, talking only to ourselves.

II. Stage Left: Backers

Faculty

The answer to the question of which faculty are respected is full of irony, contradiction, and racism. In my own case, which is not unusual, I have much faculty support on my home campus and across the country. At Brandeis, my autobiography, *Cravings*, has been taught in a course on contemporary Jewish women's voices in American Studies, and I am regularly invited to lecture in other classes as well as participate in campuswide panels on subjects relevant to my fields of expertise. Brandeis faculty and administrators often sit in on my courses and give guest lectures to my students. My professional campus academic support (including a recent MacArthur "genius grant" recipient) crosses many borders, from Sociology to Near Eastern and Judaic Studies, American Studies, Classics, African-American Studies, and Romance and Comparative Literature. All are full professors, some chairs of their departments. The irony is that when it comes to performance evaluations, the recommendations, both written and oral, from those same supportive faculty are discredited and ultimately discounted. Perhaps it is the scope and the breadth of support my work engenders that causes so much contention. It is the negative voices, those of the flackers, whose opinions are given undue weight in terms of my own evaluations (and those of others like me). This unbalanced and perhaps unfair assessment system represents a serious attempt to return the university to a more traditional canonical environment (as encouraged by Harold Bloom and company), while at the same time emphasizing form over content. Additionally it is a covert effort to reinscribe a patriarchal pedagogical paradigm even as it delegitimizes the feminist classroom, including feminism itself. But the substantial faculty support for those of us on the academic vanguard is not gratuitous or superfluous: without the support of our peer risk-takers who dare to publicly disagree with their more traditional colleagues, we academic "daredevils" would be far less effective and perhaps even less courageous. If the academy is to remain a fluid learning space, strategies must be developed in which peer support in and outside the home institution is legitimized.

Students

Anonymous student evaluation of Blacks and Jews, spring 2000:

> The class is organized in such a way that each student is availed of the opportunity to learn from one another and the instructor, after thinking analytically and critically about the information presented. The challenge in the class is precisely to broaden your perspective; the goal is to step away from previous knowledge and learn everything anew from a basis of fact and experience. In addition, the community and communication that this class created and fostered both in the classroom and outside . . . added a valuable dimension to the learning experience.

Anonymous student evaluation of Reading and Writing Autobiography, spring 1999:

> The ability to find [my] voice when given the direction, space, and encouragement is probably the most useful tool I have learned in my entire college career.

Anonymous student evaluation of Introduction to Women's Studies, fall 1998:

> I would ask for a bit more sensitivity to the experiences students have had and may be having in the class. We talk about difficult issues and the professor needs to be prepared for people needing support and/or help.
>
> Something that would be wonderful, though very difficult would be a room . . . where everyone can see each other.
>
> For the first time . . . students' ideas [were taken] seriously. We were never asked to spit back knowledge without thinking about it first and finding our [own] position and [we were] never expected to just agree with the professor. . . . There was very little power operating and each student, TA, grad student and professor was equal . . . each voice important. . . . Felman took risks in ways most . . .

professors would not. These didn't always work out, but she was still willing to take them.

When it comes down to the quality of their classroom experience, students rarely lie. If they do, it's most often the result of a personal grudge or a personality clash with the professor. The question then becomes: Why are student evaluations most often taken seriously only when the professor receives negative comments rather than when she or he receives overwhelmingly positive, often rave reviews? There is a delegitimizing process that goes on regarding student course evaluations. Excellence is held in contempt, perpetually suspected of lacking intellectual rigor because the professor is so popular. Gossip among my colleagues has it that receiving the "Teacher of the Year Award" is the poison kiss of academic death.

This poses a particular problem for both Women's Studies and those professors (campuswide) who employ feminist pedagogy in the classroom, for our best and most consistent backers are our students. They understand that the experiences they have in the feminist classroom are qualitatively different from those in other classrooms. And contrary to the campus grapevine, these classes don't guarantee the much-sought-after but highly inflated A. Instead, students comment repeatedly on the amount of work required in courses based on feminist pedagogy, and its value to the entire learning experience. In the feminist classroom students are the backbone; the class simply does not exist without their active engagement. I am consistently amazed by how much I learn from my students, and try at every opportunity to communicate the intellectual reciprocity that occurs in the classroom. Because I never assume that I know everything about the subjects I teach, space is created for student agency. And when student agency is activated in the classroom a dramatic power shift occurs, including a dynamic human transformation. As performance artist Sandra Bernhard says to her audience, so I say to my students: *Without you, I'm nothing.* I mean it. We need to develop a strategy in which the university takes its students' opinions—good and bad—of professors seriously.

Students know that their opinions with regard to specific professors are devalued, if not ignored completely. This sets up an antagonistic relationship between the students and the administration. Distrust permeates the campus, and a certain amount of lethargy is evident among the students. This is one of those "academic truisms" that is rarely verbalized: everyone understands that students, at the final point of a professor's evaluation, are irrelevant. How ironic, because as the students themselves become disempowered, ultimately so are the professors. Eventually (if it hasn't already) the classroom itself will become obsolete. The virtual classroom is much easier and far more economical to reproduce than the live performance. But in feminist pedagogy it is the human connection that is essential to a powerful and successful classroom experience.

Part of the problem of current student disempowerment is the fact that, since the Reagan-Bush era, this generation of students has moved more to the right of apathy than to the left of action. Nowhere has the impact of this passivity been stronger than on university campuses. The student protests of the mid-1960s and early 1970s helped end the Vietnam War, caused university endowments to no longer be invested in South Africa, and successfully demanded the development of new departments (such as African-American, Chicano, Native American, and Women's Studies) whose subject matter had been previously ignored or excluded from both the canon and the curricula at large. Today's students do not feel so empowered. And they are far more afraid of the negative consequences of any risk-taking they might envision that publicly challenges administrative decisions. As my students tell me repeatedly, "We just don't have any power; no one in the administration ever listens to us."

So the development of voice and agency in the classroom and beyond becomes crucial. At the same time, it is profoundly threatening to the dominant academic paradigm. Current administrations are literally banking on the fact that students' lethargy regarding institutional policy will endure for quite some time. As for me, I am empowered each time a student finds and uses her voice—and whenever a student asks me a question for which I have no answer.

The Hot-Pink Cyclamen and the Defiant Hebrew Muse

On my desk sits a hot-pink cyclamen uncharacteristically blooming its way through a scorchingly hot New England summer. Cyclamens don't usually bloom all year round. They take the late spring and early fall months off. But this cyclamen clearly is different. It was a gift from my eight teaching assistants (four graduate and four undergraduate) on the last day of 5A, the introductory Women's Studies course that we teach in tandem. When they presented the blooming plant to me, it was December, the dead of winter, and freezing outside. Then the plant had eight small blooms, just opening. Now, on my desk in July, it has at least eighteen. I have never seen a hot-pink cyclamen with so many flowers. They explode daily, surrounded by a small mass of green leaves.

Along with this plant, my TAs gave me a book, *The Defiant Muse: Hebrew Feminist Poems from Antiquity to the Present.*

"How did you know?" I was caught off guard, surprised by such a loving gesture. Although I had received individual gifts from students in the past, I have never received a "group" gift from my 5A teaching assistants.

"We hoped you didn't already have a copy," Ariel said.

"I don't, but how did you know, flowers, and feminist Hebrew poetry . . . ?" I was particularly moved by the specificity of their thoughtfulness. I wondered if they understood the meaning and the metaphor of their gift.

"There will never be fewer than eight hot-pink flowers," I promise them. "Whenever I'm watering my new plant, it will be as though I am talking to each one of you, continuing our relationship." They nod, knowing my flare for the dramatic, and knowing too just how sincere I am. In fact, the cyclamen is a delicate plant, requiring constant moisture; it must be attended to, and cannot be forgotten. It reminds me of my students, of the mutuality of our existence, teacher and student, co-learners on an invigorating, lifelong quest.

As for the accompanying bilingual book of poems, written in the language of my people by my Ashkenazi, Sephardic, and Mizrachi sisters, turning each page after glorious page, all I can say of *The Defiant Muse* is *thank you*, my colleagues, for seeing me, your teacher, your friend.

"I Went to Work as an Ostrich" Blues
by Rahel Chalfi

I went to the zoo to work as an ostrich
They told me you're not qualified to work as an ostrich
You have too many eyes and too little sand

Stop wanting to be an ostrich
How much sand how much sand do I need
To see everything I need
And a salary too I need
To work how sweet to work as an ostrich   willing
To be an ostrich even as hobby, a volunteer ostrich, if only they'd let me
     work as an ostrich

Don't you see? Running around like a huge birdie-girl cut off from the
     sand of forgetting
what difference does it make that I'm willing if they won't
     let me be an ostrich?
Your neck should be rigid your body frigid
They tell me at the zoological unemployment agency
Your gaze should fidget says the social worker at the zoo
Don't you see that until you are changed by a Change,
Change your skin bend your neck and bury your head
You won't get an ostrich job?!

Maybe at least I'll wear a dress made of ostrich feathers
it's so sensual   it's so dimensual

Na! It's not a matter of feathers, they yell at me, it's a matter of
     savvy
Of sand and savvy.

—Translated from the Hebrew by Shirley Kaufman

Power Plays
in the Master Class

i was hooked the first time I stood in front of an auditorium full of a hundred undergraduates. Twenty years ago I was the only graduate teaching assistant—there were eight of us—who had volunteered to give a lecture to the entire Introduction to Women's Studies class at the University of Massachusetts in Amherst. My topic was gender roles. I began by describing the delicate, precise process of shaving my legs with a specially designed, light-pink Lady Remington until nothing but a glistening, smooth surface remained to be smothered with Jergen's body lotion.

At the end of the first paragraph I looked up nervously. There wasn't a sound in the cavernous room. Everyone was listening to me; no one moved or coughed. We were all of us enveloped by the exquisite silence of active, engaged listening. But I didn't understand what else was happening simultaneously, and I didn't have the words to describe what I sensed beyond the compelling nature of the material. Today I comprehend all too well what happens whenever I stand behind that smooth oak podium.

"Okay, let's start." The entire room quiets down. For the next three hours, I am in charge. Sometimes I think of myself as "Queen for a Brandeis Day," and all that's missing is the solid gold crown balanced precariously on top of my lofty head. It is a moment both pompous and portentous. How am I to proceed? Closing my eyes, I hear the words of the Amazonian woman-poet-warrior Audre Lorde in *Sister Outsider*: "The master's tools will never dismantle the master's house." Slowly, fortuitously, the brilliantly bejeweled crown slips from my academic head as I realize the full magnitude of the position I hold.

This is power. The power to move, excite, exploit, anger, incite, dominate, inspire, oppress, engage, destroy, hurt, terrify, and/or transform. To teach is to have power. What this means on a day-to-day basis, week after week, semester after semester, is what concerns me. My power as the professor and the students' power to inhibit, liberate, censor, move, inspire, criticize, cheer, attack, resist, resent, reproach, enliven, and affirm me year after year.

In preparing to write this chapter, I recall my own student days and those professors who used their power with great care and insight. And those who chose to misuse it by denying me a grade or a prize that I rightly deserved, or the ones who withheld a recommendation I desperately needed. But it is the professors who understood the power inherent in their positions and ultimately used it to assist and guide their students who taught me the most. Those individuals treated me for who I was, a sensitive, precocious student requiring special attention. They invited me home for long, elaborate dinners followed by a small glass of sherry and "deep" philosophical discussions. I was even permitted to call certain professors at home. I was also, on occasion, given a better grade than I had actually earned: an English professor had sensed something about where I was headed and what I needed from her to succeed. Then there was the professor who gave me a D. He knew it was appropriate, and lucky for me no amount of pleading could make him change his mind. Both men and women modeled positive, empowering uses of power long before Women's Studies existed and feminist pedagogy had impacted the academy. It is those early personal experiences with power that I have chosen to emulate and promote in my own classroom.

Power is diffuse, fluid, and potentially explosive in Women's Studies classes today, more so than in most other disciplines, because there is an expectation on the part of the students that Women's Studies is "different." That it is nonhierarchical, nonpatriarchal, and exceptionally student-friendly—egalitarian rather than authoritarian in tone and style. Power plays harder in the feminist classroom because in addition to students' usual projections, there is a host of extra particulars. Especially when the professor is a woman. She must also be nice, nurturing, kind, sympathetic: more "motherly" and less "fatherly." And when the professor turns out to be just him or herself, and does not fulfill all the "benevolent" gendered expectations that both male and female students bring into the room, the response can be dramatic. Perilous as the response may feel, it is resolved over time:

"I was afraid of you. In the beginning," Chava says.

"No. Me?" I laugh, finding this utterly impossible.

"From the very first day, the minute you started speaking. There you were. I had never seen anything like it before."

It's midsemester. Chava has come to see me because she is upset about the language Jenetta Martin used last week in her one-woman show on race.

"You looked and sounded so tall." I am five foot one, exactly. Diminutive.

"And you looked right at us. I wanted to run out of the room, but I wasn't sitting on the aisle, so I couldn't get up. Then, you stomped out from behind the podium and started walking back and forth, pacing in those big black shoes you always wear. I was terrified. You were so . . . intimidating. I told all my friends that I was going to drop the course."

I couldn't stop laughing from embarrassment, although what Chava was describing wasn't funny to me in the least. She continued speaking as though rushing to confess. "I couldn't imagine an entire semester with you. And when you called on us—the first day—even if we didn't raise our hands, I sat there for the whole three hours, petrified that you were going to call on me. And you did. I was so mad at you."

I hear this description of myself over and over again. It never makes complete sense until I see it through a stereotypically gendered lens. Then I understand. Even though it's 2000, the sight of a strong, articulate, smart female professor *still* unnerves students, male and female. *This* knowledge unnerves me.

"So, now how do you feel?" I ask Chava, knowing ahead of time what she'll say.

"Oh, now, I can't believe I ever felt that way, you are sooooo cool and approachable. But back then, the first few weeks . . ." she's laughing.

"It's because I'm a woman, isn't it? In a position of authority?" She nods. "That's why you were afraid." She is sheepish, her cheeks slightly pink. "You've had women teachers before?" She nods again, "So what's the problem?"

"But not like you." Chava shifts and her voice for the first time is strong. She stops slouching and sits straight up, until we are eye to eye. She's ready to discuss Jenetta's use of derogatory epithets. We talk about cultural specificity. I explain how Blacks and Jews might choose different descriptors. At the end I ask, "Can you learn to tolerate the ambiguity of cultural relativity?"

"I'll try," she says, meeting my gaze head on before walking out of the office. "And thanks for everything," she adds, turning back briefly.

To teach is to influence in a myriad of conscious and unconscious ways. As an activity, teaching is not neutral. It is political by nature *and* nurture. It is political whether there is an obvious or stated agenda, or a covert one. Teaching is political because it embodies power and the negotiation of that power when the balance shifts, as it inevitably does. What happened to Chava's perception of me, and more important, what happened to Chava herself is about the shifting and growing relationship of power in the feminist classroom. At the end of the semester, I was not surprised that Chava applied to be a student teaching assistant for 5A. Feminist teaching, although never neutral, is mutual. Chava had found her own internal power when she ceased to find me—her first strong, loud, articulate, Jewish female professor—intimidating.

And me, what did I find? After teaching 5A at Brandeis for three years, I was preoccupied with the question of gendered power in the classroom, about where I was with it, and where "the power" was with me. It came home in a very direct way when I acceded to the director of Women's Studies' persistent urging to use student assistants in the class. I had been reluctant, assuming that supervising students (as assistants) would only add to my workload. But I agreed to try it for one semester. I invited previous 5A students to apply for the new positions and set up a mentoring program. Every graduate teaching assistant was paired with an undergraduate who had already taken the course. Together this pair would lead a weekly discussion section of about twenty students, then e-mail me their reflections on the section so we could dialogue about what had occurred. They would also read, discuss, and comment on the weekly student response papers, and attend a required one-hour meeting with me and the other teaching assistants right after class.

The mentoring process itself was to be completely fluid, moving continuously back and forth from me to all the teaching assistants, who simultaneously mentored each other and the students taking the class, who in turn mentored all of us. Through this reciprocal mentoring, the traditional hierarchy so central to maintaining the academy was interrupted and redirected. I had no idea how well the mentor-mentee system I put in place was going to work. As it turns out, it has become an essential part of the introductory Women's Studies class for me, the students, and all the teaching assistants. Every year students actively vie for the TA positions.

The system's success is due in large part to how everyone negotiated the various forms of power operating among us, including the principles of feminist pedagogy that I adapted for this specific use: the belief that knowledge is a shared experience and that it is not located solely in a single authority figure; and that the classic dominate/subordinate binary as a form of instruction was totally outmoded. This means that in the middle of class I may be interrupted by a graduate or undergraduate teaching assistant who has something to contribute. Or that during the break, students and/or assistants will approach me to comment on the "pulse" of the class, and then will make suggestions or observations about what might be needed next. In retrospect I see that my own "Jewishly" gendered ambivalence toward the amount of power I was quickly amassing in my own feminist classroom influenced the way I designed and implemented the mentoring program.

The cultural messages I received about growing up to be "a nice Jewish girl," rather than a wild, raging, passionate *vilde chaye*, influenced my own evolving relationship to power. I had to learn to accept *and* manage the power, rather than allow the power of the position to manage me. And I had to resist the urge to reject the power entirely, out of my own fear. Teaching at Brandeis, a predominantly Jewish institution, unexpectedly afforded me the unique opportunity to explore my own internalized, conflicted messages about being a powerful, loud, vibrant, sensuous, creative, piquant, and popular Jewish woman professor who is entitled to take up a lot of secular, institutional space. Before exploring the power relationships—the pros and cons—of the mentoring process, I want to explore my own specifically gendered and culturally informed relationship to power in the feminist classroom.

I remember vividly, when I first began teaching at Brandeis, being challenged by an African-American student in front of the whole class. We were discussing Boutros Boutros-Ghali, the then newly appointed secretary general of the United Nations. Most of the students had no idea who he was. "He's an Egyptian man in a public position of global influence and, significantly, the first Arab to head the UN," I told the class, mentally noting but not publicly adding how concerned Jews were that an Arab secretary general of the UN would administrate fairly and not further ostracize Israel. Before I had even finished speaking, a hand in the first row shot up. "Yes?"

"Mr. Boutros Boutros-Ghali is not Arab, he's Coptic," Moniika said. I had never heard the word *Coptic* before.

"What do you mean, he's not Arab?" I was testy and felt threatened but didn't know why, as students often add information to class discussions. Although I tried to appear as if everything were fine, inside I was fast becoming resentful. In an attempt to reassert my authority, I said, "Yes, that's true, but he's also Egyptian." Then I continued teaching, while Moniika stared at me. After class she approached the smooth oak podium behind which I had retreated.

"Is this how you're going to teach race?" she asked. I had no idea what she was talking about.

"What do you mean?"

"I was just wondering since you didn't seem to know who Mr. Boutros-Ghali was . . . really. I mean, the whole issue of who is an Arab and who isn't, and whether or not you see Egypt as part of Africa, is part of what you're misrepresenting here."

"Oh, no," I muttered back, disturbed that I didn't get to finish my sentence because Moniika had turned around and walked out of the room. Afterward, I went over the whole conversation in my head, trying to understand what had happened and why I felt so threatened. I wondered how to interpret the fact that Moniika had opted out of discussing what she herself had introduced, and thus abandoned the critical process of discursive engagement that she had begun during class.

At Brandeis, as in most elite private universities, many students have a strong sense of entitlement, so it is not unusual for professors in any discipline to be "interrogated" in class about facts and statistics, or to be asked for proof. The interrogation becomes an initiation ritual for both the neophyte assistant professor and the novice student, as well as characteristic of the status of the institution itself. Understanding the privileged environment in which I teach, and this type of student questioning in particular, assists me in negotiating what often turns out to be a typically covert, unconscious challenge to my authority. In Women's Studies classes these challenges happen so regularly that a large body of literature discussing "student resistance" to feminist theories has developed. (See, most recently, *Feminist Teaching in Theory and Practice*, by Becky Ropers-Hiulman.) But Moniika's behavior did not fit into this familiar behavior pattern as described in the literature. She wasn't resisting feminism per se; rather, I thought she was resisting *me*. Or, I wondered, was she actually resisting anything at all? Perhaps, I was the resister this time. Applying the multiple lens approach (looking at the world through race, class, gender, and sexuality) that I teach in all my courses, I asked myself the following questions:

1. If Moniika were Jewish, and corrected me about the background of a Jewish official, would I have reacted or felt differently?
2. If she were a lesbian, how would my response have changed, if at all?
3. If she were a man of color, a White man, or a gay man of any color, would I still feel threatened?
4. What had so unnerved me?
5. What was I afraid of?

I had to admit that it was precisely the fact that she was an African-American, heterosexual woman confronting me in public about the "authentic" identity of another person of color that made me feel threatened. Had she been a Jewish woman like Chava, a lesbian, or a gay man, I would not have felt such an extreme challenge because I could rely on our commonality, our "shared" oppression to mediate against any attack on me personally as the professor or the power I held. In this situation I felt as though Moniika was really saying that I had no right to teach anything about race, and that if I tried, whatever I said was not going to be sufficient. What upset me most was to discover, at the time, I was more disturbed by *who* made the comment than by how inadequately I had responded, or that I had not had accurate, complete information.

What happened between Moniika and me has everything to do with power and privilege between "races" in the elite White classroom—

and my own internal script. That I was afraid to name the issues stuck between us, when confronting a dissenting voice that belonged to a woman of color, was a big piece of the problem. Complicating an already difficult interaction was that I had not yet learned how to negotiate my own power in a feminist classroom. Nor had I given up the internalized pejorative fear that included being perceived as a difficult, controlling Jewish woman. Back then, I was used to falling back on the dominant, hierarchical model whenever necessary. That is, whenever I felt threatened. Instead of confronting the situation directly, as I would do now, I retreated behind that smooth oak podium, cashing in on the power and privilege—the color and status—of the profession I embodied. Looking back, I am chagrined at my own recalcitrant behavior.

It turns out that Moniika and I were both right. Boutros Boutros-Ghali is both Egyptian and Coptic. Albeit not an Arab. I reviewed all the newspaper clippings from the *New York Times* that I had saved when he was first nominated. In each one, Boutros Boutros-Ghali was referred to as the "first Arab to head the UN." Nowhere was it mentioned that he was Coptic. I had to look elsewhere for a specific definition of Coptic, which is an Afro-Asian language descended from ancient Egypt, and spoken by the Copts, who are also Christian. Were a similar situation to occur today in class, I would also discuss the "racism of omission," and our over-reliance—including my own—on the mass media for accurate information.

I would use this example to ask the class why Boutros Boutros-Ghali was being repeatedly portrayed by the U.S. media as an Arab rather than as a Copt. And I'd ask how much of the concern over his appointment by the U.S. government and prominent Jewish leaders had to do with not wanting to connect Boutros Boutros-Ghali to the pan-African liberation struggle—and also not wanting to introduce Christianity and nationalism into the equation. Is it, I would ask, because Coptic is more complex and confuses the oversimplified Western Black/White binary used to represent race? In retrospect I had yet to face my own emotional and intellectual demons: that I was unable to untangle the confusing borders governing identity, the overlaps among Jewish, Black, and Arab peoples, Moslems and Christians, and the Middle East. This was why I was so irritated with Moniika. She was right, in that she may have intuited how unprepared I was—at the time—to talk about race. Thus the nature of Boutros Boutros-Ghali's "true" identity became an intellectually compelling diversion from the real issue.

But in turning her back on me, and in refusing to engage, Moniika was concurrently refusing her own power as a student. Had she stayed to talk out the issues she herself had raised, her impact on the pedagogy and the subject matter itself would have been obvious. For what she was actually calling my attention to was the fact that I had reduced the identity of Boutros-Ghali to the rarified notion of color as the operative signifier for race. That is, to see brown in the Middle East is to see only Arab, which thus reduces the complexities and truly fluid nature of race as it is now understood in the contemporary poststructural lexicon. In leaving the room, Moniika was actually reproducing the hierarchy of knowledge I was trying so hard to dismantle. She was playing a counterdependent, subordinate role to my dominant one. By turning her back and walking out of the room in the middle of our discussion, she acquiesced to the power of the professorial position. And I let her leave. Some part of me was relieved that we weren't going to "get into it" after all.

Were this situation or a similar one to occur today, I would also set up an appointment with the particular student and discuss what had happened with all my teaching assistants in our postclass meeting. Together we would dissect and deconstruct the various elements of the student-teacher interaction, including an in-depth critique of race and representation. This is significant, because the moment I open myself to the very public scrutiny of my undergraduate and graduate teaching assistants, the power shifts. And it is this shifting that impacts directly the balance of power between us as I expose my own vulnerability in the classroom and ask for assistance in analyzing what just occurred, and then taking constructive criticism from those in a lower status position than myself within the academic hierarchy. The traditionally discreet, extremely privatized process of amassing large amounts of professorial power is thus disrupted and destabilized. In this way, maximum benefit accrues to all involved parties.

Furthermore, the intense isolation, so fostered by the internal structure of the institution and designed to be perpetuated by the role the professor is expected to perform, is finally intruded upon. Breaking through that isolation has been one of the most profound contradictions I have been able to put into practice while teaching at Brandeis. For isolation is the essential hierarchical ingredient used to maintain the superficial integrity of the institution by individual faculty members in each department. Contained within the immanent domain of our singular expertise, each professor is encouraged to protect his or her cerebral terrain with all the insidious tenacity he or she is capable of. In the end, the professor is left dangerously alone on the taut academic highwire. Within the isolation model, a professor's only recourse is to take out the singular, supreme fear of publicly falling/failing on the masses of students hovering below.

Therefore, becoming fully human before my teaching assistants allows me to break down the isolation of the institution and to be more fully myself. And when I am myself, I am able to make connections in the classroom while simultaneously transforming the power relationships between and among the students, the teaching assistants, and myself. The mentoring system is unique in that it allows the professor to actually receive and ask for support herself—not just to give it. This is critical, and part of its success. Those involved feel powerful and powerfully necessary to the learning process itself. The mentoring system permits the act of learning to be a dynamic energy force, artfully contradicting the static, stagnating antiforce it so often is.

In looking at what it means in the classroom to be both fully me— Jewish and female—and fully in my pedagogical and epistemological power, I have come to understand that I need help. That's where, by default, the mentoring program has had its most profound impact. It helped me to negotiate my own ethnically gendered power without the fear of contamination or domination. In fact, I began to thrive, achieving far greater successes in the classroom as my isolation continued to break and as I continued to ask for help from the "mentors" themselves. I began to redesign 5A based on the feedback from the postclass meetings and to expand my own capacity to accept others' insights into classroom dynamics. Depending on the mentors was only the first step. I had to learn to communicate to them that their assistance was not gratuitous in any way, but rather that it was crucial to maintaining the high-quality, dynamic classroom experience we had all come to enjoy and expect.

Equally important, by my behavior I was able to communicate to the class as a whole our growing interdependence on each other, and the relationship of that interdependence to the success of the course; as well as to their individual learning experiences. The many-faceted relationships we as a class developed together, including their interdependence on each other, were revealed to the students by the standards I set from the very beginning: requiring that we start on time; not permitting students to whisper while another student is speaking; calling on the teaching assistants in class; and incorporating student papers, comments, and critiques into my lectures. It was obvious to everyone that we worked as a team. No one was left isolated or unattended to, including me the professor. I came to look forward to the after-class meetings with the mentors, because I knew that within the act of processing, a profound bonding also occurred, challenging each one of us to understand our own interdependence and essential connection to one another. The relationships were real and fully realized. Whether we liked each other or not became irrelevant; we were truly committed to making 5A the richest, most compelling learning experience that we possibly could—not just for the students but also for ourselves. These mentors became my *compañeros*.

I asked the most recent mentors to write to me about the process, as I was curious to see how their experiences mirrored and/or contradicted my own. The following comments are excerpted directly from their responses.

Undergraduate Teaching Assistant: Jillian Gross

The true beauty of the mentoring program . . . is that it is not designed for us to learn solely from the professor. All eight of us were given the responsibilities of students as well as teachers. . . . When it began, that first evening in September, I was more nervous than I had ever been. There I was a sheltered Orthodox Jew from New York, surrounded by people who were completely different from me and whom I had never seen before. It was quite a shock and quite a first experience. I actually do not think that I realized what the program was going to be like. I . . . figured that I would glance at papers and sit quietly in the discussion section. But, from the moment we sat down, Jyl explained that this was a learning experience and we were not only there to facilitate learning but to learn for ourselves.

When it came time for Jyl to pair us up, it seemed . . . random. Only after sitting with her in meetings once a week did I realize how much goes into teaching, especially her method of teaching. She had carefully and quietly figured us all out and paired us so that we would complement each other perfectly. My partner and I were both very shy and quiet in the beginning and Jyl thought that we would learn the most from each other because neither one of us would steal the spotlight. She was 100% right. I learned from Sam so many things. . . . We come from very different backgrounds so I had the opportunity to learn about her culture [Korean] and her heritage. I was able to learn from Sam on an academic level as well. She, being nine years my senior, has had much more teaching experience than I have had. So she was able to show me how to have a presence in the classroom and how to direct a discussion. But, again, the most amazing part . . . is that Sam, the grad student, was learning from me as well. It boggled my mind in the beginning that there was something for her to learn from me but . . . she learned a lot. I was able to help her understand the students in our room. . . . Having operated solely in a patriarchal classroom, the notion of learning from the students was virtually foreign to Sam.

I find myself sitting through classes thinking about how differently the professor could have done this . . . to make it more interesting. I definitely learned more about teaching than I thought I would, but what surprised me was how much I learned about people. . . . Jyl taught us that quiet does not always mean not paying attention, or frustration does not mean no desire to learn. . . . The mentoring program was the best learning experience I had at Brandeis . . . it made me the critical thinker, reader and listener that I need to be.

Graduate Teaching Assistant: Samantha Joo

Mentorship is beneficial . . . at the first level, the class has access to three individuals, and depending on their particular needs and questions, the students are able to approach any one of them. Based on personal experience as a student and as an instructor, . . . students are . . . reluctant to approach the professor and even the TA for sheer fear of authority figures. Here, the undergraduate TA who appears more accessible and nonthreatening fills the perceived and mythic chasm between the overwhelmed students and "all-knowing" professor and graduate TA. . . .

Section dynamics dramatically change with the presence of two instructors. Rather than bouncing ideas off of one individual, who is . . . unable to respond to all the comments, the class becomes more interactive as both instructors engage in a dialogue, opening the classroom to a different model of instruction. . . . The students see an interactive discourse which they then could emulate in their own response to the topic. . . . They are no longer bound to the traditional, static, linear discourse from the instructor to the students. . . . Now the students can and do talk with each other, which enhances their learning process especially in a class on feminism. . . .

With the undergraduate TA in the classroom, they can critique each other so that section gradually improves over time. As Jyl Lynn Felman has designed the mentorship, the professor is also able to receive constructive feedback from the TAs. Right after the main class, there is a rap session where everyone is to reflect on and assess the dynamics of the class. One cannot make a general statement since Professor Felman pushes for concrete observations that allow her to decide whether certain methods should be continued or modified. . . . Therefore the class is constantly strengthened and modified for the benefit of the students' academic experience.

There are some problems within the mentorship system, mainly in the section. . . . It is hard to predict and prepare for some of the comments. . . . As a result, there may be . . . conflict in the way the undergraduate and graduate TA would want to directly respond to the students. . . . At times, I find myself leading the students in the direction that the undergraduate TA did not want to go and vice versa . . . hesitating to speak, for fear of stepping on the undergraduate TA's authority or thinking that she will speak but doesn't. Therefore, there are instances where continuity is lacking in the discussions. . . . It takes time to learn the other instructor's method of teaching and body language and by the time we do, it's almost the end of the semester.

Student Teaching Assistant: Daniel J. Franklin

When I first entered the 5A classroom a year and a half ago, I had no idea what a profound effect it would wind up having on my life. Now, looking back on having been a TA, I could not imagine the experience being anything less than life-altering.

Before this school year began, all eight of us who had been chosen as TAs met for dinner. There we met the person we would be working with for the next four months. . . . I was rather ambivalent as to whom I would be paired up with. When I learned that I was to work with Antje, it occurred to me that I knew but three things about her: she is German, she looks . . . Aryan, she has a name which I had difficulty pronouncing. . . .

Since Jyl dealt with us as two equals—not as a graduate student and an undergraduate—it was easy for us to treat each other as equals. Also of great importance, I in no way felt uncomfortable asking Antje for help when I needed it, or for assistance and guidance. Similarly, since our equality was based on our each bringing something different to the working relationship, offering guidance was merely an opportunity to share experience—not to show superiority. The pairing of a graduate student with an undergraduate takes away the competitiveness that might exist between two undergrads (even in a feminist classroom!).

Jyl also played an immense role for me this semester. Each week after class, all nine of us would meet. Section, class, and individual students, . . . feminist theories and issues were discussed. . . . Together the nine of us would talk about what had worked in class, and what we wanted for our upcoming sections. . . . All would contribute ideas and opinions, and work together to explore the problems some of us had faced with students and sections. Though Jyl's comments spoke from years of experience and learning, this in no way lessened the value of our own thoughts. . . .

Antje and I took turns e-mailing Jyl what happened that week in section—both good and bad. . . . Jyl promptly responded with words of . . . encouragement, as well as some advice to keep in mind for the future. She also offered possible explanations for why certain things happened that neither Antje nor I understood—why was nobody talking today; why did students not deal with a specific issue as we'd expected. . . . My time working with students was wonderful. However there is no way that I could have been a positive mentor and role model for them without mentors of my own. Jyl, Antje, and the mentorship program provided this for me.

Graduate Teaching Assistant: Antje Ellerman

Mentoring and the Structure of 5A (the systemic piece). The way that you have set up 5A provides a framework conducive to the development of mentoring relationship—it enables "multilevel" and "multidirectional" mentoring. Mentoring occurs on multiple levels, between professor, graduate TAs, and undergraduate TAs (and, in a different way, undergraduate students). Mentoring also takes place in multiple directions—rather than being top-down, it works between the different institutional levels, with relationships being dynamic and flexible and everybody holding the roles of teacher and "learner" at different times. The hub of these . . . relationships is the weekly meetings after class. This forum of individual feedback creates a place for everybody to move between the roles of mentor and mentees, as each perspective—helped by the structural differentiation of our roles—contributes something new. The most valuable contribution of undergraduate TAs lies in their experience of having been students themselves, and in observing how this experience interacts with their present roles and perceptions as TAs. Graduate TAs contribute their struggles to develop their own pedagogical styles as future teachers and therefore reflect on lectures based on their effectiveness in conveying and developing knowledge and building up relationships. Finally, the professor contributes her perspective as the main orchestrator watching the class from the front stage who afterwards reflects on the match between her goals for the class, on the one hand, and the outcome, on the other. Because of this plurality of perspectives, feedback rounds not only enable mutual learning, but also paint a complex and whole picture of what did take place in class.

These group dynamics not only provide multiple and complementary perspectives, they also represent various levels of the academic hierarchy which now interact in a non- or at least less-hierarchical setting. In this way, because the duality between professor and TA is disrupted by having both undergraduate and graduate TAs (in the same way the existence of TAs interrupts the duality between professor and student), it is easier to work together collaboratively and develop one's own perspective unrestricted by institutional hierarchical molds.

Mentoring and My Relationship with Jyl (a personal piece). What I have learnt most is your active interest in your students and TAs. I have come to realize that, no matter how motivated I am as a student, I will not reach my full academic potential without active mentoring by a professor. As a student I need feedback on my written work (and

I do need to write as a way of exploring my analytical capabilities) in order to know that I am listened to, to know that my hard work of writing is acknowledged and respected. Feedback as a way of encouragement strengthens my belief in my abilities—to know that what I know is worth saying, thereby developing my own voice. I also need a relationship in order to build up trust, which is essential if I want to take risks in my writing and learn from feedback. Because academia is built on the structures of hierarchical relationships, which are defined by rigid boundaries, students are infantilized. Students learn to speak only when they are asked to speak, and it is the professor who is in control of both the content and the shape of classroom discussions. Once a professor tries to change these structures, things do not simply fall into place—rather, the structures outside the classroom have not changed and carry on inside, as students' role behavior has become deeply ingrained. Therefore the professor needs to continually reach out to her students and actively engage in the building up of relationships—merely providing space (though an important achievement in itself) is not enough. I have learnt these things from you by watching you teach (and only being a TA can offer you this opportunity) and by listening to your own feedback after class, and by listening to your feedback on my class feedback. You have very consciously created an environment that not only gives space for reflection and engagement, but that also gives mentoring relationships a chance to grow.

Mentoring and My Relationship with My Undergraduate TA (another personal piece). . . . . Because Dan and I both wrote extensive comments on students' papers, and because we both read each others' comments, we had the rare opportunity to be exposed to at times differing reactions to papers, thus being pushed to reassess our own reactions and comments. . . . We both observed some convergence toward each other's grading styles, which I consider to be a reflection of us learning from each other. Students initially found it difficult to accept us as "fellow TAs," having only been exposed to graduate TAs previously. Much of this (though not all) faded away as Dan was very proactive in class discussions and paper feedback and I made a very conscious effort of giving him space to work as a TA in his own right. I think that the struggle to create an equal TA relationship often hinges on little pieces of actions. For instance, I always made sure that Dan was fully informed of everything (and vice versa), by, for instance, forwarding him the revised grade sheet every week (as the one ultimately in charge of grading), while he kept me informed of informal conversations he had with students on campus.

Although Jillian, Sam, Daniel, and Antje speak positively about their mentoring experiences, including their individual pairings, the next excerpt is less sanguine and more indicative of the issues that can occur when different sexes and/or races are partnered. Not wanting to intrude on the developing relationship between Carmen, the graduate TA, and her undergraduate partner, Ariel, yet being extremely invested in the success of their section, I wrestled with how much I should assert "my authority" into their dynamic, which did not go smoothly in the beginning. Knowing that I did not want to play social worker or therapist, and that it takes time to develop a working rhythm with a colleague in a coteaching environment, I chose not to intrude or use the power of my position to redirect the course of their working relationship. Instead, I relied on an informal approach. After our group meetings I occasionally gave Carmen a ride home. In the car, we discussed her section more intimately, and it was then that Carmen expressed her personal frustration. I chose not to share Carmen's concerns with any of the other TAs because I had asked the graduate and undergraduate TAs to meet every other week as separate groups, to discuss—without me and their partners—any personal issues that needed airing. In this way (I hoped) lateral support was regularly built into the mentorship program. In fact, just as I had hoped, Carmen did talk with Sam about race and was able to get the support she needed.

Graduate Teaching Assistant: Carmen Nge

I came into 5A this semester with a different set of expectations from last year. I was more confident about my abilities, . . . more comfortable leading section and participating actively in class, and most of all, I had the benefit of having had a wonderfully positive experience working with Yasmin last year. . . . I expected to have as good a semester as I did last time and was prepared to go the extra mile to make my section excel. I was also ready for a challenge and when I found out I was paired with a man, I was a little excited at . . . doing something I had never done before.

The racial dimension . . . I have thought about a lot. . . . As teachers who have to talk about and teach race, we hope that some of that learning gets modeled in our own lives. . . . With Ariel, we talked about race in a scholarly way . . . that allowed us to handle the discussions and to deal with the students. . . . My feeling is that Ariel's stake in the race discussions was very personal as well. Not that the personal is not a good thing but sometimes, I felt that his own personal interest in the issue—his preoccupation with rap and hip-hop music and then his own thinking about his minority friends—took center stage. . . . I would have liked to see him be more critical about the students' perceptions of race, to push them to go deeper and to think harder about their circle of friends and their own biases. But because he himself was dealing with some of these issues, I did not think he was able to extricate himself from the discussions and to concentrate on the students and their learning.

I blame some of that on myself. . . . I was unwilling to engage with Ariel about my feelings regarding race. I am sure that subliminally, as an Asian woman whose work is about race and race relations, I have had no tools with which to deal with White men. I read about them and talk about them in the context of class but when face to face with one, I still am wary and cautious about what I can or cannot say. I was willing to listen to Ariel tell me about himself and I shared a good bit about myself but the connection I shared with Yasmin [who is Afro-Caribbean] last year was not about to be replicated. It could not.

Race still continues to be a difficult topic for me and I have to be honest and say that my dealings with White men, in general, have not been positive, especially on the topic of race. I appreciated Ariel's honesty and his willingness to change things about himself, but I was also very much aware that I was unwilling to . . . work through my own discomfort of talking about whiteness. . . . My perceptions about race are also different from most Asian people; for example, when we had that incident with "Jewel" about her ignorance of being seen as Asian, I was deeply upset and very involved with that issue. Ariel tried to comfort me . . . but what I had difficulty communicating was my deep and profound sadness about the state of affairs among Asian people themselves. At that moment, I felt like Ariel understood what I was talking about but he had no way of understanding my pain. I talked to Sam . . . for a long time and there was no resolution... but I felt differently talking to her. She didn't comfort me . . . we both understood that it was not comfort we sought.

My feelings about our working relationship really colored the way I thought about our section; it influenced the level of success I perceived the students were able to achieve. . . . I am probably too hard on myself now but . . . I am only able to see this in retrospect. Plus, it is too easy to look back on last year and think that everything went so well when it probably had its ups and downs. . . .

I learned a lot from working with Ariel. Mostly . . . about the intricacies of negotiating power between two teachers and the difficulty of achieving a good balance between two very different personalities. I also learned the importance of honesty and that it is a crucial part of the process of working together. Even though I did not always share everything that was on my mind, I did share a good bit and . . . Ariel and I ended on a really good note. At least, I know that I have made a good friend—someone I never would have come to know in any other context—and for me, that has been the best part of this whole process.

Ironically, Carmen and Ariel's section worked beautifully; the student writing from their group was some of the strongest writing in the class. But I wondered whether I should have used the power of my position to insist that Carmen talk directly with Ariel about her identity as an Asian woman and her feelings about White men. I did not push this to happen based on the feminist philosophy that I had to trust Carmen's instinct, respecting her method of choice in dealing with the difficulties around race that arose for her on a personal level. However, unlike in the past, I was not afraid to talk about race, and offered my own insights to Carmen on an informal basis. Perhaps it is not surprising that in Ariel's comments there was no mention of any racial tension, although he did discuss the challenges in learning to work together as a team. His response reflected an altogether positive experience and did not echo Carmen's preoccupation with race in any way. Their dynamic, however, speaks directly to the notion of *simultaneous truths* coexisting with *contradictory realities*, concepts central to the material on race and gender covered in 5A. Disturbingly, they confirm the status quo concerning White male privilege. Although I am left feeling unsettled by their conflicting and contrasting narratives, I am also affirmed in my belief that Simone de Beauvoir's *la vie verité* is a vital part of any learning experience.

In addition to the question of when to assert my own power, an equally compelling challenge is present: to allow such a process to resolve organically without trying to control the final outcome. This is a difficult goal to achieve because it is based on trusting that all parties involved are productively powerful in their own right. That is, in this case, Carmen and Ariel will somehow muddle their way through the turbulent waters where identities—power and privilege—collide. (This collision was emotional and deeply felt, raising concern for me about the nature and extent of my emotional responsibility in the mentoring process as a whole and specifically about not abandoning Carmen in her current dilemma.) Around the issue of race, Carmen was temporarily isolated from her partner but she also found the necessary connection, emotional and intellectual support, she needed from Sam, another graduate teaching assistant and Asian woman.

This, then, is what power anchored in mutuality and based on interdependence is all about. Within the act of sharing power, there exists the possibility and the recognition of multiple meritorious solutions. Without my active direction and left to her own sagacious counsel, Carmen sought out another like herself. And in so doing, she too broke out of the traditional academic hierarchy and the insidious isolation so endemic to the institution. From this experience I learned to use the power of my position in a nontraditionally gendered way: I did not take care of Carmen, and I resisted the overwhelming urge to "fix" everyone. I did acknowledge the situation, confirming my support without diminishing in any way the difficulties she was having. But by the end I let go of my need for everything to be resolved perfectly. I realized that connection, not perfection, is the heart and soul of uncorrupted power in the feminist classroom.

The Mistress' Master Class

MASTER: a person very skilled and able in some work, profession, science expert; specif. a) a highly skilled workman or craftsman qualified to follow his trade independently and usually to supervise the work of others. 3b) an artist regarded as great
—Webster's New World Dictionary, 2nd Ed.

After receiving Carmen's original response I asked her a series of questions about the mentoring process itself. She affirms much of what I believe to be a feminist model of a "master class."

> In 5A . . . the power relations in the teacher-student dynamic changes significantly. For the first time students get to see themselves . . . in positions of authority because of the prominent role of the student TA. Graduate student TAs also interrupt the seamless power relationship between teacher and student but the role of the student TA really makes a big difference in students' ability to see themselves as masters of the material and valued members of the learning community. . . .
>
> Your ability to trust us, your TAs, with complete control of the discussion sections as well as commenting on papers, contributes significantly to the students' trust in the TAs. . . . You constantly reiterate your working relationship with your TAs and how important we are to your teaching, and also how you cannot do this without us. . . . That sends an important message to the students . . . that as a teacher, you are not the receptacle of all information and all knowledge. You show them that the teaching, as well as learning process, happens within a community of diverse individuals. . . . This is a really important point to stress because in a large classroom of 60–80 students, learning happens in a community as well. So, in many ways, the community of teachers reflects the community of students and a symbiotic relation develops between the two.
>
> You value questioning and thinking but by the same token, you do not give the students an easy ride—at the end of the day, the classroom is not a place where anything goes but it is a place where students feel safe to take risks and to engage in the process of learning in a very real way, yet, at the same time, it is also a place where they value others and the learning processes of individuals different from themselves.

In a patriarchal model the goal is to master the subject matter and the class, while in the feminist performative model the goal is to provide all participants with mastery of the power dynamic itself. This, then, is the artist at work. Carmen's analysis of the mentoring process reflects a deep understanding of this complicated pedagogical artistry.

Out of respect for my own relationship with Carmen, I was concerned that we have a more concrete closure around the question of race. And after the semester I didn't want any unfinished business to stifle our future connection. So I asked her the following questions:

> *Do you think it was Yasmin's personality and that she is a woman of color that you worked so well together? What about a White woman? A Jewish or even another Asian woman? I know you don't essentialize, but do you think you work better with women of color in general?*

The issue that affects me the most is not so much race but culture and that the dichotomy between what it means to be American and not-American is greater than being White and not-White. I think Yasmin is able to understand some of that complexity.

And about Ariel I wanted to know:

> *Do you have any regrets about not talking up front more to Ariel about the race issue? His paper does not reflect the tension that yours does . . . although he talks about it taking a long time to find your groove together. He said the party at his house was great. Was that your experience?*

I am . . . not regretful for not talking to Ariel more honestly about my feelings about the race issue. . . . For me, race is not always the most important thing to work through in a thoroughgoing manner. . . . It was a lot more important for me that Ariel and I negotiate teaching together and that we were able to talk more honestly about the delegation of power and responsibility and not all of that had to do with race. Also, . . . I wanted to make sure the semester ended on a positive note, so that it would then set the stage for more productive interactions between me and Ariel in the future.

The last time Ariel and I met, and had dinner together and went over the grades . . . was a wonderful experience. . . . He told me a lot of things about himself and his family and . . . he asked me "What about your narrative?" in a totally honest and down-to-earth manner. I liked that very much and . . . was pleased that he was able to take the initiative and find out more about me too. . . . That marked an important point in our relationship because I was able to tell him my story . . . to talk about some of the things I had alluded to during the semester. He was . . . thoughtful and listened . . . carefully . . . [w]e solidified our trust during that time. . . . I agree with him that my experience during the party as well as our last meeting was great. I really do value our relationship as co-teachers as well as our friendship.

The main difference between the master's class and the mistress' is in the quality of the relationships formed at every level of the teaching experience. As Carmen so articulately expresses, she valued her relationship with Ariel enough to make choices in the classroom that would facilitate future connection. Because she did not view Ariel merely as a one-semester coworker, she consistently left open the possibility of healing some of the early ruptures that had occurred between them. For me, Carmen and Ariel illustrate the critical role that bona fide human connecting facilitates in creating a positive learning environment. Through their struggles it becomes obvious how intellectual distance and emotional detachment from the "live" interactions occurring in the classroom actually detract from the quality of the learning experience. And in the end, the detachment itself serves to perpetuate the old model of power through domination. Although a model based on the mutuality of shared power is much more work, it is additionally more satisfying. The lessons students and professors learn endure as the power of the pedagogy radiates far into the future.

At the close of the hour, the master's lecture is done; his or her work is finished. But for the mistress, the work is never done. Because the relationships built throughout the course last a lifetime. Invariably, I carry with me the presence of last year's students and TAs into a new semester. Their spirits ground me. Vibrant memories of their voices guide me through the rough spots of a totally different class. Whenever I get an e-mail from a former student, I ask her to reflect on her experience. *Tell me what worked for you, and what didn't. What remains, if anything, important to you from our class?* I never stop wanting to know what my students think. The class may be over and the semester long finished, but the connections that are made continue to inform my relationship to power in the feminist classroom. Just when I think I have it all figured out, I come face to face with a new student who is not so unlike my precocious self over twenty years ago. At the height of our classroom encounter I am forced to reconsider, once again, my approach. This is the true power of the pedagogy.

Further Reading

"A Wedding on a Caribbean Mountaintop," *New York Times*, July 10, 1994, 39.

Bateson, Mary Catherine. *Composing a Life*. New York: Plume, 1990.

Biale, David, Michael Galchinsky, and Susannah Heschel, eds. *Insider/Outsider: American Jews and Multiculturalism*. Berkeley: University of California Press, 1998.

Boal, Augusto. *Legislative Theatre*. London: Routledge, 1998.

Bornstein, Kate. *Gender Outlaw*. New York: Vintage, 1995.

Boyarin, Daniel. *Unheroic Conduct*. Berkeley: University of California Press, 1997.

Boyarin, Daniel, and Jonathan Boyarin, eds. *Jews and Other Differences*. Minneapolis: University of Minnesota Press, 1997.

Case, Sue-Ellen, ed. *Split Britches*. London: Routledge, 1996.

Cohee, Gail E., et al., eds. *The Feminist Teacher Anthology*. New York: Teachers College Press, 1998.

Collins, Patricia Hill. *Black Feminist Thought*. 2nd. ed. New York: Routledge, 2000.

Culley, Margo, and Catherine Portuges, eds. *Gendered Subjects*. New York: Routledge, 1985.

Davis, Angela Y. *Women, Race, and Class*. New York: Vintage, 1983.

Douglas, Susan J. *Where the Girls Are*. New York: Times Books, 1994.

Felman, Jyl Lynn. *Hot Chicken Wings*. San Francisco: Aunt Lute Books, 1992.

———. *Cravings*. Boston: Beacon, 1997.

Frye, Marilyn. *The Politics of Reality*. New York: The Crossing Press, 1983.

Gallop, Jane. *Feminist Accused of Sexual Harassment*. Durham, N.C.: Duke University Press, 1997.

———. ed. *Pedagogy: The Question of Impersonation*. Bloomington: University of Indiana Press, 1995.

Garber, Marjorie. *Vested Interests*. New York: Harper Perennial, 1993.

Gates, Henry Louis, Jr., and Manning Marable. "A Debate on Activism in Black Studies," *New York Times*, April 18, 1998, B1, B13.

Golden, Carla. "The Radicalization of a Teacher." In *The Feminist Teacher Anthology*, ed. Gail E. Cohee et al. New York: Teachers College Press, 1998.

Gómez-Peña, Guillermo. *Dangerous Border Crossers*. London: Routledge, 2000.

Goodman, Lizbeth. *The Routledge Reader in Gender and Performance*. London: Routledge, 1998.

hooks, bell. *Teaching to Transgress*. New York: Routledge, 1994.

Jenoure, Theresa. *Navigators: African American Musicians, Dancers, and Visual Artists in Academe*. Albany: State University of New York Press, 2000.

Jones, Bill T. *Last Night on Earth*. New York: Pantheon, 1995.

Kaufman, Shirley, Galit Hasan-Rokem, and Tamar S. Hess, eds. *The Defiant Muse: Hebrew Feminist Poems from Antiquity to the Present*. New York: Feminist Press, 1999.

Kimmel, Michael S., and Michael A. Messner, eds. *Men's Lives*. Boston: Allyn and Bacon, 2000.

Lorde, Audre. *Sister Outsider*. New York: The Crossing Press, 1984.

Makosky, Vivian P., and Michele A. Paludi. "Foundations for a Feminist Restructuring of the Academic Disciplines." In *Feminism and Women's Studies in the Academy*. New York: Haworth, 1990.

Matsua, Mari J. *Where Is Your Body? And Other Essays on Race, Gender, and the Law*. Boston: Beacon, 1997.

Mayberry, Maralee, and Ellen Cronan Rose, eds. M*eeting the Challenge: Innovative Feminist Pedagogies in Action*. New York: Routledge, 1999.

Mintz, Beth, and Esther D. Rothblum, eds. *Lesbians in Academia.* New York: Routledge, 1997.

Ortner, Sherry B. *Making Gender.* Boston: Beacon, 1996.

Painter, Nell Irvin. *Sojourner Truth.* New York: W. W. Norton, 1996.

Pipher, Mary. *Reviving Ophelia.* New York: Ballentine, 1994.

Plimpton, George, ed. *Writers at Work: The Paris Review Interviews.* 2nd ser. New York: Viking, 1963.

Ropers-Hilman, Becky. *Feminist Teaching in Theory and Practice.* New York: Teachers College Press, 1998.

Shandler, Sara. *Ophelia Speaks.* New York: Harper Perennial, 1999.

Simon, Roger. "Face to Face with Alterity: Postmodern Jewish Identity and the Eros of Pedagogy." In *Pedagogy: The Question of Impersonation*, ed. Jane Gallop. Bloomington: University of Indiana Press, 1995.

Somerville, Siobhan B. *Queering the Color Line.* Durham, N.C.: Duke University Press, 2000.

Tatum, Beverly Daniel. "*Why Are All the Black Kids Sitting Together in the Cafeteria?*" New York: Basic Books, 1997.

Thomas, Laurence Mordekhai. *Vessels of Evil.* Philadelphia: Temple University Press, 1993.

Walker, Alice. *The Same River Twice.* New York: Scribner, 1996.

Relevant Films

20/20: Gay and Lesbian Marriage
20/20: The Gender Wars: Nature vs. Nurture
A Place of Rage
A Sense of Place: Japanese American Women
Africans' America: Americans' Journey through Slavery
All God's Children
America and the Holocaust: Deceit and Indifference
Amistad
bell hooks: Cultural Criticism and Transformation
Beyond Black and White
Blacks and Jews
Complaints of a Dutiful Daughter
Crooklyn
Daughters of Dykes
Dialogues with Madwomen
Do the Right Thing
Double Shift
Female Perversions
Fires in the Mirror: Crown Heights
From Swastika to Jim Crow
Gentleman's Agreement
Hair Piece
Hairspray

Halving the Body

Hidden Faces

History and Memory: Akiko and Takashige

Hollywoodism: Jews, Movies, and the American Dream

Identifiable Qualities: Toni Morrison

If Only I'd Been Born a Kosher Chicken

Investigative Reports: Transgender Revolution

Iraqi Women

Juggling Gender

L'Operacion

Maya Lin: A Strong Clear Voice

Mirror Mirror

Mo' Better Blues

Nappy Hair

Nothing but a Man

Punch Me in the Stomach

Remembering Wei Yi-fang, Remembering Myself

Roe v. Wade

Secret Daughter

Secret Life of Barbie

Shattering the Silence

Skin Deep

Still/Here: Bill T. Jones with Bill Moyer

Stonewall

Stuart Hall: Race as a Floating Signifier

Thank God I'm a Lesbian

The Ballad of Little Jo

The Color Purple

The "F" Word

The Lion King

The Longest Hatred

The Price of the Ticket: James Baldwin

The Search for American Character: Anna Deavere Smith

The Women Next Door: Israeli and Palestinian Women

Index

Felman, Jyl Lynn, 24–25, 51, 58,
      69, 71, 79, 88, 91, 97, 120,
      126, 135, 161, 169–70, 174,
      186, 201–5
   Cravings, 125–27, 134, 185
   Hot Chicken Wings, 125
femaleness, 32, 58–61, 84–85
feminine hesitancy, 85
Femininist Teacher Anthology, The,
      152
femininities, 65, 96
   performing, xvii, 83–104
   Western White, 72
femininity, 58, 61–62, 66, 71, 73,
      78, 143–44
   academic, 62
   Black, 102
   Jewish, 102
feminism, 4, 9, 11, 20, 33, 38, 44,
      59, 63, 76, 79, 81, 164, 179,
      182, 185, 197, 203, 209
   academic, 166
   liberal, 179
   radical, 92, 179
feminist: academy, 91
   classroom, xvi, xviii, xix, 22,
      26, 29, 31, 38–40, 42, 50,
      52, 62, 82, 99, 141, 147,
      149, 152, 154, 156, 168,
      185, 187, 194–95, 198,
      211, 213
   discourse, 31
   master class, 210–13
   performance, 158, 211 (*see also*
      feminist classroom)
   space, 85–86
   theory, 45, 59, 66, 72, 91, 135,
      152, 166, 168, 197, 204

feminist pedagogy, xv, xix, 23, 29,
      42, 44, 46, 48, 64, 85,
      94–95, 103, 123, 125, 145,
      158, 175, 180–82, 187–88,
      192, 195
   performance of, 3, 211
feminists, 9, 59–60, 79, 99, 105,
      176, 178, 181
   Black, 117
   Jewish, 164
   men, 20–21, 66, 68, 82, 113
Femme 2000 course, 63, 65–66,
      68, 78–79, 81, 166, 167
Fierstein, Harvey: *Torch Song
      Trilogy*, 33
Film Studies, 178
Franklin, Daniel J., 203–4, 207
Freud, Sigmund, 176
Frye, Marilyn: *The Politics of
      Reality*, 83–85

Gallop, Jane: *Feminist Accused of
      Sexual Harassment*, 106, 114,
      119, 125
Garber, Marjorie, 114, 141
Gates, Henry Louis Jr., 165
gays. *See* homosexuality; lesbians;
      students, homosexual
gaze, the, 31, 146–47, 155
gender, xvii–xviii, 7, 31, 38–39,
      45, 52, 58–59, 62, 64, 78,
      89, 98, 103, 109–13, 135,
      140–42, 144, 159, 162,
      177, 182, 193–94, 197,
      200, 209
   barriers, 39, 62, 102
   identity, 147